Second Edition

Classroom Strategies for Interactive Learning

Doug Buehl

Madison Metropolitan School District
Madison, Wisconsin, USA

INTERNATIONAL
Reading
Association

800 Barksdale Road, PO Box 8139
Newark, Delaware 19714-8139, USA
www.reading.org

The International Reading Association attempts, through its publications, to provide a forum for a wide spectrum of opinions on reading. This policy permits divergent viewpoints without implying the endorsement of the Association.

Director of Publications Joan M. Irwin
Editorial Director, Books and Special Projects Matthew W. Baker
Special Projects Editor Tori Mello Bachman
Permissions Editor Janet S. Parrack
Associate Editor Jeanine K. McGann
Production Editor Shannon Benner
Publications Coordinator Beth Doughty
Production Department Manager Iona Sauscermen
Art Director Boni Nash
Supervisor, Electronic Publishing Anette Schütz-Ruff
Electronic Publishing Specialist Cheryl J. Strum
Electronic Publishing Specialist Lynn Harrison

Project Editor Janet S. Parrack

Photo Credits Depression era photo, page 150. Dorothea Lange, 1938. From the Library of Congress American Memory Collection. Available: www.memory.loc.gov

Library of Congress Cataloging-in-Publication Data
Buehl, Doug.
    Classroom strategies for interactive learning / Doug Buehl.—2nd ed.
        p.   cm.
Includes bibliographical references.
ISBN 0-87207-284-3 (pbk. : alk. paper)
    1. Reading comprehension.   2. Content area reading.   3. Active learning.   I. Title.
LB1050.45.B84   2000
371.3—dc21   00-011872

Eleventh Printing, May 2005

Contents

SECTION 1
Developing Strategic Readers and Learners

SECTION 2
Classroom Strategies for Teaching and Learning

Foreword

I love books written by classroom teachers, especially a book written by one of the finest teachers I have ever known. And even more impressive, he is a secondary reading teacher. I have known Doug Buehl as a great friend and colleague for most of my grown-up life. He works every day as a high school reading specialist at Madison East High School in Wisconsin. He knows students; he knows teachers. He also understands the kinds of books we practitioners love to keep handy on our desks. *Classroom Strategies for Interactive Learning* just happens to be one of those books.

The first edition of this book, originally published by the Wisconsin State Reading Association, was a gem. In fact, it didn't take much urging for me to convince the curriculum director of my school district to buy a copy of Doug's book for each one of our middle and high school teachers.

I also thought that IRA should figure out some way to publish his next edition of this book. I talked to Doug about the possibility and even called Joan Irwin, Director of Publications, to see if she could use her magic to put some gentle pressure on Doug. Apparently, I wasn't the first person to make this call. Joan was well aware that this was a book IRA simply had to have.

The timing of this publication is perfect. With the current surge of interest in adolescent literacy, *Classroom Strategies for Interactive Learning* fills an important niche. Reading specialists and classroom teachers have many available resources for the beginning stages of reading development but few tools for older students, particularly at the middle and high school level. This book has broad appeal. It is an important resource for anyone including elementary teachers involved in teaching students how to become independent learners.

Classroom Strategies for Interactive Learning is comprehensive and organized perfectly for use in college classes and for inservice programs. Doug has a gift for writing clearly and succinctly. He avoids jargon and has a talent for making something complicated accessible to a wide audience of preservice and practicing teachers from all content areas. In one tidy volume, he places his personal stamp and voice on decades of work in comprehension. Included are ideas for developing vocabulary, promoting discussion, encouraging writing, and teaching study skills. This work transcends grade levels and content areas.

I have already made plans to use the second edition of *Classroom Strategies for Interactive Learning* for staff development. After modeling a particular lesson for teachers, such as Questioning the Author or K-W-L Plus, I would ask teachers to turn to the explanation of these same strategies in this book. Doug's work provides a wonderful resource to back up and extend practically any inservice I could imagine on comprehension and learning. No longer do I have to sort through my endless files and photocopy stacks of articles as inservice handouts. Doug has done it for me. It's all here. Thank you Doug for sharing your wisdom with us.

Carol Minnick Santa
Director of Education
Montana Academy
Marion, Montana, USA

Acknowledgments

A number of individuals deserve recognition for their roles in this publication. Bill Hurley, editor of the *WEAC News & Views*, developed the concept of a regular column in that newspaper that would appeal to classroom teachers looking for ideas useful to their teaching. His support for my monthly column, "The Reading Room," has allowed these strategies to be shared with teachers throughout Wisconsin since 1990. My colleague at Madison East High School, Sharon McPike, thoughtfully read and critiqued each strategy before it went to press. I continue to value her professional input in "reality-testing" what I write. Doug Vance, my former colleague in the Madison Metropolitan School District, reacted to portions of this manuscript and contributed his usual insightful feedback. My collaborations with Doug over the years on numerous workshops and projects laid the groundwork and provided the inspiration for this project. In addition, Doris Cook, formerly Reading Supervisor for the Wisconsin Department of Public Instruction, receives my gratitude for involving me in the creation of the 1989 curriculum guide, *Strategic Learning in the Content Areas*, which has been the impetus for much of my subsequent professional writing. My wife, Wendy Buehl, reviewed this manuscript, with a keen eye trained for detecting convoluted prose and unclear description. Her encouragement, support, and love has made this book possible. And finally, students I have worked with over the years at Madison East High School deserve special mention for helping me figure out how I could better teach them. I would like to thank two students in particular, my sons Jeremy and Christopher, who could put up with their father as a teacher and who constantly provide me with ideas and insight about this business of teaching reading.

I dedicate this book to Wendy.

Introduction

Picture the following scene in your classroom: A student is leaning over an open textbook, her eyes scanning the pages. At times she is writing in her notebook. From all appearances, she seems to be completing the assignment. But if she is like many students, this will not be a smooth process for her. She may be having difficulty focusing on what is important in the reading. She may be only superficially skimming the textbook, looking for answers needed to satisfy an assignment. She may feel frustrated by the vast amount of information she is encountering and think that she will never learn it all. She may have decided that none of the material has anything to do with her, so she will merely get the work done, only to forget most of it once the unit is over.

Teachers are well aware that many students do not successfully learn their course content. Conversations around the copy machine and in the teacher lounge frequently focus on dissatisfaction with student performance. Because many students founder with classroom reading demands, teachers may lose confidence at times in reading assignments. Instead of having students read, we may resort to telling them what they need to know or we may turn to other media for instruction. Yet significant portions of our curricula are necessarily print-based, and teachers know that students need to develop effective reading behaviors in order to survive and be successful in school.

In recent years we have witnessed a resurgence in interest in the reading and writing needs of adolescents. As state and national standards for achievement have been developed in reading, writing, social studies, mathematics, science, and other curricular areas, educators have begun to rediscover the importance of developing the literacy skills of older students. In an extensive review of the literature on the literacy needs of adolescent learners, the Commission on Adolescent Literacy of the International Reading Association concluded that

(1) adolescents deserve instruction that builds both the skills and desire to read increasingly complex materials, [and that]

(2) adolescents deserve expert teachers who model and provide explicit instruction in reading comprehension and study strategies across the curriculum. (Moore, Bean, Birdyshaw, & Rycik, 1999, pp. 5, 7)

Classroom Strategies for Interactive Learning, Second Edition, is intended to assist classroom teachers as they become better prepared to meet these two important goals for their students. This edition features 45 classroom teaching strategies that can be adapted for students from elementary school through high school, and that are appropriate for helping students learn in all curricular areas from language arts to mathematics, science to foreign language, and vocational subjects to social studies. The appeal of these classroom strategies is grounded in their effectiveness in developing students who are active, purposeful, and increasingly independent learners. These strategies also provide innovative ideas for teachers working with diverse classrooms and with students who exhibit a variety of learning needs.

The first edition of *Classroom Strategies* (1995) was an outgrowth of a 10-year collaboration between the Wisconsin State Reading Association (WSRA) and Wisconsin Education Association Council (WEAC). During this time, my column "The Reading Room" appeared in WEAC's monthly newspaper, *News and Views*, which circulates to state public school teachers. My purpose in writing the column was to provide classroom teachers with sufficient information for using strategies with students without becoming immersed in a lot of educational jargon. This book adapts those strategies, which were selected from a variety of sources including professional journals, books, and presentations.

Although this book is not an exhaustive compendium of classroom strategies, it does streamline discussion of strategies so that classroom teachers can readily discern the benefits to their students and learn how to implement them in their curriculum. Teachers who want more in-depth treatment of a strategy can consult the resources listed at the end of each strategy description.

References

Buehl, D. (2000). *The Reading Room* [Online]. Available: http://www.weac.org/News/reading.htm

Moore, D., Bean, T., Birdyshaw, D., & Rycik, J. (1999). *Adolescent literacy: A position statement for the Commission on Adolescent Literacy of the International Reading Association*. Newark: DE: International Reading Association.

SECTION 1

Developing Strategic Readers and Learners

4. How does the character change?

History Memory Bubbles

Essential Knowledge

Who/What

Solutions

Fact

CHAPTER 1

An Interactive View of Reading and Learning

Reading comprehension—the process of obtaining meaning from print—is fundamental to learning in the subjects we teach. As teachers we see students engaged in reading activities almost daily. Although some students appear to handle school reading demands successfully, many students experience breakdowns in their attempts to make sense of the print they encounter in the classroom. How can we explain the dynamics involved with being an effective reader? What needs to be happening in a student's mind if reading comprehension is to result? How can we use classroom strategies to develop readers who can learn from a wide variety of print materials?

Reading as a Constructive Process

In the past, reading comprehension was described more as a skill than as an active mental process. We conceived reading to be the skill of recognizing letters and words, which led to the ability to connect words into sentences, sentences into paragraphs, and paragraphs into longer discourse that represented various themes or ideas. We regarded getting the main idea, identifying the important details, making inferences, and other such behaviors as the gist of comprehension. If a student could describe what was in the text or in other words reproduce what an author had written, then we concluded that comprehension had occurred. If a student could not, then we explained the situation by saying that the student was lacking in reading ability, the student had poor study skills, or the text was too difficult.

Recent research in the psychology of reading has led to the development of a much different description of what it means to comprehend written text. The key concept of this new definition of comprehension is that a reader constructs meaning from a text rather than merely reproducing the words on the page. Meaning is something that is actively created rather than passively received. No two people will have exactly the same comprehension of a text, because no two people will be reading a text under exactly the same conditions. The interactions among four conditions determine what meaning a reader will construct from a text (see Figure 1.1):

(1) what the *reader* brings to the reading situation; (2) the characteristics of the written *text*; (3) the learning *context* that defines the task and purpose of the reader; and (4) the *strategies* consciously applied by the reader to obtain meaning. (Cook, 1986, 1989)

The Reader

The constructivist definition of reading emphasizes that it is too simplistic to look at readers solely from the perspective of whether they have developed specific reading skills (for example, applying phonics, using context, and identifying main idea), which are certainly important. But equally important are other traits of the reader. Because comprehension is essentially a mental construction of what is on the page based on what is already known, then the background knowledge of the reader is a primary determinant of how a text will be understood. The more a student knows about a topic, the better she will be able to

---

FIGURE 1.1

Interactive Model of Reading Comprehension

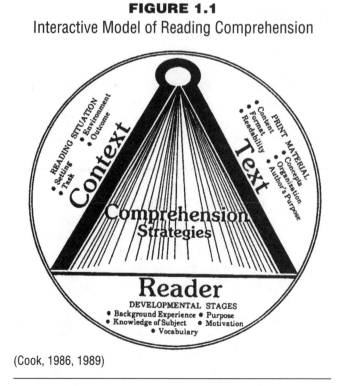

(Cook, 1986, 1989)

---

comprehend printed material on that topic. If her background knowledge includes much of the content vocabulary that appears, for instance, in a passage on medieval cathedrals or in an article on creatures that live in the ocean, then comprehension is enhanced correspondingly. Also, comprehension is influenced greatly by personality characteristics such as a student's personal reasons for reading a piece of print and her willingness or motivation to do so.

The Text

Traditionally, teachers have talked readability scores and appropriate grade levels when referring to difficulty of reading material. But readability formulas and grade-level designations are not helpful in predicting how individual students will react to reading a specific piece of prose. Other factors about what impact print has on reading comprehension need to be considered: the way the content is presented, the density of the concepts, and the study aids that help students focus on important ideas. In addition, the language in which the text is written and the text's organizational structure, from the sentence level up through entire chapters or units, play a critical role in the process of constructing meaning. (See Chapter 2 for a discussion of the impact of organizational text frames on reading.) Clearly, some texts are written and organized in ways that are more reader friendly than others, as anyone who has struggled through a computer manual can attest.

The Context

A reader's comprehension is also influenced by situations in which the reading occurs. Contextual factors may include physical conditions such as noise level in the room, time elements such as early morning or late at night, and family circumstances such as parental support for a child's learning. In the classroom, a teacher has a great deal of influence in creating the environment for reading. The teacher's expectations as well as the instructions for a specific reading determine the way a student approaches a reading task. Does the assignment require a careful examination for mastery of details, or will a general understanding of the major ideas be sufficient? Will the information be discussed the next day, tested a week later, or used to complete a project? After the reading, will students complete a worksheet, answer inferential questions, write an essay, or conduct a lab experiment? Are students expected to get everything they need on their own, or can they collaborate in their reading with other students? Student comprehension of a text will vary considerably depending on the messages the teacher sends through the context of the reading assignment.

The Strategies

Because comprehension can be seen as a result of sophisticated interaction among the reader, the specific text, and the context for reading, effective readers employ strategies in order to maneuver meaningfully through this interaction. The strategies a reader selects depend on why she thinks she is reading the selection, how familiar she is with the content of the selection, and of course, what strategies she is skilled in applying. Proficient readers employ a variety of effective comprehension behaviors as they monitor their understanding: predicting, connecting with prior knowledge, determining importance, self-questioning, clarifying, and summarizing (Duke & Pearson, 2000). Previewing a selection, rereading a difficult passage, underlining pertinent information, using context to figure out new vocabulary, creating a graphic organizer of a chapter, quizzing oneself, skimming, and taking notes are all examples of effective reading strategies at work. The more a reader understands when certain strategies are effective and why they work, the more likely she will become a strategic reader in the classroom.

The following three principles summarize reading as an interactive process among reader, text, and context. Classroom strategies that embody these principles are more likely to develop students who can effectively learn from print materials.

1. Students learn best when they have adequate background knowledge about a topic. The more teachers help students to understand concepts prior to reading about them, the better students will read. By "frontloading" instruction—shifting teaching to before student reading—teachers can accomplish a number of important objectives. They can discover what students already know or do not know about a topic, build relevant background with students who are beginning a reading with insufficient knowledge, spotlight key vocabulary, and pique student interest in reading about a topic.

2. Turning students from passive receivers to active constructors of meaning involves asking them to use reading rather than "do" reading. Classroom strategies that encourage students to actively think about what they are reading and to apply what they have learned lead to students more deeply engaged in making sense from print. Activities that permit students to interact with other students tend to increase both motivation to learn and as a result, active involvement.

3. Students learn best when they become strategic readers. Ultimately, teachers want students to

grow from dependence to independence in learning. Students need to discover which learning strategies work best for them and when to apply them. Classroom strategies that guide students in assessing the learning situation, setting their own purpose, choosing the most effective actions, and evaluating their success lead to more self-sufficient individuals capable of becoming lifelong learners.

Frontloading

Does the following sentence make sense to you?

There's a bear in a plain brown wrapper doing flip-flops on 78, taking pictures, and passing out green stamps.

What does this sentence seem to be about? How confident are you of your interpretation? Is there anything difficult about this text? Do you understand all the vocabulary? If I provide a hint—Citizen Band (CB) radios—can you make sense of the sentence? Many will recognize immediately the sentence as CB lingo, used by truckers and travelers and popularized in the 1970s by a series of *Smokey and the Bandit* movies featuring Burt Reynolds. You could confidently translate the passage:

There's a state patrol officer in an unmarked car going back and forth across the median on highway 78, using radar and passing out speeding tickets.

Shaky initial comprehension of this sentence was not due to poor reading skills, difficult vocabulary, or complex sentence structure. Instead, the sentence did not make sense due to confusion about the text. You probably asked, What do I know that can help me figure out this passage? You were struggling to make a meaningful connection to the material.

Many students have similar problems when they launch into a reading assignment "cold." They may be unsure of what the material is about and may have not taken measure of what they already know about the topic, which could guide their understanding. They glide along—reading words, noticing details, picking out pieces of information—but may be clueless about what they are attempting to read.

The importance of frontloading—the teaching done before students begin a reading assignment—is underscored in many of the classroom strategies outlined in this book. The following analogy emphasizes this importance.

Imagine a student's background knowledge as a gray file cabinet standing in the corner of your classroom. The file cabinet represents a memory bank of everything a student knows about the world—his experiences, his perceptions, and his definitions of reali-

ty. The contents of the cabinet provide the basis for the student's understanding of what is happening around him. The knowledge in the cabinet is divided into drawers, then into sections within the drawers, and finally into file folders within the sections. Sometimes new information is integrated into the mental file folders. If a folder is already bulging with knowledge about a particular topic, reading about that topic will add new pieces of information to an already well-understood topic. However, if a folder is empty or no folder exists for a topic, then reading comprehension will be imprecise, incomplete, and confused. By practicing frontloading techniques, teachers help students to extract relevant information from their folders in their memories and to integrate new information into those folders. Frontloading fosters strategic reading behaviors that will lead to successful construction of the meaning of texts.

Using Effective Classroom Strategies

Teachers are incredibly resourceful, always on the lookout for good ideas and potential materials they can use with their students. Yet teachers are frequently frustrated with the classroom strategies they see modeled at workshops and conferences or discussed in professional journals. Although the strategies seem to work perfectly when they are demonstrated by the "expert," teachers may find it difficult to make them work with their students in real classroom situations. Three rules will help teachers avoid becoming discouraged when using new strategies with their students.

First, what the students are learning is more important than which strategy is used. Once you decide what you want students to learn, you can consider how you want to set up instruction. A classroom strategy may work well with some objectives and materials, but very poorly with others. Make sure the teaching strategy is aligned with your learning goals.

Second, it is the students' thinking that counts, not the specific classroom strategy. Merely following the steps of a strategy does not guarantee that students will engage in the kind of thinking that leads to meaningful learning. Students may fall into a routine of "going through the motions." Be alert for students just "doing" rather than thinking. The classroom strategies in this book do not lead magically or inevitably to success.

Third, tailor what you are doing to match your students and your goals. Although classroom strategies are often described in a series of "all-important" steps, be aware of the thinking you want to stimulate in your students and respond accordingly. Avoid becoming so involved in following a formula that you lose sight of

FIGURE 1.2
Classroom Teaching Strategies Indexed by Student Activities

Developing Vocabulary
Analogy Graphic Organizer
Concept/Definition Mapping
Frayer Model
Magnet Summaries
Mind Mapping
Possible Sentences
Question Dissection
Semantic Feature Analysis
Story Impressions
Vocabulary Overview Guide
Word Family Trees

Brainstorming of Ideas
Analogy Graphic Organizer
Anticipation Guides
Brainstorming Prior Knowledge
Character Quotes
Frayer Model
History Change Frame
Inquiry Charts
K-W-L Plus (Know/Want to
   Know/Learned)
Mind Mapping
Possible Sentences
Problematic Situations
Story Impressions
Vocabulary Overview Guide
You Ought to Be in Pictures

Learning Cooperatively
Anticipation Guides
Character Quotes
Different Perspectives
Discussion Web
Follow the Characters
Inquiry Charts
Interactive Reading Guides
Jigsaw
Paired Reviews
Point-of-View Study Guides
Problematic Situations
Read Alouds
Save the Last Word for Me
SMART (Self-Monitoring
   Approach to Reading and
   Thinking)

Promoting Discussion
Analogy Graphic Organizer
Anticipation Guides
Brainstorming (Prior Knowledge)
Character Quotes

Different Perspectives
Discussion Web
Follow the Characters
Interactive Reading Guides
Jigsaw
K-W-L Plus (Know/Want to
   Know/Learned)
Paired Reviews
Problematic Situations
Pyramid Diagram
Save the Last Word for Me
Semantic Feature Analysis
You Ought to Be in Pictures

Interactive Reading
Anticipation Guides
Character Quotes
Chapter Tours
Different Perspectives
Discussion Web
Elaborative Interrogation
Guided Imagery
History Change Frame
Inquiry Charts
Interactive Reading Guides
Jigsaw
Math Reading Keys
Point-of-View Study Guides
Power Notes
Problematic Situations
Proposition/Support Outlines
Pyramid Diagram
Questioning the Author
Read Alouds
Save the Last Word for Me
Science Connection Overview
SMART (Self-Monitoring
   Approach to Reading and
   Thinking)
Story Mapping
Structured Notetaking
You Ought to Be in Pictures

Encouraging Writing
Discussion Web
Inquiry Charts
K-W-L Plus (Know/Want to
   Know/Learned)
Learning Logs
Magnet Summaries
Point-of-View Study Guides
Possible Sentences
Power Notes

Proposition/Support Outlines
Pyramid Diagram
Question Dissection
RAFT
   (Role/Audience/Format/Topic)
Story Impressions
Template Frames

**Representing Information
Graphically**
Analogy Graphic Organizer
Concept/Definition Maps
Different Perspectives
Discussion Web
Follow the Characters
Frayer Model
History Change Frame
History Memory Bubbles
Inquiry Charts
K-W-L Plus (Know/Want to
   Know/Learned)
Mind Mapping
Power Notes
Proposition/Support Outlines
Pyramid Diagram
Science Connection Overview
Semantic Feature Analysis
Story Mapping
Structured Notetaking
Vocabulary Overview Guide
Word Family Trees

Building Study Skills
Chapter Tours
Elaborative Interrogation
Follow the Characters
History Change Frame
History Memory Bubbles
Inquiry Charts
Interactive Reading Guides
Learning Logs
Magnet Summaries
Math Reading Keys
Paired Reviews
Power Notes
Question-Answer Relationships
Question the Author
Question Dissection
Science Connection Overview
Story Mapping
Structured Notetaking
Template Frames

the learning that you want happening in your classroom. Be flexible and adjust strategies to fit your needs.

Strategies for Interactive Learning

Effective classroom teaching strategies involve students in a wide variety of interactive practices. The 45 classroom strategies highlighted in this book are categorized into eight student activities (see Figure 1.2): developing vocabulary, brainstorming of ideas, learning cooperatively, promoting discussion, interactive reading, encouraging writing, representing information graphically, and building study skills. Note that some teaching strategies may include several student activities as integral components and therefore are cross-referenced in more than one student-activity category.

For example, the Discussion Web strategy (see page 47) is indexed under five student activities: learning cooperatively, promoting discussion, interactive reading, encouraging writing, and representing information graphically. It is an excellent strategy for fostering discussion among students and makes extensive use of cooperative learning activities. Students record pertinent information in a graphic outline that can be used subsequently as a blueprint for various writing exercises. The Discussion Web involves students in a directive and purposeful rereading of assigned material.

Strategies That Stimulate Thinking

The classroom teaching strategies featured in this book are also categorized according to the kinds of thinking in which students become involved when engaged in the lesson. The cognitive behavior elicited by a strategy is correlated to the three phases of instruction: (1) preparing students to encounter new content (before reading activities), (2) guiding students in their learning (during reading activities), and (3) enhancing or building on the learning (after reading activities).

We want to encourage different types of thinking in students, depending on whether they are learning new material, processing while reading, or consolidating new learning into their existing memory banks. Figure 1.3 identifies the cognitive mind-set of effective learners during each phase of learning. Before reading, effective learners activate what they know about the topic, and they focus their attention on learning for a specific purpose. During learning, effective learners are actively engaged in selecting from the text what they deem important to know, and they undertake some method to organize this information. To consolidate their learning, effective learners use strategies that help integrate the new information into

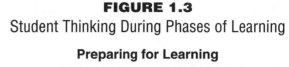

FIGURE 1.3

Student Thinking During Phases of Learning

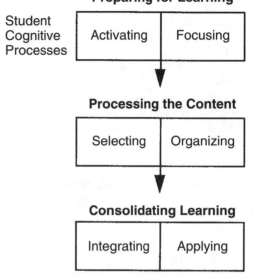

what they already know. They also look for ways to apply this new information to meaningful situations.

As you use the classroom strategies described in this book, notice how they encourage these cognitive behaviors (see Figure 1.4). For example, a frontloading strategy such as K-W-L Plus (page 75) is an excellent way to prepare students for new learning because it encourages them to activate what they know and focus their attention on questions for new learning. A strategy such as Structured Notetaking (see page 138) prompts students to selectively read and to meaningfully organize important information. A Role/Audience/Format/Topic (RAFT) writing exercise (see page 114) helps students integrate new concepts into their previous understandings by having them personalize their learning. A RAFT assignment also provides students with a creative way to apply what they have learned.

Building Independent Learners

As teachers, we know that students will not learn everything they need to know in the 13 years leading up to graduation from high school. In daily work with students, we strive to encourage them to become lifelong learners who will continue to deepen their understandings related to the various subject areas we teach. By using classroom strategies that teach students to activate, focus, select, organize, integrate, and apply as they learn, we foster the development of individuals who are purposeful thinkers and independent learn-

FIGURE 1.4
Classroom Teaching Strategies Indexed by Cognitive Processes

Preparing For Learning
Activating/Focusing Strategies
- Analogy Graphic Organizer
- Anticipation Guides
- Brainstorming Prior Knowledge
- Chapter Tours
- Character Quotes
- Concept/Definition Mapping
- Frayer Model
- Guided Imagery
- History Change Frame
- Inquiry Charts
- K-W-L Plus (Know/Want to Know/Learned)
- Learning Logs
- Math Reading Keys
- Mind Mapping
- Possible Sentences
- Problematic Situations
- Science Connection Overview
- Semantic Feature Analysis
- Story Impressions
- You Ought to Be in Pictures

Processing the Content
Selecting/Organizing Strategies
- Analogy Graphic Organizer
- Anticipation Guides
- Chapter Tours
- Character Quotes
- Concept/Definition Mapping
- Elaborative Interrogation
- Frayer Model
- History Change Frame
- History Memory Bubbles
- Inquiry Charts
- Interactive Reading Guides
- Jigsaw
- K-W-L Plus (Know/Want to Know/Learned)
- Math Reading Keys
- Mind Mapping
- Point-of-View Study Guides
- Possible Sentences
- Power Notes
- Problematic Situations

- Proposition/Support Outlines
- Pyramid Diagram
- Question-Answer Relationships
- Questioning the Author
- Read-Alouds
- Science Connection Overview
- Semantic Feature Analysis
- SMART (Self-Monitoring Approach to Reading and Thinking)
- Story Mapping
- Structured Notetaking

Consolidating Learning
Integrating/Applying Strategies
- Analogy Graphic Organizer
- Concept/Definition Mapping
- Different Perspectives
- Discussion Web
- Follow the Characters
- Frayer Model
- Guided Imagery
- History Memory Bubbles
- Inquiry Charts
- K-W-L Plus (Know/Want to Know/Learned)
- Learning Logs
- Magnet Summaries
- Paired Reviews
- Point-of-View Study Guides
- Power Notes
- Question-Answer Relationships
- Question Dissection
- Pyramid Diagram
- RAFT (Role/Audience/Format/Topic)
- Save the Last Word for Me
- Semantic Feature Analysis
- SMART (Self-Monitoring Approach to Reading and Thinking)
- Story Mapping
- Story Impressions
- Structured Notetaking
- Template Frames
- Word Family Trees
- Vocabulary Overview Guide
- You Ought to Be in Pictures

---

ers. The classroom strategies outlined in this book should help your students understand, remember, and apply key information and concepts. They are also designed to accomplish a gradual increase in student self-responsibility for learning. Effective strategies build in students a discipline for learning that enables them to become independent learners.

References

Cook, D. (Ed.). (1986). *A guide to curriculum planning in reading*. Madison, WI: Wisconsin Department of Public Instruction.

Cook, D. (Ed.). (1989). *Strategic learning in the content areas*. Madison, WI: Wisconsin Department of Public Instruction.

Duke, N., & Pearson, P.D. (2000, June). Effective practices for developing reading comprehension. Paper presented at Madison Literacy Institute, Madison, WI.

CHAPTER 2

Guiding Thinking Through Text Frames

It is a quiet evening. You are settled in a comfortable chair, anticipating a few hours pleasantly lost in the latest Tony Hillerman or P.D. James mystery. As you open the book to initially appraise it, what is your frame of mind? What are you expecting from this novel? To put it another way, why have you chosen to read a mystery? Undoubtedly, you are looking for the kind of reading experience that a mystery novel will satisfy. And your "frame of mind" is organized around a set of questions that a well-written mystery novel would be expected to answer: What mystery in this book needs to be solved? What character in the book is searching for the solution? What clues can be identified? What false leads must we be wary of? Who are the suspects? What are their motives? What steps should be taken to solve this mystery? As you consider these questions, you set the perfect frame of mind to approach the reading of this book.

Text Frames: A Mental Approach to Reading

Effective readers approach print with an active, purposeful attitude. They know why they are reading a selection and what they are looking for. In other words, effective readers have an appropriate frame of mind that will structure their reading of a particular piece of writing. They read to answer relevant questions about the material—questions that relate directly to their purpose for reading the material.

Researchers use the term *frame* to describe sets of questions that are expected to be answered in a specific piece of reading (Anderson & Armbruster, 1984). A frame provides a sense of structure, outlines boundaries, and delineates shape. Eyeglass frames, picture frames, and window frames all serve to hold things together in a certain functional shape or form. Authors use frames to provide a sense of coherence to writing. By considering what questions their writing needs to answer, authors provide themselves with a "text frame" to guide in selecting and organizing the most appropriate information to include in the text.

Jones, Palincsar, Ogle, and Carr (1987) highlight six text frames typically used by authors to organize information: compare/contrast, concept/definition, cause/effect, problem/solution, proposition/support,

and goal/action/outcome. Each text frame signals to a reader the most effective way to approach the reading of a specific piece of material. A U.S. history passage about the Great Depression might be read most successfully using a problem/solution frame. A section in a chemistry textbook might follow a cause/effect frame. A newspaper editorial read during language arts instruction might follow a proposition/support frame. A geometry chapter about characteristics of different triangles may require a compare/contrast frame. Figure 2.1 highlights the questions implied in each text frame, which guides reading and organizing of text so it makes sense.

When we read a mystery we shift to a problem/solution frame, which prompts us to search for clues, suspects, motives, and alibis. When we pick up the sports section from the daily newspaper, we shift to a cause/effect frame, which prompts questions about the latest athletic events: Who won the game? What events were significant in leading to the win? Were there any notable individual performances? How did the game effect team standings? Was the outcome effected by any special occurrences such as errors, injuries, or coaching decisions? Will the game influence future games?

Students have developed the know-how to successfully read mystery stories and sports pages. Their experiences first learning and later reading these genres, as well as their years of watching television mysteries and sports events, have prepared them to generate the same questions as other readers so. But what kind of writing do students encounter in textbooks? What frame of mind should they assume when reading a biology passage about microorganisms? Or a health section about smoking? Or a social studies chapter about the Roman Empire? What are the significant questions implied in each of these different texts? What text frames are represented in social studies, science, math, and other content materials?

Metaphors for Text Frames

Thinking within a text frame during reading helps students become more directive and purposeful in their learning. A text frame establishes students' frame of mind toward an assignment (see Figure 2.2, page 13).

FIGURE 2.1
Determining Text Frames—What Is the Point of the Material?

1. That a problem needs solving? (Problem/Solution Frame)

- What is the problem?
- Who has the problem?
- What is causing the problem?
- What are the effects of the problem?
- Who is trying to solve the problem?
- What solutions are recommended or attempted?
- What results from these solutions?
- Is the problem solved? Do any new problems develop because of the solutions?

2. That certain things result from certain conditions? (Cause/Effect Frame)

- What is it that happens?
- What causes it to happen?
- What are the important elements or factors that cause this effect?
- How do these factors or elements interrelate?
- Will this result always happen from these causes? Why or why not?
- How would the result change if the elements or factors are different?

3. That certain things are similar or different? (Compare/Contrast Frame)

- What is being compared and contrasted?
- What categories of characteristics or attributes are used to compare and contrast these things?
- How are the things alike or similar?
- How are the things not alike or different?
- What are the most important qualities or attributes that make them similar?
- What are the most important qualities or attributes that make them different?
- In terms of the qualities that are most important, are these things more alike or more different?
- What can we conclude about these things?

4. That someone is trying to do something for a specific reason? (Goal/Action/Outcome Frame)

- What is the goal? What is to be accomplished?
- Who is trying to achieve this goal?
- What actions/steps are taken to achieve this goal?
- Is the sequence of actions/steps important for achieving this goal?
- What are the effects of these actions? What happens?
- Were these actions successful for achieving the goal?
- Are there unexpected outcomes from these actions?
- Would other actions have been more effective? Could something else have been done?

5. That a concept needs to be understood? (Concept/Definition Frame)

- What is the concept?
- To what category does it belong?
- What are its critical characteristics or attributes?
- How does it work?
- What does it do?
- What are its functions?
- What are examples of it?
- What are examples of things that share some but not all of its characteristics?

6. That a viewpoint is being argued and supported? (Proposition/Support Frame)

- What is the general topic area or issue?
- What proposition (viewpoint, theory, hypothesis, thesis) is being presented?
- How is this proposition supported?
- Are examples provided? Do the examples support the proposition?
- Are data provided? Does the data support the proposition?
- Is expert verification provided? Does it support the proposition?
- Is a logical argument provided? Does it support the proposition?
- Is a sufficient case presented to warrant acceptance of the proposition?

For example, while reading a mystery with a problem/solution text frame, students are apt to think like a detective or assume the attitude of a troubleshooter—someone who determines what is wrong, why it is wrong, and how it can be fixed. A cause/effect text frame invites students to think like a scientist, asking what happens and why it happens. Students reading concept/definition material might imagine themselves as a news reporter, asking who, what, where, when, and how questions. Students reading compare/contrast material might adopt a shopper's frame of mind, weighing how products are alike and different. Students might best approach a proposition/support text frame like a judge, who analyzes arguments and evaluates the strength of corroborating evidence. And with a goal/action/outcome text frame, students may assume a coach's perspective, identifying the actions players need to take to meet team goals and evaluating these actions in terms of their results.

Figure 2.3 provides a framework for identifying text frames in classroom materials. For example, sci-

FIGURE 2.2
Metaphors for Text Frames

Text Frame	Frame of Mind
Problem/Solution	Troubleshooter
Cause/Effect	Scientist
Compare/Contrast	Shopper
Proposition/Support	Judge
Concept/Definition	News Reporter
Goal/Action/Outcome	Coach

FIGURE 2.3
Framework for Identifying Text Frames

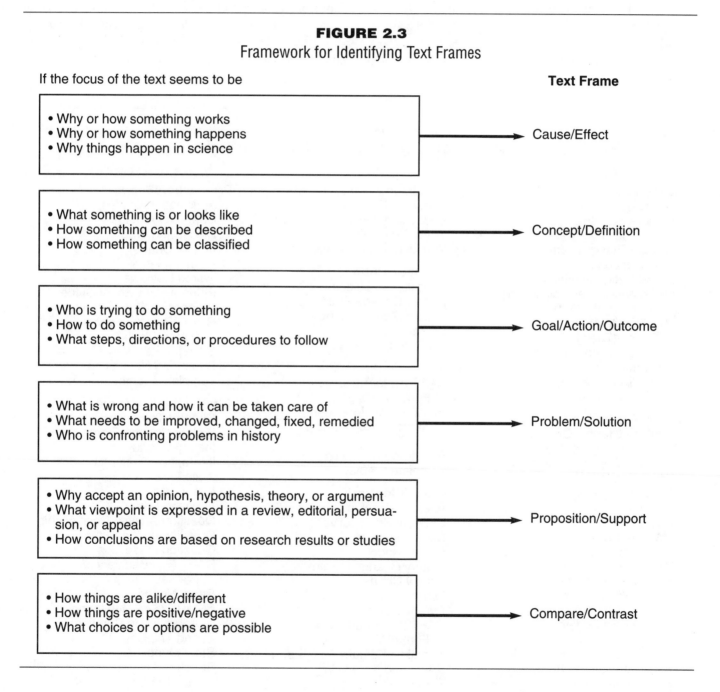

If the focus of the text seems to be | Text Frame

- Why or how something works
- Why or how something happens
- Why things happen in science

→ Cause/Effect

- What something is or looks like
- How something can be described
- How something can be classified

→ Concept/Definition

- Who is trying to do something
- How to do something
- What steps, directions, or procedures to follow

→ Goal/Action/Outcome

- What is wrong and how it can be taken care of
- What needs to be improved, changed, fixed, remedied
- Who is confronting problems in history

→ Problem/Solution

- Why accept an opinion, hypothesis, theory, or argument
- What viewpoint is expressed in a review, editorial, persuasion, or appeal
- How conclusions are based on research results or studies

→ Proposition/Support

- How things are alike/different
- How things are positive/negative
- What choices or options are possible

→ Compare/Contrast

ence texts frequently emphasize cause/effect relationships; students focus on how certain scientific phenomena lead to specific results, whether a chemical reaction, a law of physics, or a principle in earth science. Problem/solution relationships predominate in history texts, which tend to focus on the stories about people who are confronted with problems and changes. Material that outlines a chronology, such as the story of a family immigrating to a new country, or a sequence of steps, such as the directions for operating woodworking equipment, a protocol for setting up a Web page, or a recipe for baking a spice cake, involve goal/action/outcome thinking. An article that presents a series of choices or options requires a compare/contrast frame of mind. A political speech, movie review, or a research article involves proposition/support thinking, by providing conclusions predicated on the author's basis for justification. Finally, highly descriptive texts, such as in biology, mandate a concept/definition frame of mind for reading.

Strategies That Frame Instruction

A text frame organizes the most important arguments or information in a piece of writing so that the reader gets the point and can make sense of the material. So how can we encourage students to read with an active frame of mind when they tackle textbooks and other print material we use in our classrooms? The answer lies in the classroom strategies we use when involving students in reading assignments. We can employ strategies that tip off students to the appropriate frame for reading (see Figure 2.4).

FIGURE 2.4
Text Frames and Corresponding Teaching Strategies

Cause/Effect
Anticipation Guides
Elaborative Interrogations
Follow the Characters
History Change Frame
Learning Logs
Problematic Situations
Question-Answer Relationships
Questioning the Author
RAFT (Role/Audience/
    Format/Topic)
Science Connection Overview
Story Impressions
Structured Notetaking
Template Frames

Concept/Definition
Analogy Graphic Organizer
Brainstorming Prior Knowledge
Concept/Definition Mapping
Frayer Model
Guided Imagery
Learning Logs
Magnet Summaries
Math Reading Keys
Mind Mapping
Paired Reviews
Possible Sentences
Power Notes
Pyramid Diagram
RAFT (Role/Audience/
    Format/Topic)
Science Connection Overview
Semantic Feature Analysis
Story Impressions

Structured Notetaking
Template Frames
Vocabulary Overview Guide
Word Family Trees
You Ought to Be in Pictures

Problem/Solution
Anticipation Guides
History Change Frame
History Memory Bubbles
Learning Logs
Math Reading Keys

Problematic Situations
RAFT (Role/Audience/
    Format/Topic)
SMART (Self-Monitoring
    Approach to Reading
    and Thinking)
Structured Notetaking
Template Frames

Compare/Contrast
Analogy Graphic Organizer
Different Perspectives
Discussion Web
Frayer Model
History Change Frame
Inquiry Charts
Learning Logs
Pyramid Diagram
RAFT (Role/Audience/
    Format/Topic)
Semantic Feature Analysis
Structured Notetaking
Template Frames

Proposition/Support
Anticipation Guides
Character Quotes
Discussion Web
Inquiry Charts
Learning Logs
Paired Reviews
Point-of-View Study Guide
Proposition/Support Outline
RAFT (Role/Audience/
    Format/Topic)
Save the Last Word for Me
Structured Notetaking
Template Frames

Goal/Action/Outcome
Chapter Tours
History Change Frame
Inquiry Charts
Interactive Reading Guides
Jigsaw
K-W-L Plus
Learning Logs
Question-Answer Relationships
Questioning the Author
Question Dissection
RAFT (Role/Audience/
    Format/Topic)
Read-Alouds
SMART (Self-Monitoring
    Approach to Reading
    and Thinking)
Story Mapping
Structured Notetaking
Template Frames

For example, if students are to read a passage about snowshoe hares, first determine which text frame will best structure their thinking. If the passage emphasizes environmental hardships that the snowshoe hare encounters, work your strategy around problem/solution questions. If the passage describes similarities and differences between the hare and various types of rabbits, structure the assignment around compare/contrast questions. If the passage discusses the reasons why hares are returning to some regions, work within a cause/effect frame. If the passage presents a theory as to why the hares have survived but other species have not, stress proposition/support relationships. If the article focuses on the Sierra Club's efforts to save the hare, then structure a goal/action/outcome assignment. If the passage is a general informational segment about snowshoe hares, then concept/definition questions should predominate.

The classroom strategies presented in this book can be used effectively to signal text frames to students and to provide the support they need in order to read in the right frame of mind. In addition, strategies that direct student thinking toward a specific text frame can help them overcome text that is poorly written, confusing, or challenging. Struggling readers, in particular, benefit from strategies that provide them with an organized way of thinking about information that otherwise may be overwhelming.

References and Suggested Reading

Anderson, T., & Armbruster, B. (1984). Studying. In P.D. Pearson (Ed.), *Handbook of reading research*. New York: Longman.

Buehl, D. (1991). Frames of mind. *The Exchange. Newsletter of the IRA secondary reading interest group, 4*(2), 4–5.

Jones, B., Palincsar, A., Ogle, D., & Carr, E. (1987). *Strategic teaching and learning: Cognitive instruction in the content areas*. Alexandria, VA: Association for Supervision and Curriculum Development.

CHAPTER 3

Setting Priorities With Fact Pyramids

"If you remember only one thing about this, it ought to be...." For many students, the remembering of a single thing about a unit, a chapter, or a lesson would be a tall order. Unfortunately, they seem to conceptualize learning in school as a short-term process. Students steel themselves each day for a steady barrage of information, and they cope by trying to remember it only long enough to pass a test. Then it is on to the next material. Teachers find it discouraging that so many students seem to retain little of what they supposedly "learned" in school.

Of course, we also realize that losing some of what is learned is a natural phenomenon. Each of us can think of personal instances of selective forgetting. We all have experienced moments when we have to admit to a student (or a son or daughter) that we cannot recall enough information to help him or her with the homework for another teacher's class. Ideally, we have retained the central concepts of the material, but like most people, we have forgotten the specific details.

The Forest and Acres and Acres of Trees

One reason students seem so readily disposed to quickly forget much of the information they encounter in school is due to the nature of the material itself. We want students to be able to differentiate and prioritize as they process material. We want them continually making determinations as to what is most important and worthy of knowing over time. But often textbooks make selective processing a demanding task for students. In a critical analysis, Kennedy (1991) faults textbooks for burying "big ideas"—those most worthy of being remembered—underneath a tremendous array of what she terms "factlets." Textbooks are often poorly organized and do not cue students satisfactorily as to how to maneuver through all the factual information so that they can make sense of the material. Textbooks tend to be written to expose students to information rather than to help them truly understand it.

Figure 3.1 is a visual representation of the challenge facing students when they attempt to learn from textbooks. Many students become mired in the "factlets" as they read, their minds perhaps ticking them off one by one:

Here's a fact. Here's another fact. Here's a capital letter fact (it's in bold print!). Here's another fact. Another capital letter fact.

And so on through the remainder of a passage. But what do all these facts mean? At the end of a passage students may have accumulated a mass of disorganized information for which they have little use.

Understanding occurs when students are able to connect facts, to organize information into a coherent message in order to make sense of it. In Chapter 2, the term *text frame* refers to the mental frameworks used for meaningfully organizing information. When students are able to perceive how the information fits together, that the point of a passage is a cause/effect relationship, for example, which binds together all those facts, they are able to think about the implications of what they are reading. They can draw conclusions, make generalizations, and develop broad conceptual understandings of important content.

School for many students is construed as an overwhelming onslaught of factual information that is never sorted into anything useful or worth remembering. The old adage that they "can't see the forest for the trees" becomes a daily occurrence for students immersed in the factual detail of their textbooks. As a consequence, activities that help students see the point of new material are especially important. Questions that guide students toward sorting through factual information and making meaningful connections will more likely lead to the kind of long-term associations that make learning memorable.

Unfortunately, this primary means of guiding students through new information—asking them to respond to questions—often does not help students with their learning. Klein (1988) summarizes the research on classroom questioning and reports that few questions are actually designed to assist students as they learn. Most questions merely assess what students have learned. Klein observes that most questions are asked after rather than during reading, and that questions predominately target a literal level of understanding. Furthermore, most questions could be answered with a rote, paraphrase level of processing and often with only a single word or short phrase. Finally, most questions, especially those that appear in

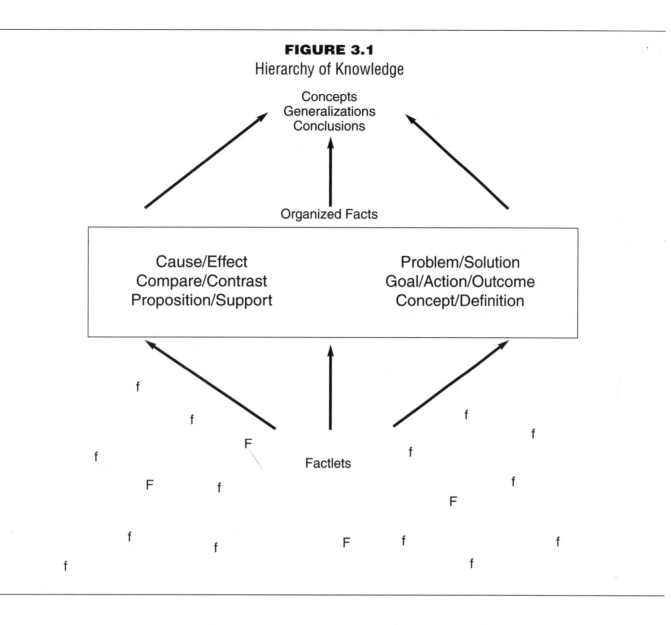

FIGURE 3.1

Hierarchy of Knowledge

Concepts
Generalizations
Conclusions

Organized Facts

Cause/Effect
Compare/Contrast
Proposition/Support

Problem/Solution
Goal/Action/Outcome
Concept/Definition

Factlets

textbooks, have no clear and coherent focus. In contrast to a natural set of questions that ask students to think about information in terms of specific text frames, many textbook questions seem to be random, making it unlikely that readers will recognize central relationships in the material. Students resignedly assume that anything that appears on a page of text is fair game for a question, whether it is truly important or not.

World Brains and School Brains

Many students operate in school as if they possessed not one, but two brains. These two brains do not correspond with the familiar right-hemisphere/left-hemisphere dichotomy. Instead, imagine the mind split into a *world brain* and a *school brain*. The *world*

brain can be visualized as taking up most of the room in the student's skull. In it are stored all of what the student knows and understands about the world, all of life's experiences and personal explanations of *what is, why,* and *how.* The student relies on this world brain to make sense of the world (see Chapter 1 for further discussion of students' background knowledge).

Now imagine the *school brain,* located in an out-of-the-way corner of the mind and occupying only a small cavity. Think of the school brain as carefully insulated from the world brain—very little that enters it ever gets transferred into the brain that makes sense of things. The school brain has a minuscule storage capacity, but that is quite all right—information does not need to stay there very long. The most distinctive feature of the school brain is an ever-open chute, ready to dump yesterday's lesson quickly and irrevocably into oblivion. Students use the school brain for short-term storage of the daily stuff of school; as soon as the test is over or a new chapter started, they flush out the backlog of old facts and stray information and ready themselves for another cycle of short-term learning.

Certainly some of our students are very adept at perceiving the connections between what they already know and what they are learning in the classroom. They are able to integrate new information successfully into their existing mental structures, and they find that new information does indeed help them to make more sense of their world. But for many students, school has little to do with the real world, and their failure to make connections virtually ensures that much of what they learn in school will be lost—relegated to the dead-end depot of the school brain.

Prioritizing Factual Information

How can student activities be structured so that real learning takes place, so that a true conceptual change occurs in the mind, so that important information is retained over time and not merely long enough to pass tests? Classroom strategies that guide students into making connections between their background knowledge (world brain) and what they are studying in class (school brain) will increase the probability that the new information will find a place in long-term memory.

Imagine the following scenario: Five years from now as you stroll down the street, you chance upon a student you are teaching now. What does this person still remember from your class? You realize that much of the specific information the student had encountered will be forgotten. But what learning has he retained (lest you be bitterly disappointed)? What should this former student remember about the New Deal, or cell division, or congruent triangles, or *Animal Farm*? Did this former student get the point from these various units of instruction?

It is unlikely that you would be crestfallen if your former student could not recite the provisions of the National Industrial Recovery Act or identify former Vice President Henry Wallace. But the New Deal, as an extensive governmental reaction to the Great Depression that engendered a variety of support programs for U.S. citizens, should have significant associations for this individual. Likewise, you probably would not expect your former student to name the various stages of mitosis or recall specific theorems. You would, however, expect a basic understanding of cell division and the basic principles of triangles. You would accept that your student has forgotten most of the characters and plot details of *Animal Farm*, but you would hope that George Orwell's basic premises of the oppressed becoming the oppressors and the corruption of power would be remembered.

Essentially, you would concede that much factual information is forgotten over time, but that other, more transcendent information must be remembered if one is to be regarded as a literate individual. Fact Pyramids (Buehl, 1991) provide teachers with a structured way of analyzing information so that our teaching guides students' focus toward big ideas—those few facts and concepts that we truly want them to remember over time. Fact Pyramids graphically categorize text information into three levels: (1) essential knowledge, (2) short-term facts, and (3) supportive detail (see Figure 3.2).

Essential knowledge is those concepts or ideas that one would expect a literate person to remember over time: If you remember only one thing about a lesson or unit, this is it. Essential knowledge is still with us years later. It represents the "point" of the lesson, which resides in the point of the fact pyramid.

Short-term facts comprise the necessary information that allows concepts to be learned with some level of sophistication but will generally be forgotten over time. These facts make up much of the language of class discussion and instruction, the key vocabulary and major details, but ultimately they are not important as ends in themselves. Students use short-term facts to construct a deeper understanding of a concept or idea. Short-terms facts allow us to make generalizations and draw conclusions that become memorable, but this baseline of information gradually drifts away.

Supportive detail represents the more specific information that provides the depth to flesh out an understanding but that does not need to be learned for its own sake. Certainly a rich text supplies the reader with more than headlines and boldface vocabulary. Supportive detail comprises the "semantic glue" for a text, the elaborations and examples that help to illuminate understanding. Supportive detail can be an asset in textbooks, but such information should not be emphasized as "factlets" that draw students' attention away from central ideas.

Integrating Fact Pyramids Into Teaching

Using the concept of Fact Pyramids can help teachers make decisions about which classroom strategies best differentiate among the levels of information delivered in a chapter. By categorizing information in terms of the three levels, teachers can identify shortcomings in a textbook's organization and questions. Are the elements of the text that you regard as essential readily apparent? Or will your students have to dig for them? Will students become overwhelmed by the fac-

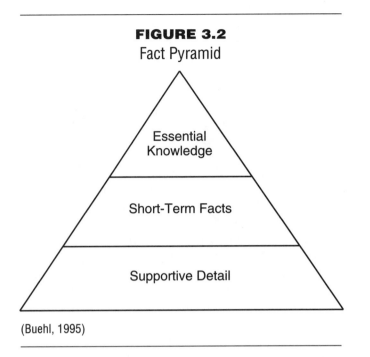

FIGURE 3.2

Fact Pyramid

Essential
Knowledge

Short-Term Facts

Supportive Detail

(Buehl, 1995)

tual information and cope by completing answers to questions without realizing the point of the material? Will students be able to learn what is essential, or will they stumble lost through forests of factual information?

The questions for student learning provided in textbooks frequently divert attention away from essential concepts. Unfortunately, many textbook questions ask students to focus on supportive detail information. For example, the following question from a U.S. history textbook involves students in processing supportive detail to complete an assignment:

> Identify the following: (a) Benjamin Wade, (b) Henry Davis, (c) John Wilkes Booth, (d) Thaddeus Stevens, and (e) Charles Sumner.

Such a question sends a faulty message to students. First, they are led to believe that all historical figures mentioned in a text are equally important. John Wilkes Booth, the assassin of Abraham Lincoln, is an important historical figure, but most literate adults would have scant idea of the importance of the others. Students are given no direction in evaluating which information is most deserving of emphasis. Second, students know they will forget the facts about these people within a short period of time, so they begin to regard all information they encounter in history as equally forgettable. A Fact Pyramid would help clarify important text information for students to write about and remember.

Fact Pyramid for History

A history teacher might construct a fact pyramid to identify essential knowledge about the post–Civil War period (see Figure 3.3). The teacher might decide that primary focus for activities in this unit—what literate people should remember over time—should center on three concepts:

> Reconstruction was a federal government action to monitor bringing the southern states back into the union,
>
> black codes were passed to deny the newly freed slaves their rights, and
>
> disagreements over Reconstruction led to the impeachment of a president.

Short-term facts for this unit might include the major players in this controversy, President Andrew Johnson and the Radical Republicans. The major provisions of the Reconstruction Act of 1867 will probably become hazy for most students over time, but a sense that the federal government, through use of troops, controlled the southern states, will perhaps remain. Although many students will forget which amendment did what, most should realize that Constitutional amendments abolished slavery and guaranteed "due process."

Specific information about people such as Benjamin Wade or Charles Sumner, or pieces of legislation such as the Tenure of Office Act, represent

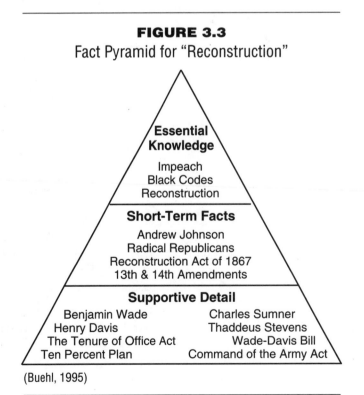

FIGURE 3.3

Fact Pyramid for "Reconstruction"

Essential Knowledge
Impeach
Black Codes
Reconstruction

Short-Term Facts
Andrew Johnson
Radical Republicans
Reconstruction Act of 1867
13th & 14th Amendments

Supportive Detail
Benjamin Wade   Charles Sumner
Henry Davis   Thaddeus Stevens
The Tenure of Office Act   Wade-Davis Bill
Ten Percent Plan   Command of the Army Act

(Buehl, 1995)

supportive detail useful only to broaden and enrich the understanding of this unit's major ideas. Few adults would be able to successfully identify most of this information. Direct questions on supportive detail information should thus be avoided.

Fact Pyramid for Health

A Fact Pyramid created for a health textbook chapter on nutrition is featured in Figure 3.4. The chapter contains a great deal of detailed information on the six nutrients found in food and is packed with biology terminology that would be difficult for most students. What would a health teacher expect a former student to remember about this material 5 years from now? Certainly not the fact that complex carbohydrates consist of long chains of glucose. Or the differences between fat-soluble and water-soluble vitamins. Specific facts about amino acids are also not likely to last over time.

Three priorities could emerge from this material. First, there is a connection between what you eat and how your body functions. Second, different nutrients supply different important ingredients to a healthy diet. Third, specific nutrients are found in a variety of different foods. Essential knowledge, then, could include the six nutrients—fats, proteins, carbohydrates, minerals, vitamins, and water—and the contribution of each to a healthy diet. *Calorie* is a frequently used concept, so students also need to have a meaningful understanding of that term.

The short-term facts include more specific information related to the nutrients, which play a role in the discussion of nutrition but do not need to be learned for their own sake. Most adults probably are murky on the particular distinctions between simple and complex carbohydrates, complete and incomplete proteins, and polyunsaturated and saturated fats.

Most of the health chapter is made up of supportive details, many of which are difficult to understand. Information related to terms such as *hemoglobin, pantothenic acid, enzyme activities*, and *thyroid gland* is too specific to warrant student attention. Most students would have insufficient background to adequately absorb such information. An emphasis on learning these details distracts students from the overall point of the material.

Fact Pyramids are constructed by teachers to spotlight what is important and worthy of being remembered over time. They allow teachers to adapt their textbooks and target questions to help students be selective and get the point (the "tip" of the pyramid).

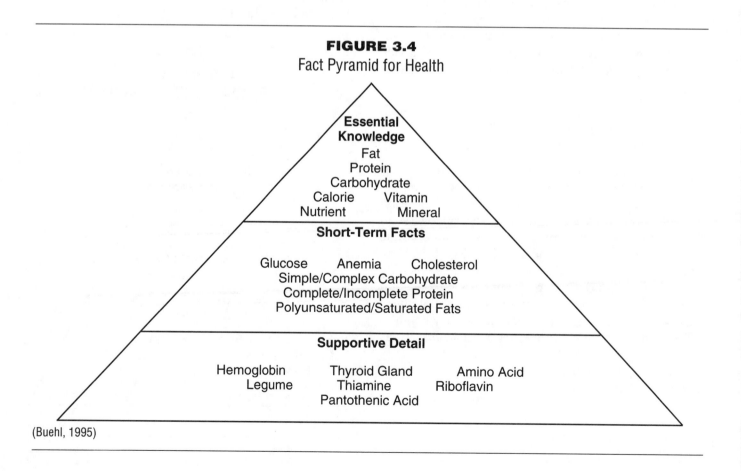

FIGURE 3.4
Fact Pyramid for Health

Essential
Knowledge
Fat
Protein
Carbohydrate
Calorie   Vitamin
Nutrient   Mineral

Short-Term Facts

Glucose   Anemia   Cholesterol
Simple/Complex Carbohydrate
Complete/Incomplete Protein
Polyunsaturated/Saturated Fats

Supportive Detail

Hemoglobin   Thyroid Gland   Amino Acid
Legume   Thiamine   Riboflavin
Pantothenic Acid

(Buehl, 1995)

Fact Pyramids lead to using classroom strategies that engage students in successfully handling material that contains a wealth of detail.

References

Buehl, D. (1991). Fact pyramids. *New perspectives: Reading across the curriculum, 7*(6), 1–2. Madison, WI: Madison Metropolitan School District.

Buehl, D. (1995). *Classroom strategies for interactive learning.* Madison, WI: Wisconsin State Reading Association.

Kennedy, M. (May, 1991). Policy issues in teacher education. *Phi Delta Kappan, 72*(9), 658–665.

Klein, M. (1988). *Teaching reading comprehension and vocabulary: A guide for teachers.* Englewood Cliffs, NJ: Prentice Hall.

Classroom Strategies for Teaching and Learning

Matching Strategies to Your Instruction

When is the best time to use the classroom teaching strategies described in this section? Each classroom strategy will feature a Strategy Index, which is found in the lower right corner of the page on which the strategy is introduced, to help identify the strengths of the strategy in terms of cognitive processes, text frames, and student activities.

Cognitive processes refer to the kinds of thinking in which students will be engaged during instruction. As discussed in Chapter 1, strategies that prepare students for learning activate background knowledge and focus attention on important concepts. Strategies that help students during reading involve selecting and organizing information. Strategies that help students to consolidate learning after reading include exercises that integrate new learning into their memories and apply new learning in useful contexts.

Text frames refer to the way thinking is organized during reading and learning activities. Chapter 2 outlined six basic text frames that condition a student's frame of mind during the lesson: cause/effect, concept/definition, problem/solution, compare/contrast, proposition/support, and goal/action/outcome. Text frames help students ask themselves the right questions about the material as they learn.

Student activities refer to the various ways a classroom strategy can involve students in learning. Chapter 1 detailed eight student activities that connect to instructional goals for students during their learning: developing vocabulary, brainstorming of ideas, learning cooperatively, promoting discussion, interactive reading, encouraging writing, representing information graphically, and building study skills.

Within each category of the Strategy Index, the cognitive processes, text frames, and student activities most emphasized by the strategy are highlighted. Notice that several strategies emphasize more than one cognitive process, text frame, or student activity. Use the Strategy Index in your instructional planning as a guide for identifying the particular strengths of each classroom strategy.

For example, the first classroom strategy in this section is the Analogy Graphic Organizer (page 26). In the Strategy Index under Cognitive Processes, all the cognitive processes are highlighted because the Analogy Graphic Organizer can be used with students before, during, and after reading. The two highlighted boxes under Text Frames, concept/definition and compare/contrast, indicate that the Analogy Graphic Organizer involves students in developing understanding of concepts and stimulates them to make compare and contrast decisions. Under Student Activities, four boxes are highlighted indicating that the Analogy Graphic Organizer is a strategy that helps students to develop vocabulary, brainstorm from background knowledge, promote discussion among themselves, and create graphic representations of information.

STRATEGY INDEX
Cognitive Processes
Activating/Focusing
Selecting/Organizing
Integrating/Applying
Text Frames
Cause/Effect
Concept/Definition
Problem/Solution
Compare/Contrast
Proposition/Support
Goal/Action/Outcome
Student Activities
Developing Vocabulary
Brainstorming of Ideas
Learning Cooperatively
Promoting Discussion
Interactive Reading
Encouraging Writing
Graphic Representation
Building Study Skills

Analogy Graphic Organizer

"You mean it's like...?" Their eyes light up. The concept you are teaching comes alive. An analogy that relates to your students' lives has helped them make a connection. Teachers know that analogies are a powerful way to help students understand new information or concepts. For example,

> Cells are the building blocks of your body like bricks are the building blocks of this school.

> The judicial branch of government is like umpires in baseball.

> Punctuation marks in a sentence are like traffic signs.

Analogies help students link new information to familiar concepts. The Analogy Graphic Organizer (Buehl & Hein, 1990) is a strategy that provides a visual framework for students to analyze key relationships in an analogy. The compare/contrast text frame serves to broaden their understanding of important concepts or vocabulary. An Analogy Graphic Organizer (see example) can be used with students to introduce a topic, to guide comprehension while reading, or to extend the learning after reading.

Using the Strategy

The Analogy Graphic Organizer uses analogy to help students perceive similarities and differences between a new concept and something familiar in their lives. Using this strategy involves the following steps:

1 Determine what students already know to establish an analogous relationship to the concept being introduced. Selecting a familiar concept can act as a bridge to the new concept. For example, students studying the colony concept in history class can relate it to a situation with which they are familiar—being a dependent child in a family.

2 Introduce the Analogy Graphic Organizer on an overhead transparency (see Appendix, page 152). Brainstorm with students specific characteristics or properties common to both concepts. Enter these in the Similarities column. Students might offer that a colony and a child in a family share the following characteristics: they are dependent on a parent figure for their needs, they must follow rules or laws set by others, they are related or connected to the parent fig-

ure, and they have feelings of resentment and a desire to be independent.

3 Ask students how the two concepts are different and enter these in the Differences column. Initially, Steps 2 and 3 need to be modeled by the teacher, but after students develop more independence, have them complete individual copies of a blank Analogy Graphic Organizer in cooperative groups. Students may note the following: (a) that a colony usually is separated geographically from the parent figure, while a child usually lives with the parent figure in a family group; (b) that a colony is regarded as a negative system, while families are not; and (c) that a colony's independence is often associated with violence, which is not characteristic of children coming of age in most families.

4 Discuss with students further categories that make up the basis for the comparison. For example, some Similarities (both rely on the parent for protection and other basic needs, and both are at an early stage of development) might be labeled as *Dependence on Others*, while other Similarities might be labeled as *Kinship or Family Background*, and *Control/Self-Determination*.

5 Have students write a summary about the similarities of the new concept and the familiar concept using the Analogy Graphic Organizer. Students may write about how children and colonies often depend a great deal on the parent, how they eventually grow up or mature and want to assume control over themselves, how they may feel exploited, or how resentments lead to arguments or violence in the process of gaining independence.

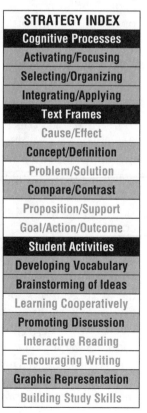

STRATEGY INDEX
Cognitive Processes
Activating/Focusing
Selecting/Organizing
Integrating/Applying
Text Frames
Cause/Effect
Concept/Definition
Problem/Solution
Compare/Contrast
Proposition/Support
Goal/Action/Outcome
Student Activities
Developing Vocabulary
Brainstorming of Ideas
Learning Cooperatively
Promoting Discussion
Interactive Reading
Encouraging Writing
Graphic Representation
Building Study Skills

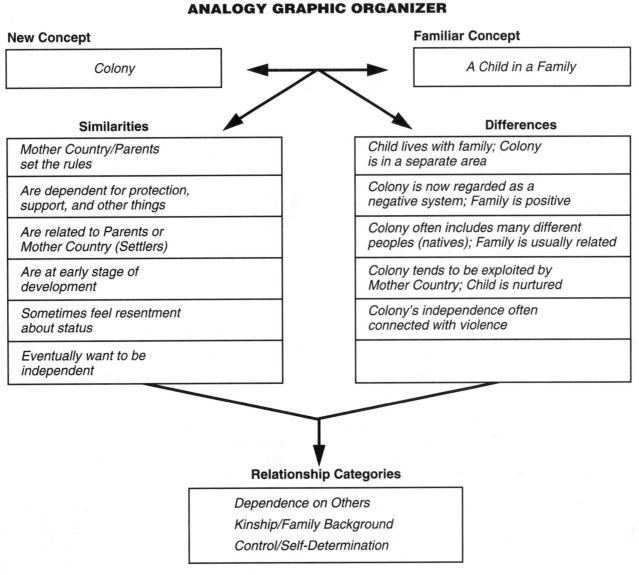

ANALOGY GRAPHIC ORGANIZER

New Concept

| Colony |

Familiar Concept

| A Child in a Family |

Similarities

| Mother Country/Parents set the rules |
| Are dependent for protection, support, and other things |
| Are related to Parents or Mother Country (Settlers) |
| Are at early stage of development |
| Sometimes feel resentment about status |
| Eventually want to be independent |

Differences

| Child lives with family; Colony is in a separate area |
| Colony is now regarded as a negative system; Family is positive |
| Colony often includes many different peoples (natives); Family is usually related |
| Colony tends to be exploited by Mother Country; Child is nurtured |
| Colony's independence often connected with violence |

Relationship Categories

| Dependence on Others
Kinship/Family Background
Control/Self-Determination |

(Buehl, 1995; adapted from Buehl & Hein, 1990)

Advantages

- Students enhance their understanding of new concepts or vocabulary through the analysis of familiar analogous concepts.

- Students make connections to new material by activating related experiences and background.

- Students gain practice in writing well-organized summaries that follow a compare/contrast text frame.

This strategy can be adapted for use with elementary through secondary level students, and is appropriate for all content areas.

References and Suggested Reading

Bean, T., Singer, H., & Cowan, S. (1985). Analogical study guides: Improving comprehension in science. *Journal of Reading, 29*, 246–250.

Buehl, D. (1995). *Classroom strategies for interactive learning.* Schofield, WI: Wisconsin State Reading Association.

Buehl, D., & Hein, D. (1990). Analogy graphic organizer. *The Exchange. Newsletter of the International Reading Association Secondary Reading Special Interest Group, 3*(2), 6.

Cook, D. (Ed.). (1989). *Strategic learning in the content areas.* Madison, WI: Department of Public Instruction.

Anticipation Guides

Suppose you are going out for dinner at a gourmet restaurant. As you anticipate the meal, which of the following statements reflect your expectations?

> Gourmet meals are very expensive.
>
> Gourmet meals feature foods that are difficult to prepare at home.
>
> Gourmet dining is a relaxed and very pleasurable experience.
>
> Gourmet meals feature small portions.
>
> Gourmet foods are delicious but fattening.

After dinner as you drive home from the restaurant, you will probably think about whether your experience was consistent with your expectations.

The Anticipation Guide (Herber, 1978) is a strategy that forecasts the major ideas contained in a passage through the use of statements that activate students' thoughts and opinions. Before reading a selection, students respond to several statements that challenge or support their preconceived ideas about key concepts in the passage. Students then explain or elaborate on their responses in small-group or class discussion. This process arouses interest, sets purposes for reading, and encourages higher level thinking—all important aspects of prereading motivation. The Anticipation Guide can then be used when students have completed their reading in order to evaluate how well the material has been understood and to ensure that misconceptions have been corrected.

Using the Strategy

Anticipation Guides can be used in almost any learning situation in any content area and is effective with nonprint media as well as with written materials. Using this strategy involves the following steps:

1 Identify the major ideas and concepts in the text that the students will be reading. For example, students studying acid rain in science class should focus attention on the following ideas as they read:

- Acid rain has a harmful effect on aquatic life.
- Acid rain destroys bridges, buildings, and statues.
- Acid rain has multiple causes including auto and factory emissions.

- Acid rain prevention involves economic trade-offs.
- Acid rain problems are increasing in certain regions of the United States.

2 Consider students' experiences and beliefs, which will be either supported or challenged by the reading. Determine what students already know about the topic, which will ensure that they are able to respond to an Anticipation Guide about the reading. Otherwise, they may adopt an "I don't know" posture as they go through the statements on the guide. Most students will have heard of acid rain and its negative effect on our lakes. Some may have opinions about its impact in different parts of the world, including their own region. Some students will know that acid rain is connected to the burning of fossil fuels, and that the control of fossil fuel consumption is controversial.

3 Create an Anticipation Guide with three to six statements that challenge or modify students' preexisting understandings of the material. Include statements that will elicit agreement between students and the information in the text. The most effective statements are those about which students have some knowledge but do not necessarily have a complete understanding. If possible, include a statement that taps into possible misconceptions about the topic (see Anticipation Guide for Science). To prepare students in a literature class for the major themes of the novel *The Call of the Wild*, create an Anticipation Guide that elicits student opinions on ideas explored by the author (see Anticipation Guide for Literature).

4 Present the Anticipation Guide on a chalkboard, an overhead projector, or as individual student handouts.

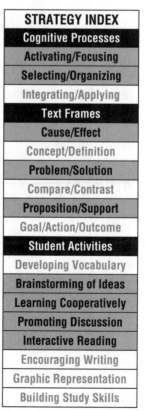

STRATEGY INDEX
Cognitive Processes
Activating/Focusing
Selecting/Organizing
Integrating/Applying
Text Frames
Cause/Effect
Concept/Definition
Problem/Solution
Compare/Contrast
Proposition/Support
Goal/Action/Outcome
Student Activities
Developing Vocabulary
Brainstorming of Ideas
Learning Cooperatively
Promoting Discussion
Interactive Reading
Encouraging Writing
Graphic Representation
Building Study Skills

ANTICIPATION GUIDE FOR SCIENCE
Acid Rain

Directions:

- Read the following statements concerning problems associated with acid rain.

- Put a check next to each statement with which you agree.

- Be prepared to support your views about each statement by thinking about what you know about acid rain and its effects. You will be sharing this information with other members of your group when you discuss the following six statements:

_____ 1. Acid rain kills fish.

_____ 2. The major cause of acid rain is fuel emissions from automobiles.

_____ 3. Stopping acid rain will cause some people to lose their jobs.

_____ 4. Acid rain problems are not yet serious in our region of the United States.

_____ 5. Acid rain is made up of sulfur oxides.

_____ 6. If acid rain is not controlled, we will experience a major environmental disaster.

(Buehl, 1995)

ANTICIPATION GUIDE FOR LITERATURE
Call of the Wild

Directions:

- Read the following statements about the book *Call of the Wild*.

- Compare your opinions about these statements with those of the author, Jack London.

- Check the column labeled *You* for those statements with which you agree. Be prepared to support your opinions with examples.

- Check the column labeled *Jack London* for those statements with which you feel he would agree.

You	Jack London	
_____	_____	1. Only the strong survive in this world.
_____	_____	2. People must live in harmony with their environment.
_____	_____	3. Greed makes people cruel.
_____	_____	4. The primitive instinct exists in all people.
_____	_____	5. Much of what happens to people is the result of fate.
_____	_____	6. People will adapt to their surroundings and survive.

(Developed by Sarah Conroy, 1993, Madison East High School, Madison, WI, USA.)

Leave space on the left for individual or small-group response. As each statement is discussed, have students provide justification for their opinions. First, you may wish to have students complete the guide individually and then defend their responses in small-group or class discussions. Another variation is to have students rank statements, starting with 1 for the statement that they agree with most and so forth, until the highest number is given to the statement with which they agree least.

5 Have students read the selection. Ask them to focus on the information in the reading that confirms, elaborates, or rejects each of the statements in the Anticipation Guide. If students are reading material that can be marked, instruct them to underline or highlight sections that are germane to each statement as they read. Or they can affix sticky notes to textbook pages, alongside information that supports or rebuts each statement.

6 After students complete the reading, have them return to the statements in the Anticipation Guide to determine whether they have changed their minds regarding any of them. In cooperative groups, have them locate the information from the text that supports or rejects each statement. Students then rewrite any statement that needs to be altered based on the selection they have read.

Another option is to include two columns in the Anticipation Guide for responses—one for students and one for the author. After reading the passage, students then compare their opinions on each statement with those of the author. This is especially effective when responding to ideas presented in literature (see Anticipation Guide for Literature). In this case, students determine the extent to which they accept Jack London's basic premises on human nature as he illustrates them in his novel.

Advantages

- Students are cued into the major ideas of a selection before they start reading.
- Students activate their background knowledge about a topic before they read, which they can share with classmates.
- Students are motivated to read in order to determine whether the text will confirm their opinions and ideas and disprove those of their classmates.
- Student misconceptions about a topic are addressed openly and are more likely to be changed after reading and discussing the new material.

This strategy can be modified and used successfully with elementary through high school level students.

References and Suggested Reading

Buehl, D. (1995). *Classroom strategies for interactive learning.* Madison, WI: Wisconsin State Reading Association.

Herber, H. (1978). *Teaching reading in content areas* (2nd ed.). Englewood Cliffs, NJ: Prentice-Hall.

Readence, J., Bean, T., & Baldwin, R. (1989). *Content area reading: An integrated approach* (3rd ed.). Dubuque, IA: Kendall/Hunt.

Other Work Cited

London, J. (1995). *Call of the wild.* New York: Simon & Schuster.

Brainstorming Prior Knowledge

What do you know—about Antarctica? Earthworms? Ultraviolet light? Ernest Hemingway? Chances are, if you were going to read a passage about any of these topics you would spend a few moments collecting what you already knew before you begin. You would take stock of your prior knowledge.

Suppose as you paged through a magazine you found an article titled "Lasers: The Promise of a Space-Age Technology." What would you anticipate about this article? Laser weapons? Laser surgery? Computer printers and other laser tools? Laser disks? Spectacular light shows? The principles behind lasers as a beam of light?

Like any mature reader, you would predict the article's content by recalling pertinent information that might connect to new material in the article. Effective readers activate what they know before they start reading. Activities that guide students in identifying relevant prior knowledge are an excellent way to jump-start learning about a topic. The knowledge and experiences students bring to the classroom greatly determine their success in learning new material. Many researchers feel that a student's prior knowledge about material is the single most important variable in reading comprehension. How can teachers assess what students already know about a topic and help them access this useful knowledge? The key is to work with students before they read a passage so that what they know is revealed and connected to what they will be learning.

Using the Strategies

Brainstorming strategies provide a useful framework for eliciting students' prior knowledge before learning. Several classroom variations are available: LINK, List-Group-Label, and Sequential Roundtable Alphabet.

LINK

List, Inquire, Note, and Know (LINK) (Vaughan & Estes, 1986) is a brainstorming strategy that encourages student-directed discussion about their prior knowledge of a topic. Using this strategy involves the following steps:

1 Decide on a key word or concept related to the material that will trigger responses from your students. Write this "cue" on the chalkboard or overhead transparency. Allow 3 minutes for the students to list on paper their associations for the cue. For example, the cue term *solar system* might be appropriate for a sixth-grade class preparing to read a science selection related to this topic. Next, ask students for associations and write them around the cue term. Start with less active students to increase their involvement and ensure that all students contribute. Limit responses to one per student. When everyone has offered an association, allow students to respond with further ideas. During this stage, list student contributions without comment from either you or the students, including those offering the associations. Sixth graders, for example, will offer a rich assortment of associations for the cue term *solar system* (see LINK for Solar System, page 32).

2 Encourage students to inquire about the items listed on the chalkboard or overhead transparency. They may ask for clarification or elaboration of some items or ask for examples or definitions. They may challenge some items. However, all inquiries are directed to fellow students, not the teacher. Langer (1981) advocates that the teacher model this process by selecting responses and asking questions such as, What made you think of...? The purpose of the prompts is to condition students to converse with one another as they explore the topic.

3 During the inquiry process, students interact both to share and to extend their understandings of the cue word or concept. To help students assume this responsibility, establish some classroom ground rules. For

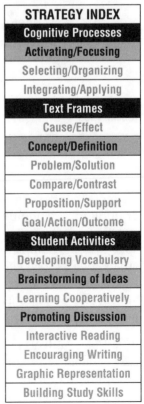

STRATEGY INDEX
Cognitive Processes
Activating/Focusing
Selecting/Organizing
Integrating/Applying
Text Frames
Cause/Effect
Concept/Definition
Problem/Solution
Compare/Contrast
Proposition/Support
Goal/Action/Outcome
Student Activities
Developing Vocabulary
Brainstorming of Ideas
Learning Cooperatively
Promoting Discussion
Interactive Reading
Encouraging Writing
Graphic Representation
Building Study Skills

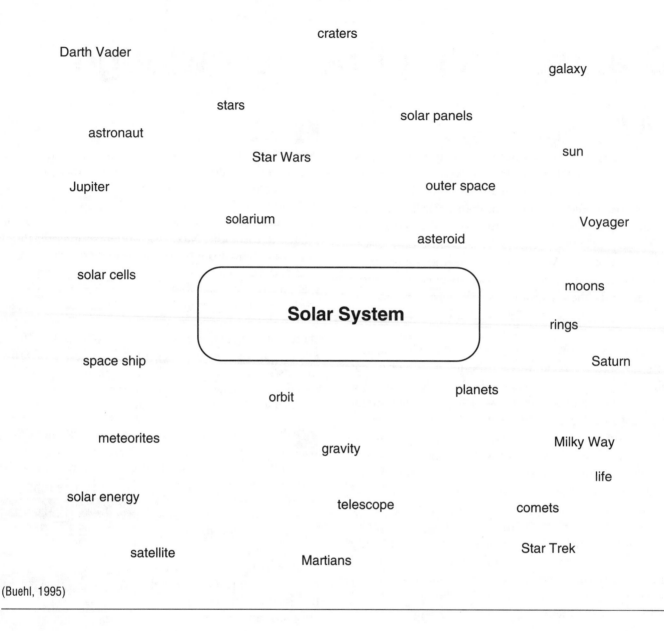

LINK FOR SOLAR SYSTEM

craters

Darth Vader

galaxy

stars

solar panels

astronaut

Star Wars

sun

Jupiter

outer space

solarium

Voyager

asteroid

solar cells

Solar System

moons

rings

space ship

Saturn

orbit

planets

meteorites

gravity

Milky Way

life

solar energy

telescope

comets

satellite

Star Trek

Martians

(Buehl, 1995)

example, remind students to be respectful of each other during their inquiries, taking care not to embarrass or belittle classmates as they examine the items. In the solar system example, students might question associations such as solar cells or solarium. The resulting discussion could establish a connection between the solar system (the sun and its orbiting bodies) and other important links with the sun (solar energy).

4 When students have completed their inquiries and comments about the items, erase the chalkboard or turn off the overhead. Instruct students to turn over their papers and note what they have learned about the

cue word. One variation is to have them write a definition for the concept. What they write can be based on both their prior experience and the class discussion during the inquiry. Students are now ready to read the passage. After reading, ask them to note what they know since encountering new material.

List-Group-Label

List-Group-Label (Taba, 1967) is a more involved brainstorming strategy that is effective for students who have an adequate baseline of information about a topic. Using this strategy involves the following steps:

1 Decide on an appropriate cue word and give students 3 minutes to write as many words as they can associated with the term. For example, ask students to jot down associations for *amphibian* before studying this topic. List the associations on a chalkboard or overhead transparency. Ask for a quick justification for how each word or expression relates to the topic. For example, a list might include frog, salamander, lives near water, toad, eats bugs, cold-blooded, ponds, aquarium, and slimy skin.

2 When you have a sufficient list, have students work in cooperative teams to group items by common characteristics. Provide teams with small slips of paper so they can record items and physically shift them into groups. Students should aim for at least three items per group, although there may be misfit items that do not correspond with the others.

3 The final stage of this brainstorming activity involves categorization. Have students examine their groupings and decide on an appropriate label, which can be written on a slip of paper and used as a title for each sublist. Each team shares its categories and explains the rationale for organizing the lists. Labels for amphibian could include *types*, *where they live*, and *characteristics*.

Sequential Roundtable Alphabet

The Sequential Roundtable Alphabet (Ricci & Wahlgren, 1998) is effective for students who have extensive background knowledge. The resulting chart serves as a prompt for remembering terms, facts, or events like the example shown here for a history class studying the 1960s. Using this strategy involves the following steps:

1 Give each student or cooperative group a blank copy of the Sequential Roundtable Alphabet chart (see Appendix, page 165).

2 Have students generate a related term or association that begins with each letter of the alphabet. Ask students to fill in as many boxes as possible within a designated time period.

3 Ask students or groups to share their terms with the entire class. In particular, students will want to hear if other groups came up with associations for difficult letters. In the 1960s example, some groups might have thought of "Malcolm X" for the *X* slot on the chart.

Advantages

- Students prepare for the study of new material and anticipate the content based on what they already know. Students are more motivated to

---

SEQUENTIAL ROUNDTABLE ALPHABET—1960s

A	B	C	D	E	F	G
Apollo	Beatles	Civil Rights	Drugs	Easy Rider	Flag Burning	
H	I	J	K	L	M	N
Hippies		Jimi Hendrix	Kennedy	Long Hair	Moon Walk	Nixon
O	P	Q	R	S	T	U
	Protests		Rock Music	Sexual Revolution		
V	W	X	Y	Z		
Vietnam	Woodstock			Mao Zedong		

(Adapted from Ricci & Wahlgren, 1998)

---

read material that is related to something they already know.

- Students with extensive background knowledge share so that all students begin the study with familiarity of the topic. Students with little background knowledge build their information base through class discussion before encountering the topic.

- Student misconceptions about the material are corrected during instruction.

- Students assume responsibility for raising questions, seeking clarifications, and engaging in discussion about the topic.

- Students review after learning. Lists can be revisited to add new information or to correct erroneous information.

References

Buehl, D. (1995). *Classroom strategies for interactive learning.* Madison, WI: Wisconsin State Reading Association.

Langer, J. (1981). From theory to practice: A prereading plan. *Journal of Reading, 25,* 152–156.

Ricci, G., & Wahlgren, C. (1998, May). *The key to know "PAINE" know gain.* Paper presented at the 43rd Annual Convention of the International Reading Association, Orlando, FL.

Taba, H. (1967). *Teacher's handbook for elementary social studies.* New York: Addison-Wesley.

Vaughan, J., & Estes, T. (1986). *Reading and reasoning beyond the primary grades.* Boston, MA: Allyn & Bacon.

Chapter Tours

Notice how this next painting exhibits several characteristics of Monet's later masterpieces. The subject (water lilies), the brush technique, and the use of color—all are associated with canvases completed by Monet in the 1920s....

Recall being escorted on a guided tour of an art gallery, a museum, a national park, or a historical site. A guided tour provides a knowledgeable introduction to what is being viewed, helps you focus on what is interesting or important, offers insights or experiences that enhance appreciation, and provides a framework for understanding. In contrast, unless you are already quite knowledgeable, you will probably miss significant elements of the experience if you wander about by yourself. This is also true of students struggling to make sense of textbook readings in their classes. Chapter Tours can provide them with enough direction and background so that they can successfully learn what is important in their reading.

Using the Strategy

Chapter Tours, a frontloading technique, guides or talks readers through a chapter and points out features of the text that warrant special attention. Using this strategy involves the following steps:

1 To underscore the importance of frontloading before reading, provide students with a selection that might appear obscure if they had not been alerted to the general topic. For example, display the following passage on an overhead transparency and provide students with enough time for a single reading.

> Your first decision is to choose the size you desire. Once you have made your selection, examine the general shape to determine where to start. The initial incision is always at the top, and you should continue until you can lift it cleanly. The removal of the interior portion can be fun, although some people regard this as the least enjoyable aspect. Once the shell is empty, you can begin to craft a personality. Some prefer a forbidding likeness, while others follow a more humorous direction. Finally, arrange for a source of illumination. Enjoy your results while you can, for your work will soon begin to sag.

2 Ask volunteers for hunches about the passage. As students offer their ideas, have them remember clues from the passage that triggered their theories. A variety of explanations about the selection may be offered and justified. Allow students to reread the passage with the prompt *Halloween*. Students will quickly recognize that the passage describes carving a pumpkin into a jack-o-lantern.

3 Discuss with students any frustrations they encountered when trying to read the passage without frontloading. Because students were not sure what part of their memory to access, they were not able to make sense of the text without the Halloween clue. Follow up with similar passages, each time encouraging students to search their memory banks for connections to apply to the material. Students will realize that reading will be much more efficient and successful if they frontload before tackling the text.

4 Preview a typical textbook chapter to identify salient features that students might overlook during their reading. Many textbooks present information in a variety of visual formats other than print, and offer numerous study aids that highlight important points in a chapter. Yet, unless attention is specifically called to these text features, students often skip them while reading to complete an assignment. As part of the preview process, take special notice of ways the chapter forecasts text structure—cause/effect, for example—and how it signals key concepts and ideas.

Create a Chapter Tour that guides students toward noticing these features as they use the book. For example, students reading a

STRATEGY INDEX
Cognitive Processes
Activating/Focusing
Selecting/Organizing
Integrating/Applying
Text Frames
Cause/Effect
Concept/Definition
Problem/Solution
Compare/Contrast
Proposition/Support
Goal/Action/Outcome
Student Activities
Developing Vocabulary
Brainstorming of Ideas
Learning Cooperatively
Promoting Discussion
Interactive Reading
Encouraging Writing
Graphic Representation
Building Study Skills

history textbook can easily become immersed in details and miss major themes or ideas. A Chapter Tour can help them focus on *changes* and *problems*, two concepts that predominate in history (see Chapter Tour for History).

5 Have students complete a Chapter Tour as an introduction to the textbook. An effective way of using a Chapter Tour is to allow the students to work with partners so they can verbalize what they are discovering about the way a specific textbook works. Develop variations of the Chapter Tour for subsequent chapters to remind students of critical elements in the text and to include additional aspects that you want brought to their attention.

6 Ask students to create their own Chapter Tours, which will show their understanding of key ideas.

CHAPTER TOUR FOR HISTORY

Facts! Facts! Facts! History textbooks are crammed with a never-ending series of facts: names, dates, places, and events. Chapter Tour will help students see beyond the facts—to identify important changes that people have experienced and problems they have confronted. Learning about changes in the past can help us better understand who we are and the changes we have to deal with today.

This tour of a chapter will help you discover the major ideas that are emphasized. A Chapter Tour avoids paying close attention to the details. Instead, ask, What's the point of all this? What are the important changes in the lives of these people?

Surveying a Chapter Before Reading

To find out what a chapter is about, take a survey first. The following will help determine what to look for while reading.

1. What is the title of Chapter 6 (Boyer & Stuckey, 1998)?
   Chapter 6 is organized into three sections. List those sections below.

2. Go to the first page of Chapter 6. Locate the time line in red at the bottom of the page. Note an important invention that happened during this time period and write it below.

3. Find a red triangle with the *focus*. Each chapter begins with a main idea focus statement that introduces major changes emphasized in the chapter. What changes occur in Chapter 6?
   Notice that major themes in history are listed under the focus statement. Read these and list one problem discussed in the chapter.

4. Locate the introductory paragraphs on the opposite page, which will feature a quote from a *primary source*, material that was written during the time period covered by the chapter. There are many primary source quotes throughout the textbook. Quickly skim the introduction, which will help to focus attention on what is included in the chapter. What person is quoted in this passage?

5. Look at the chapter section that begins on page 142, Industry's Golden Age. Each section begins with an *advance organizer*, questions that help to identify what to look for in each section. These focus questions are highlighted in bold print. Read the three focus questions on page 142.
   a. What group of people is the focus of this section?
   b. What problem does the government deal with in this section?

6. Quickly flip through the pages of the first section of Chapter 6. Notice that the material is divided into smaller topics, each identified by a heading. Write the three headings for this section. (Don't confuse headings [red] with subheadings [blue].)

7. Find the statement about "steel" in large blue print on page 143. These "essential points" summarize important ideas in the chapter. Locate the three other essential points in blue in this first section. List the page numbers for these statements.

8. Look over the pictures in this chapter. Look back at the changes you listed in question 3. How do these pictures relate to the changes you identified?

9. This chapter also contains a feature article, a separate article within a chapter that expands on an item of interest during this time period. Locate the feature article in this section. (Feature articles are presented in yellow.) Skim the feature article. What problem is discussed and who has it?

10. Turn to the end of the chapter where it concludes with two pages of review material. At the top of the pages (in red) is a time line that includes more information from the chapter. Find one event that sounds like a problem and write it below. Note the year that the event occurred.

In conjunction with this process, reinforce the necessity of getting a "first read" before undertaking any reading task. Use a football analogy with students:

> Before a quarterback runs a play, he takes time at the line of scrimmage to "read" the defense. He wants to know what to expect and he wants to make predictions of what might happen. He also wants to anticipate strategies he can use during the play to be successful.

A first read, or preview, is a self-guided Chapter Tour. This initial sweep through the material requires an active and aggressive mind-set that targets the following:

- **Topic**—What is the selection about? What do I already know about this topic? What do I predict I should know after reading this?

- **Main Idea**—What is the point of this material? Why did the author write this? How might this material be useful to me? What should I focus on?

- **Major Themes**—What are the key arguments or conclusions? If this material were summarized, what are the central thoughts that connect most of the details? What does this author apparently believe?

- **Structure**—How is this material put together? How is it sectioned or subdivided? Where do I need to allocate my most careful attention?

- **Salient Details**—Are there any facts that I definitely should pay attention to? What stands out in the material? Is there text in bold or italic type, quotations, or capital letters? Are there any key phrases that seem important? How familiar is this material? What details do I already know?

- **Style**—What do I notice about writing style? Complexity of sentences? Density of vocabulary? How smoothly does the prose flow? How easy will this be to read?

- **Tone/Attitude/Mood**—Does the author have an attitude toward this material? Can I detect any emotion in the material? What tone can I sense? Anger? Humor? Enthusiasm? Criticism? Sarcasm? Irony? Reasoning? Persuasion? Inspiration? Explanation? If the author were doing a live presentation of this material, what would it be like?

Advantages

- Students learn to become frontloaders when they read.

- Students are conditioned to make predictions about a passage, and then read to confirm or reject predictions.

- Students are provided with an "expert guide" to alert them to what is most important in a chapter and to make more systematic use of reading aids provided within a textbook.

This strategy can be applied to text materials in all content areas and is appropriate for students from elementary through high school levels.

Suggested Reading

Cunningham, D., & Shablak, S. (1975). Selective reading Guide-o-rama: The content teacher's best friend. *Journal of Reading, 18*, 380–382.

Wood, K.D., Lapp, D., & Flood, J. (1992). *Guiding readers through text: A review of study guides.* Newark, DE: International Reading Association.

Other Work Cited

Boyer, P., & Stuckey, S. (1998). *The American nation in the 20th century.* Austin, TX: Holt, Rhinehart, and Winston and Harcourt Brace.

Character Quotes

- Give me liberty or give me death!
- Ask not what your country can do for you; ask what you can do for your country.
- We have nothing to fear but fear itself.
- I have a dream that one day this nation will rise up and live out the true meaning of its creeds—we hold these truths to be self-evident that all men are created equal.

Or

- I'm the most terrific liar you ever saw in your life. It's awful.
- One of my troubles is, I never care too much when I lose something—it used to drive my mother crazy when I was a kid.
- It was one of the worst schools I ever went to. It was full of phonies. And mean guys. You never saw so many mean guys in your life.
- Just because somebody's dead, you don't just stop liking them, for God's sake—especially if they were about a thousand times nicer than the people you know that're alive and all.

The power of expressive language! From the stirring rhetoric of historical figures to the introspective musings of Holden Caulfield in J.D. Salinger's *The Catcher in the Rye*, spoken words are a significant way in which we reveal ourselves to others. Character Quotes (Buehl, 1994; adapted from Blachowicz, 1993) is a strategy that helps students develop insights about a character by what he or she says.

Using the Strategy

Character Quotes can be used to examine fictional characters in literature or real-life individuals in social studies books. Using this strategy involves the following steps:

1 Preview the reading to identify several quotes by a character that illustrate different elements of the character's personality. Select quotes that encourage students to develop varying descriptions of the kind of person this character might be. Write each quote on a separate slip of paper or index card. For example, students preparing to read Roald Dahl's *The BFG* will encounter a memorable Big Friendly Giant who has a penchant for hilariously mangled language. Quotes from his dialogue with the young girl Sophie provide students with an advance opportunity to explore his personality (see Character Quotes From *The BFG*). Students in a history class studying the period of development of the American West can be introduced to a Native American point of view through quotes taken from Chief Joseph's speech of surrender to government troops in 1877 (see Character Quotes From Chief Joseph).

2 Organize students into cooperative groups of three or four. Give each group a different quote to consider and to generate as many words as possible that might describe a character based on the quote. For example, groups working on quotes from *The BFG* might come up with *silly, sensitive, peace-loving, unintelligent, funny, lacks education, tries hard, crazy, looks at people as individuals, likes people, does nice things, lazy, a big guy, from another country*, or *likes to dream*.

3 After each group has generated a list of descriptors, ask a member from each group to (1) read the group's quote to the entire class, and (2) share the list of character qualities and traits that the group associates with that character. Write the qualities and traits on the chalkboard or overhead transparency as they are presented by each group. At this time, inform the students that all the quotes were uttered by the same individual.

4 Involve students in making generalizations about the character or individual. Have the students work in their cooperative groups to write a preliminary personality profile of this character

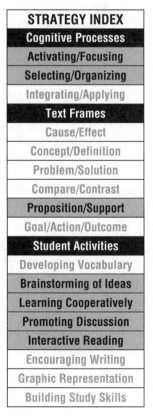

STRATEGY INDEX

| Cognitive Processes |
| Activating/Focusing |
| Selecting/Organizing |
| Integrating/Applying |
| **Text Frames** |
| Cause/Effect |
| Concept/Definition |
| Problem/Solution |
| Compare/Contrast |
| Proposition/Support |
| Goal/Action/Outcome |
| **Student Activities** |
| Developing Vocabulary |
| Brainstorming of Ideas |
| Learning Cooperatively |
| Promoting Discussion |
| Interactive Reading |
| Encouraging Writing |
| Graphic Representation |
| Building Study Skills |

Character Quotes From *The BFG*

- I would so much love to have a jumbly big elefunt and go riding through green forests picking peachy fruits off the trees all day long.

- I is never having a chance to go to school. I is full of mistakes. They is not my fault. I do my best.

- Every human bean is diddly and different. Some is scrumdiddlyumptious and some is uckyslush.

- If I come along and I is picking a lovely flower, if I is twisting the stem of the flower till it breaks, then the plant is screaming. I can hear it screaming and screaming very clear.

- Human beans is squishing each other all the time. They is shootling guns and going up aerioplanes to drop their bombs on each other's head every week. Human beans is always killing other human beans.

- I know exactly what words I am wanting to say, but somehow or other they is always getting squiff-squiddled around.

- I is a dream-blowing giant.... I is scuddling away to other places to blow dreams into the bedrooms of sleeping children. Nice dreams. Lovely golden dreams. Dreams that is giving the dreamers a happy time.

From Dahl, R. (1982). *The BFG*. London: Puffin.

Character Quotes From Chief Joseph

- I want to have time to look for my children and see how many I can find. Maybe I shall find them among the dead.

- I am tired; my heart is sick and sad. From where the sun now stands, I will fight no more forever.

- You might as well expect the rivers to run backward as that any man who was born free should be contented penned up and denied liberty to go where he pleases....

- Good words will not give my people good health and stop them from dying. Good words will not get my people a home where they can live in peace and take care of themselves. I am tired of talk that comes to nothing.

- We only ask an even chance to live as other men live. We ask to be recognized as men. We ask that the same law shall work alike on all men.

- All men were made by the same Great Spirit Chief. They are all brothers. The earth is the mother of all people, and all people shall have equal rights upon it.

- Let me be a free man—free to travel, free to stop, free to work, free to trade where I choose, free to choose my own teachers, free to follow the religion of my fathers, free to think and talk and act for my-self—and I will obey every law, or submit to the penalty.

From Bailey, T. (Ed.) (1963). *The American spirit: United States history as seen by contemporaries.* Lexington, MA: Heath.

by using the qualities and traits listed by the entire class. The profile should contain four or five statements that integrate important qualities from the list.

Provide an opening stem as a template to assist students in organizing their personality profile (see Template Frames, page 141). The following is the opening stem for a profile on Chief Joseph's quotes:

> Chief Joseph was the type of person who _____.
> He also seemed to be _____. Other traits
> of his personality included _____.

5 Have students begin reading the story, novel, or other text assignment. After completing their reading, have students return to their personality profiles to discuss what new qualities or traits they might add and how they would change the profile to make it better match their understanding of the character. Ask students to select further quotes from the text that provide

new information about their character, or have them identify representative quotes that lead to understanding a second character or individual. In addition, have students explore character qualities in their journal writing.

Advantages

- Students are introduced to several important facets of a character or individual's personality before they begin reading.

- Students are involved in actively predicting major themes and issues of a story or selection.

- Students develop a fuller sense of the complexity of individuals by examining their words.

The strategy may be adapted for use with students in the elementary grades through high school.

References

Blachowicz, C. (1993, November). *Developing active comprehenders*. Paper presented at the Madison Area Reading Association, Madison, WI.

Buehl, D. (1994). You said it: Colorful quotes can be the voice of a character's soul. *WEAC News & Views, 29*(11), 21.

Other Works Cited

Bailey, T. (Ed.). (1963). *The American spirit: United States history as seen by contemporaries*. Lexington, MA: Heath.

Dahl, R. (1982). *The BFG*. London: Puffin.

Salinger, J.D. (1951). *The catcher in the rye*. New York: Little Brown.

Concept/Definition Mapping

Let's see...harbinger...um...presage...forerunner, herald...a person sent in advance to secure accommodations. I'm still not sure that I have a feel for this word harbinger.

"Look it up in the dictionary!" Students are conditioned throughout their schooling to follow this advice. But for many students, using the dictionary results in using very narrow and sometimes vague statements to define a word. These dictionary statements contain little elaboration and may not connect at all to what students may already know about a word or concept.

Concept/Definition Mapping (Schwartz & Raphael, 1985) is a strategy that helps enrich a student's understanding of a word or concept. Concept Definition Maps are graphic structures that focus students' attention on the key components of a definition: the class or category, the properties or characteristics, and illustrations or examples. The strategy also encourages students to integrate their personal knowledge into a definition.

Using the Strategy

Concept/Definition Mapping is an excellent strategy for teaching key vocabulary and concepts in all content areas. Using this strategy involves the following steps:

1 Display a blank Concept/Definition Map on an overhead projector (see Appendix, page 154). Point out questions that a complete definition would answer: What is it? What is it like? What are some examples of it? Model how to use the Concept/Definition Map by selecting a familiar concept and soliciting the relevant information for the map from the class. For example, students responding to a map for *cheese* might identify it as *food* or a *dairy product*. Properties such as *is usually soft*, *is usually yellow or white*, *is made from milk*, and *is kept cold* could be entered into the boxes under What is it like? (see Concept/Definition Map, page 42). As examples of cheese, students might offer *cheddar*, *Swiss*, *mozzarella*, and *limburger*.

2 Present a new key term or concept from material students are learning. Have students work in pairs to create a Concept/Definition Map for the new concept.

Instruct them to use information from the reading passage, a glossary or dictionary, or their own background knowledge to complete the map. For example, science students studying different climatic regions of the earth might be given the concept *tundra* to map (see Concept/Definition Map for Science, page 43). The textbook identifies *tundra* as one of several characteristic geographical regions. Have students note the properties of a tundra from the reading: has no trees; vegetation consists mostly of grasses, mosses, and lichens; has temperatures below freezing most of the year; and has permanently frozen ground called permafrost. Some students may draw from their background knowledge that reindeer and caribou are found in tundra regions. Have students locate examples of tundra from a world map in the textbook showing the different geographic regions: The tundra region is indicated in the arctic areas of Alaska, Canada, Europe, and Russia.

3 When students have finished constructing their Concept/Definition Maps, have them use the maps to write a complete definition for the concept. Emphasize that the definition should include the category of the word, its properties or characteristics, and specific examples, and will comprise several sentences instead of simple dictionary statements. For example,

> The tundra is a region of the earth that has temperatures below freezing most of year. No trees grow there—only grasses, mosses, and lichens. The cold temperatures cause permafrost. The tundra is located in the far north, in Alaska, Canada, and Siberia.

4 Assign students to create Concept/Definition Maps for other key terms and concepts from their reading that can be used as review and study for tests.

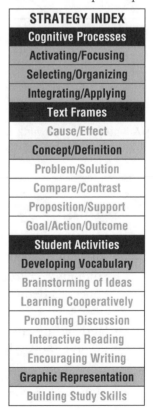

STRATEGY INDEX
Cognitive Processes
Activating/Focusing
Selecting/Organizing
Integrating/Applying
Text Frames
Cause/Effect
Concept/Definition
Problem/Solution
Compare/Contrast
Proposition/Support
Goal/Action/Outcome
Student Activities
Developing Vocabulary
Brainstorming of Ideas
Learning Cooperatively
Promoting Discussion
Interactive Reading
Encouraging Writing
Graphic Representation
Building Study Skills

CONCEPT/DEFINITION MAP

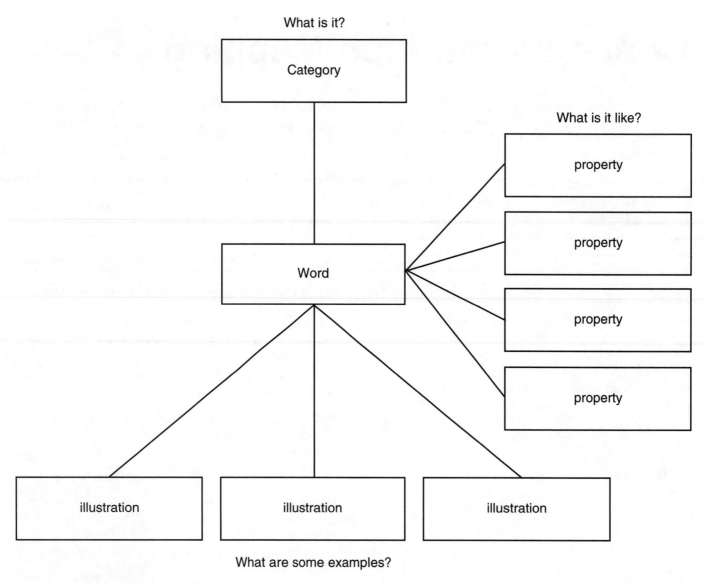

What is it?

Category

What is it like?

property

property

property

property

Word

illustration

illustration

illustration

What are some examples?

(Adapted from Schwartz & Raphael, 1985)

Advantages

- Students expand their understandings of key vocabulary and concepts beyond simple definitions.
- Students construct a visual representation of a concept's definition that helps them in remembering.
- Students are encouraged to integrate their background knowledge into a definition.

This strategy may be used with students from elementary through secondary levels.

Reference and Suggested Reading

Buehl, D. (1995). *Classroom strategies for interactive learning*. Madison, WI: Wisconsin State Reading Association.

Santa, C., Havens, L., & Macumber, E. (1996). *Creating independence through student-owned strategies*. Dubuque, IA: Kendall/Hunt.

Schwartz, R., & Raphael, T. (1985). Concept of definition: A key to improving students' vocabulary. *The Reading Teacher, 39*, 198–205.

CONCEPT/DEFINITION MAP FOR SCIENCE
Tundra

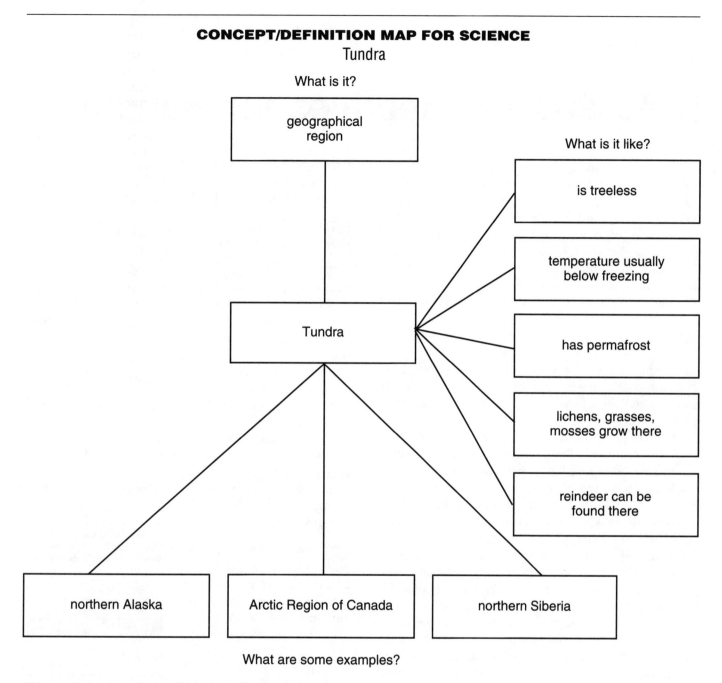

What is it?

geographical region

What is it like?

is treeless

temperature usually below freezing

has permafrost

lichens, grasses, mosses grow there

reindeer can be found there

Tundra

northern Alaska

Arctic Region of Canada

northern Siberia

What are some examples?

(Buehl, 1995; adapted from Schwartz & Raphael, 1985)

Different Perspectives for Reading

"That's not what I got out of that article!" A frequent occurrence, two individuals sparring over a piece of text that both have read. Look at the potential for spirited discussion that arrives each day in the morning newspaper—an editorial about the glass ceiling for women executives, an exposé on the flaws of capital punishment, a movie review of the most recent action blockbuster, an article about substituting holistic health practices for drug treatments, a discussion of the mayor's comments about raising bus fares, a travel column recommending must-see spots in Europe, a feature article on the need for higher standards in schools, a report about a group of teenagers who are lobbying the city for a skateboard park, an analysis of the role of "soft" money in politics—the list goes on.

What might your impressions be in each of these reading situations? Chances are, you automatically would read using a variety of personal "lenses," which would create a personal perspective made up of your experiences, values, and attitudes to aid in comprehension and making meaning of the text. Socioeconomic status, gender, political persuasion, age, ethnic identity, marital status, career history, educational background, specific life experiences—all factor into your perspective as you read. Thus, two people can read the same article and come away with different but equally valid interpretations of what the text means.

Because students, too, are individuals with different background experiences, beliefs, and understandings about the world, no two students will read and comprehend a passage in the same way. A student whose grandfather is a dairy farmer will understand a passage about Holsteins in a decidedly different way than a student whose only connection to cows may be a cartoon. Likewise, a student who has been to Arizona will comprehend a story about the desert with a different appreciation than a student who has never left New York City. Strategies that broaden perspective about a topic will help students to read with a greater depth of comprehension and appreciation.

Using the Strategy

Different Perspectives for Reading (McNeil, 1984) is a teaching strategy that guides students through multiple readings of material in a way that makes them consider ways of thinking other than their own. Using this strategy involves the following steps:

1 Have students read through a story, article, or selection for the first time.

2 Identify perspectives to use with students that could be connected to the important ideas or concepts of the passage. For example, different perspectives in a history textbook passage about the building of the Transcontinental Railroad in the United States might include those of a Native American, a fur trapper, a homesteader, and perhaps a buffalo. For fictional material, assign students the perspective of characters other than the narrator in a story. For example, in the novel *To Kill a Mockingbird* by Harper Lee, the perspective is that of the young girl, Scout; however, other perspectives to consider are her brother, Jem; the family cook, Calpurnia; the elderly neighbor, Mrs. Dubose; the lawyer, Atticus Finch; the wronged man, Tom Robinson; or the phantom neighbor, Boo Radley.

3 Divide the class into cooperative groups of three or four and assign each group a different perspective. Ask students to identify the issues, feelings, effects, or concerns surrounding a particular perspective. For students studying the Transcontinental Railroad, use a Different Perspectives Graphic Outline to provide structure for this activity (see Appendix, page 155). Have students fill in answers to the following questions: Why would the railroads be a concern to a Native American? A fur trapper? How would the railroads affect the needs of the buffalo? A homesteader? Students might decide that Native

STRATEGY INDEX
Cognitive Processes
Activating/Focusing
Selecting/Organizing
Integrating/Applying
Text Frames
Cause/Effect
Concept/Definition
Problem/Solution
Compare/Contrast
Proposition/Support
Goal/Action/Outcome
Student Activities
Developing Vocabulary
Brainstorming of Ideas
Learning Cooperatively
Promoting Discussion
Interactive Reading
Encouraging Writing
Graphic Representation
Building Study Skills

DIFFERENT PERSPECTIVES GRAPHIC OUTLINE

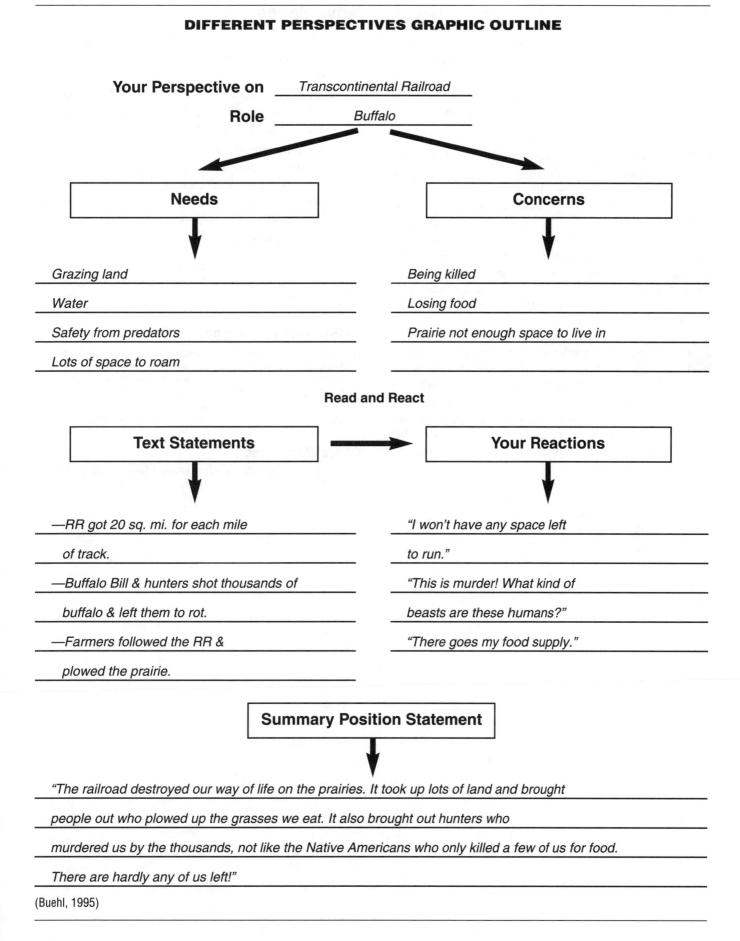

Your Perspective on _Transcontinental Railroad_

Role _Buffalo_

Needs

Grazing land

Water

Safety from predators

Lots of space to roam

Concerns

Being killed

Losing food

Prairie not enough space to live in

Read and React

Text Statements

—RR got 20 sq. mi. for each mile

of track.

—Buffalo Bill & hunters shot thousands of

buffalo & left them to rot.

—Farmers followed the RR &

plowed the prairie.

Your Reactions

"I won't have any space left

to run."

"This is murder! What kind of

beasts are these humans?"

"There goes my food supply."

Summary Position Statement

"The railroad destroyed our way of life on the prairies. It took up lots of land and brought

people out who plowed up the grasses we eat. It also brought out hunters who

murdered us by the thousands, not like the Native Americans who only killed a few of us for food.

There are hardly any of us left!"

(Buehl, 1995)

45

Americans would need their land, their food supply (the buffalo), and peace. Native Americans would be concerned about too many settlers arriving on the railroads, the loss of the buffalo, and increasing conflicts. Settlers would need supplies, markets for their products, and protection from the Native Americans. They would be concerned about railroad monopolies and high prices.

4 Have students re-read the material to look for specific statements or information that would be of special interest to their perspective. Have them write this information on the graphic outline, along with comments about their assigned perspective. For example, students re-reading the history passage from a buffalo's perspective might react as follows: With the railroad obtaining 20 square miles of land for every mile of track, the buffalo would soon run out of grazing land. The slaughter of their species by Bill Cody and other hunters might elicit reactions about genocide.

5 Discuss with students new insights gained through looking at material from a variety of viewpoints. To bring their thoughts together, ask students to write a position statement summarizing the feelings of an individual with a particular perspective. Include this statement on the bottom portion of the graphic outline (see Different Perspectives Graphic Outline).

Advantages

- The strategy reinforces that a number of legitimate conclusions and generalizations may be drawn from a specific text.
- Students read with more emotional attachment while using this strategy and develop empathy for points of view other than their own.
- Students are given a structure to re-read materials and to pick out ideas and information that they may have overlooked in the first reading.
- Students are given practice in selecting specific information that relates to alternative ways of looking at a text.

This strategy can be tailored to students from elementary to high school levels and can be applied across many content areas.

References and Suggested Reading

Buehl, D. (1995). *Classroom strategies for interactive learning*. Madison, WI: Wisconsin State Reading Association.

Cook, D. (Ed.). (1989). *Strategic learning in the content areas*. Madison, WI: Department of Public Instruction.

McNeil, J. (1984). *Reading comprehension: New directions for classroom practice*. Glenview, IL: Scott, Foresman.

Other Work Cited

Lee, H. (1960). *To kill a mockingbird*. Philadelphia and New York: Lippincott.

Discussion Web

Consider the array of political discussions in which you have participated. At times you undoubtedly have been involved in passionate and highly emotional exchanges—at other times, quietly reasoned, earnestly argued conversations have taken place. All such discussions reflect a basic underlying principle, that oft-repeated truism: There are two sides to every question. Through exchanges with others we have the opportunity to refine our thinking, respond to challenges to our viewpoints, and acknowledge alternative ideas and opposing information.

Teachers know that classroom discussions are an important way to encourage students to think. But involving the entire class in discussion is difficult to accomplish. Too often, only a few students are willing to contribute, and as a result they monopolize the conversation. What starts as a discussion ends as a dialogue between the teacher and a handful of students. Meanwhile, the rest of the class sits passively—either not listening to or not paying attention to what is being said. However, the Discussion Web (Alvermann, 1991) is a strategy designed to include all students in active participation in class discussion.

Using the Strategy

The Discussion Web incorporates four language arts (reading, writing, speaking, and listening) and takes advantage of cooperative learning ideas to give students multiple opportunities to interact. The strategy is especially useful for discussions in literature and the social studies. Using the strategy involves the following steps:

1 Choose a selection for student reading that develops opposing viewpoints such as a story that elicits conflicting opinions of a character's actions or that deals with controversial issues. Prepare students for reading by activating relevant background knowledge for the selection and setting their purposes for reading (see Brainstorming Prior Knowledge, page 31).

2 After students read the selection, introduce the Discussion Web and a focusing question for discussion. Students reading a history textbook passage on the Industrial Revolution might be asked, Did the Industrial Revolution help working people? (See Discussion Web for the Industrial Revolution, page 48.) Students in a literature class reading *The Red Badge of Courage* by Stephen Crane might be asked, Was Henry Fleming a coward for running? Middle school students reading the novel *Hatchet* by Gary Paulsen might be asked, Could Brian have survived in the wilderness without the hatchet?

3 Assign students to work in pairs to develop opposing sides of a question. As they work, have them flesh out the arguments on both sides of a blank Discussion Web (see Appendix, page 156), going back to the reading as needed. During this phase, the emphasis is on making the strongest possible arguments on both sides of the Web. Remind students to set aside momentarily their personal beliefs to ensure that both positions are represented fairly.

After analyzing the actions of the main character in *The Red Badge of Courage*, students may determine the following about cowardice: Henry ran at the beginning of the battle, he misled others about his running, and he felt shame for running. However, Henry was experiencing his first battle, he had never before been under fire, and there was much confusion during the battle.

4 After students share viewpoints and write them on the Discussion Web, group each set of partners with another pair and ask them to work toward a consensus on the question. Additional arguments on both sides of the question are added to the Discussion Web at this time. The group's conclusion is written at the bottom of the Web. For example, a group might conclude that in *Hatchet*, although Brian could have gotten fire from other means and may have adapted to his plight by using different strategies, he proba-

DISCUSSION WEB FOR
THE INDUSTRIAL REVOLUTION

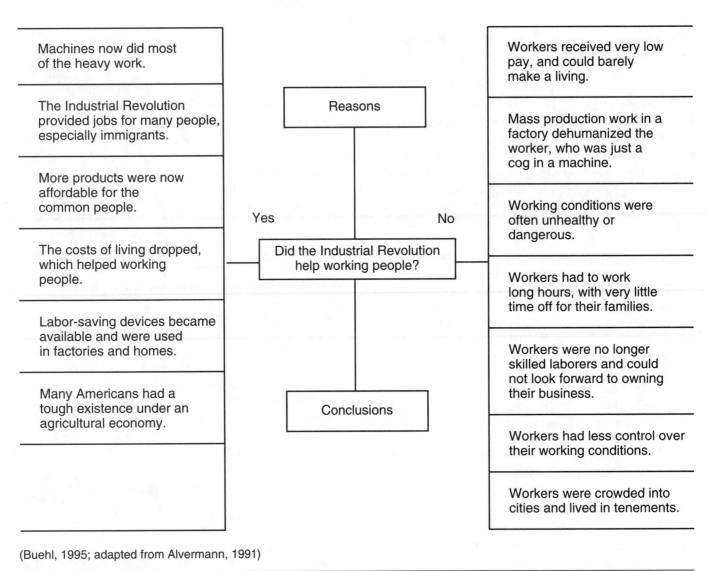

| Machines now did most of the heavy work. | | Workers received very low pay, and could barely make a living. |

Reasons

| The Industrial Revolution provided jobs for many people, especially immigrants. | | Mass production work in a factory dehumanized the worker, who was just a cog in a machine. |

| More products were now affordable for the common people. | | Working conditions were often unhealthy or dangerous. |

Yes — Did the Industrial Revolution help working people? — No

| The costs of living dropped, which helped working people. | | Workers had to work long hours, with very little time off for their families. |

| Labor-saving devices became available and were used in factories and homes. | | Workers were no longer skilled laborers and could not look forward to owning their business. |

Conclusions

| Many Americans had a tough existence under an agricultural economy. | | Workers had less control over their working conditions. |

| | | Workers were crowded into cities and lived in tenements. |

(Buehl, 1995; adapted from Alvermann, 1991)

bly would not have survived without the hatchet. A second group might argue that Brian's ingenuity and common sense toward using the hatchet could have been applied in other ways, which would have helped him survive without the hatchet.

5 Each group of four students is now ready to present its conclusions to the entire group. Allow 3 minutes for a spokesperson from each group to discuss one reason for their conclusion, which reduces the likelihood that the last groups to report will have no new ideas to offer. Encourage spokespersons to mention any dissenting viewpoints from their group discussions. In a discussion about the Industrial Revolution, some groups will decide that the revolution was progress and that working people ultimately benefit-

ed from innovations in industry. Other groups will likely deplore the unsafe and unhealthy conditions in which people worked and their exploitation by factory owners.

6 Students are now prepared to write their own personal responses to the focusing question. The Discussion Web provides an organized guide to information and arguments that may be included in the writing. Students are thus able to develop their own ideas as well as reflect on the contributions of their classmates as they write about the question.

Advantages

• Students are active participants in discussion and develop cooperative learning skills.

- Students have a framework for evaluating both sides of an issue or question, and they are encouraged to process opposing evidence and information before asserting their viewpoints.
- Student write using well-organized and developed support for positions.

The strategy is especially useful for discussions in literature and the social studies, and it is appropriate for elementary through high school level students.

References

Alvermann, D. (1991). The discussion web: A graphic aid for learning across the curriculum. *The Reading Teacher, 45,* 92–99.

Buehl, D. (1995). *Classroom strategies for interactive learning.* Madison, WI: Wisconsin State Reading Association.

Other Works Cited

Crane, S. (1942). *The red badge of courage.* Boston: McGraw-Hill.

Paulsen, G. (1987). *Hatchet.* New York: Bradbury Press.

Elaborative Interrogation

Consider the following pieces of factual information. The temperature of absolute zero is −273°C. Leonardo da Vinci painted the *Mona Lisa*. Foxes, owls, and sharks are predators. Los Angeles, California, is the largest metropolitan area in the United States. The first permanent European settlement in North America was founded by the Spanish at St. Augustine, Florida. Charles Darwin discussed his theory of evolution in his book, *The Origin of Species.* If one angle of a triangle equals 90°, then the sum of the remaining angles also equals 90°.

But why? Why is it called absolute zero? Why is the *Mona Lisa* regarded as a great painting? Why do some animals live as predators and others do not? Why has Los Angeles, California, become such a gigantic urban area? Why did the Spanish pick Florida for a settlement? Why did Darwin come to believe in evolution? Why do angles have this relationship? Why?

Why is perhaps the most significant question in education. We all have experienced this persistent question in our dealings with students. *Why* seems to be perpetually on the minds of young children as they attempt through questioning to make sense of the world around them. Why are things the way they are? Why does something happen? Why do people (or characters in a story) do what they do?

Unfortunately, many students become less inclined to ask why as they move through school. They come to regard information as arbitrary and static, learned merely for its own sake, and then perhaps forgotten. Helping students refocus on why information is significant can rekindle that inquisitive attitude toward learning, which makes it meaningful and memorable.

Using the Strategy

Pressley and his colleagues argue that Elaborative Interrogation—teaching students to ask appropriate why questions—is a powerful strategy for enhancing student learning (Pressley et al., 1988). Elaborative Interrogation engages students in activating and using their prior knowledge about a topic in order to improve their comprehension and memory. Using this strategy involves the following steps:

1 Model for students appropriate *why* questions about the material the class is studying. Select a series of factual statements from the material and present them to the students. For example, the following excerpt about the habits of skunks provides an excellent opportunity for teaching the generation of significant why questions.

> The Western Spotted Skunk lives in a hole in the ground. The skunk's hole is usually found on a sandy piece of farmland near crops. Often the skunk lives alone, but families of skunks sometimes stay together. The skunk mostly eats corn. It sleeps just about any time except between 3 o'clock in the morning and sunrise. The biggest danger to this skunk is the great horned owl. (Wood, Pressley, & Winne, 1990, p. 744)

After students review the statements, ask a series of why questions that will focus student attention on implied cause/effect relationships in the material: Why would these skunks live in a sandy area? Why do you think they eat mostly corn? Why would the great horned owl be the biggest danger to a skunk? As students ponder possible responses, emphasize that the information may give hints to the answers, but that they must also "use their heads" and consider things they already know (see Question-Answer Relationships, page 106).

In the example, students might note that because skunks have an easier time digging holes in sandy ground, they tend to live in such areas; the fact that skunks live near farmland probably explains why corn is so important to their diet; and that because owls are nocturnal, skunks, who only venture out at night, are frequent victims of great horned owls.

STRATEGY INDEX
Cognitive Processes
Activating/Focusing
Selecting/Organizing
Integrating/Applying
Text Frames
Cause/Effect
Concept/Definition
Problem/Solution
Compare/Contrast
Proposition/Support
Goal/Action/Outcome
Student Activities
Developing Vocabulary
Brainstorming of Ideas
Learning Cooperatively
Promoting Discussion
Interactive Reading
Encouraging Writing
Graphic Representation
Building Study Skills

2 Present students with a formula for conceptualizing elaborative interrogations (see Formula for Answering Why Questions). Why questions prompt students to add, What I am learning now, and What I already know, in order to discover a possible cause/effect relationship. As a result, students elaborate on text material in two ways: (1) by looking for hints in the reading that connect information, and (2) by activating relevant prior knowledge that might help to explain why.

Students may express frustration that they do not know enough or are not told enough to come up with plausible answers to why questions. Reassure them that they will not always be able to determine unambiguous or exact answers to why questions they might pose. The strength of the Elaborative Interrogation strategy lies in the process of analyzing important information for possible relationships. By asking why, students are engaged in a much deeper level of processing than if they merely read the material; they are making connections and drawing possible conclusions.

3 As students study new information, have them work with partners to generate why questions about the material and to brainstorm possible responses to their questions. Initially, it might be helpful to provide students with important factual statements from the material or story, which will guide them on the types of information worthy of consideration. For example, the following excerpted and adapted information from a history textbook dealing with the post–World War I period could be modeled as an Elaborative Interrogation exercise:

> Fear of communism reached a fever pitch in 1919 and 1920, a period known as the Red Scare. Peace groups came under particularly strong attack. Most of those arrested as "radicals" were poor immigrants newly arrived in the country, although there was no real evidence against them. During the Red Scare hundreds of foreigners suspected of radical activities were deported to

> Russia. Among the deportees was Emma Goldman, a noted feminist, writer, and speaker. (Boyer & Stuckey, 1998, pp. 281–282)

As students work with their partners, they could raise questions about why the Red Scare occurred at this time in U.S. history, why peace groups and foreigners were targeted, and why people were arrested with little evidence against them.

When students become practiced in asking good why questions, they can create their own why questions for their classmates. Pair students and have them create a series of why questions for one section of a passage. Then have them exchange their questions with those of another student pair, who developed questions on a different section. Each pair will then reread the appropriate sections to hypothesize answers to their classmates' questions.

4 Eventually students should feel comfortable generating why questions on their own with a variety of materials they encounter. The Elaborative Interrogation strategy can work just as successfully with fiction as with nonfiction. Reinforce throughout this process that relationships between information (or actions) are what is important, and that material is more meaningful and memorable if the why element is addressed and analyzed.

Advantages

- Students are engaged in a more active form of questioning, which goes beyond questions that target a literal level of understanding.

- Students come to expect connections among information they might formerly have regarded as isolated facts.

- Students are encouraged to adopt a more aggressive self-questioning attitude as they learn new material or think about a story. Why ques-

---

FORMULA FOR ANSWERING WHY QUESTIONS

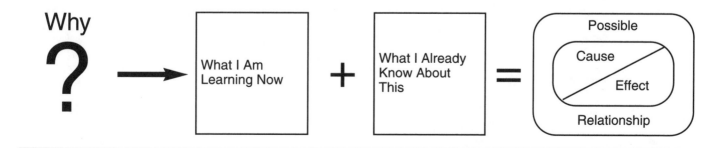

Why **?** → What I Am Learning Now **+** What I Already Know About This **=** Possible Cause / Effect Relationship

---

tions lead to the asking of other important questions.

- Students remember better factual information and details when they are able to discern significant relationships.

Elaborative Investigation works for young children as well as adults and is appropriate across all content areas.

References

Pressley, M., Symons, S., McDaniel, M., Snyder, B., & Turnure, J. (1988). Elaborative interrogation facilitates acquisition of confusing facts. *Journal of Educational Psychology, 80*(3), 268–278.

Wood, E., Pressley, M., & Winne, P. (1990). Elaborative interrogation effects on children's learning of factual content. *Journal of Educational Psychology, 82*(4), 741–748.

Other Work Cited

Boyer, P., & Stuckey, S. (1998). *The American nation in the 20th century*. Austin, TX: Holt, Rinehart and Winston.

Follow the Characters

"And the Oscar goes to...." Recent Academy Awards for best picture have recognized movies that delivered powerful messages to viewers. *American Beauty* deals with a man approaching middle age, disillusioned with his life, and grasping for ways to redefine himself. *Titanic* is a coming-of-age chronicle of two young people from vastly disparate backgrounds who learn to bridge their differences amidst the backdrop of a horrible disaster. *The English Patient* unfolds the tragedy and suffering of a young man caught in the turmoil of World War I. *Schindler's List* tells the story of a mercenary opportunist who came to risk everything in order to save the lives of Jewish workers during the Holocaust. In different ways, each of these movies communicates important ideas about how characters experience change in the face of conflict.

Change and conflict are two constants of life that underlie fictional literature. By examining how characters handle change and conflict, students can develop insight into the author's point of view. Follow the Characters (Buehl, 1994) is a strategy that helps students to understand stories through character analysis.

Using the Strategy

Follow the Characters involves organizing key information about a character into a grid. The resulting visual outline helps students decide on the author's theme or message in a story (see Follow the Characters, page 54). The strategy works with both short stories and longer works of fictional literature. Using this strategy involves the following steps:

1 Review the basic components of story structure (see Story Mapping, page 135). Establish that stories have a setting, characters, plot events, a conflict and its resolution, and an author's theme.

2 Use the role of detective as a metaphor to help students conceptualize the process of character analysis. Ask students how a detective goes about solving a mystery, and they will likely answer that a detective looks for clues and investigates people. Emphasize the detective frame-of-mind as a way to discover the theme of the story. For clues about an author's viewpoint in a story, students should "follow the characters" by tuning in to what a character does or says and what others do or say about the character. Students should pay special attention to the role of the character in the story's conflict and whether this role changes the character in any way.

3 Place a blank Character Analysis Grid (see Appendix, page 153) on the overhead projector and model with students using a familiar story, such as a fairy tale or a selection students have read previously. For example, most younger students will recall the story of Aladdin, perhaps through the animated movie version. They may know that the major conflict in this fairy tale is between Aladdin and the evil Jafar. Elicit information about Aladdin from the students to fill in the grid. Record his actions (steals things, performs daring acts, and fights to save the princess); record his thoughts and words (he lies to the princess, regrets his lie, and tells the genie what he desires for his life); record others' views of Aladdin (he is a thief, a low-status person, a liar, a victim, and a hero); and record the changes he makes during the story (he comes to value honesty, places another's well-being ahead of his own). Help students to articulate a theme for the story, such as "A person should be true to himself."

4 Students are now ready to apply the Character Analysis Grid to a work of literature. For example, students in an English class who read the short story "Duel" by Richard Matheson would analyze the major character, Mann, who is menaced by an unknown trucker on a deserted highway (see Character Analysis Grid for "Duel," page 55). After students read the story, have them work with partners to complete the conflict ring and first three quadrants:

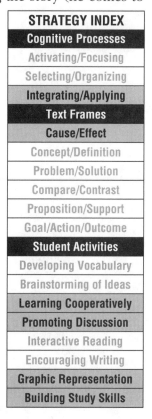

STRATEGY INDEX

Cognitive Processes

Activating/Focusing

Selecting/Organizing

Integrating/Applying

Text Frames

Cause/Effect

Concept/Definition

Problem/Solution

Compare/Contrast

Proposition/Support

Goal/Action/Outcome

Student Activities

Developing Vocabulary

Brainstorming of Ideas

Learning Cooperatively

Promoting Discussion

Interactive Reading

Encouraging Writing

Graphic Representation

Building Study Skills

What does the character do? What does the character say or think? How do others feel about the character? Note that "others" might also include the author, story narrator, and other characters in the story.

5 Team each pair of students with a second set of partners to form cooperative groups of four to work on the fourth quadrant: How does the character change? Ask students to use the information recorded in the first three quadrants to formulate the changes experienced by the character listed as *before/after* comparisons. As students examine Mann's actions and thoughts, they will find that his conflict with the trucker changes him. He is gradually transformed from a quiet, unassuming sales person into an aggressive risk-taker who accepts the challenges of a dangerous adversary on the highway. Have each student group write a version of a possible theme of the story based on their analysis of the character's changes. Emphasize that authors communicate important insights to readers through the ways in which characters change. Students might express the theme of "Duel" as, "You can only push people so far before they fight back," or "We all have a survival instinct that makes us want to defend ourselves."

6 Ask students to complete additional Character Analysis Grids for works, such as novels, which feature more than one major character.

Advantages

- Students are provided with a systematic way to attack a story to help them articulate possible meaning and the author's themes.
- Students learn to recognize the central roles that conflict and change play in character development.
- Students develop a visual outline of major elements in a story on which they can rely to help articulate the author's theme or point of view.

This strategy can be modified for use with students at all levels from elementary through high school.

References and Suggested Reading

Beck, I., & McKeown, M. (1981). Developing questions that promote comprehension: The story map. *Language Arts, 59*, 913–918.

Buehl, D. (1994). Persona: Character analysis sheds light on story's meaning. *WEAC News & Views, 29*(10), 21.

Buehl, D. (1995). *Classroom strategies for interactive learning.* Madison, WI: Wisconsin State Reading Association.

Other Work Cited

Mattheson, R. (1971). *Duel.* (This short story appears in many anthologies.)

FOLLOW THE CHARACTERS

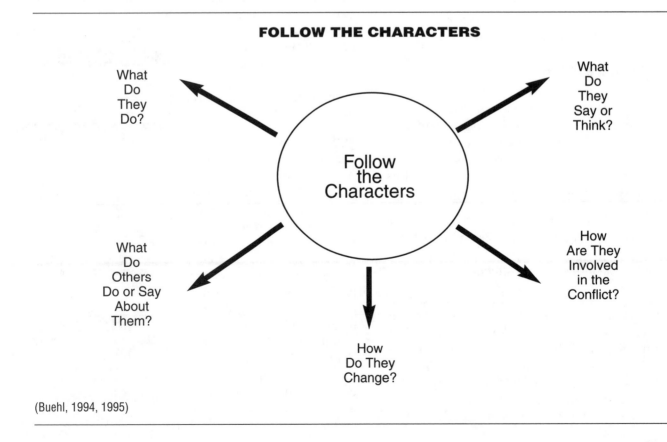

(Buehl, 1994, 1995)

CHARACTER ANALYSIS GRID
Story: _Duel_

1. What does the character do?

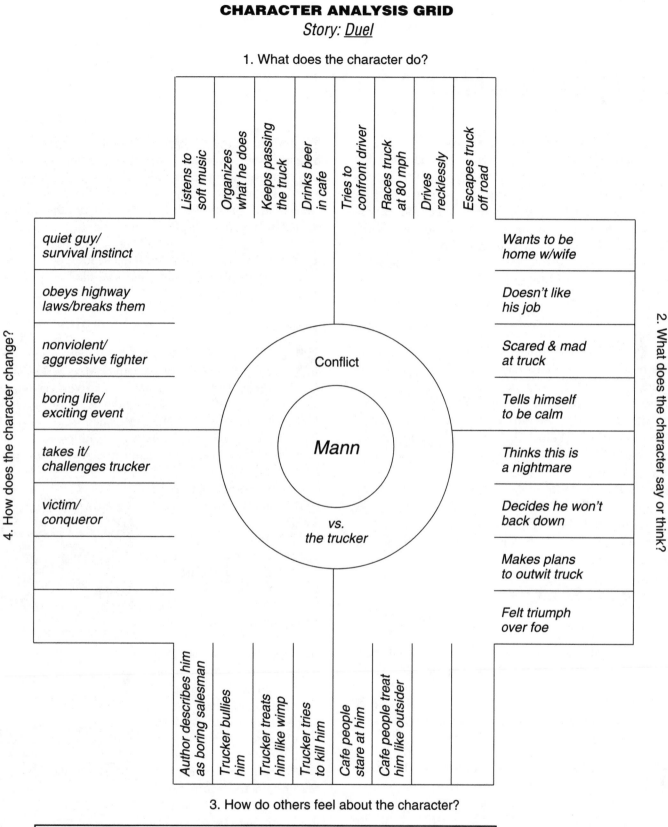

What does the character do (top labels):
- Listens to soft music
- Organizes what he does
- Keeps passing the truck
- Drinks beer in cafe
- Tries to confront driver
- Races truck at 80 mph
- Drives recklessly
- Escapes truck off road

4. How does the character change? (left labels):
- quiet guy/ survival instinct
- obeys highway laws/breaks them
- nonviolent/ aggressive fighter
- boring life/ exciting event
- takes it/ challenges trucker
- victim/ conqueror

Center: Conflict — **Mann** — vs. the trucker

2. What does the character say or think? (right labels):
- Wants to be home w/wife
- Doesn't like his job
- Scared & mad at truck
- Tells himself to be calm
- Thinks this is a nightmare
- Decides he won't back down
- Makes plans to outwit truck
- Felt triumph over foe

3. How do others feel about the character? (bottom labels):
- Author describes him as boring salesman
- Trucker bullies him
- Trucker treats him like wimp
- Trucker tries to kill him
- Cafe people stare at him
- Cafe people treat him like outsider

5. Author's Theme or Point of View:
We all have a survival instinct that makes us willing to defend ourselves.

(Buehl, 1994, 1995)

Frayer Model

Imagine that you are watching a sporting event for the first time. How do you figure out the rules that govern that sport? Simply being told the rule is probably not adequate if you really want to understand it. You need to see the rule in operation. By observing play you begin to infer how the rule works as you notice when a rule is enforced or not enforced.

For example, football fans can come to understand the rule of pass interference by viewing games over time, which refines their understanding of the rule. Tackling a receiver before the ball is caught is pass interference, but tackling after the ball arrives is not.

Providing experiences with examples and nonexamples, which share some but not all necessary characteristics, help students to construct rich and sophisticated meanings of important concepts. The Frayer Model (Frayer, Frederick, & Klausmeier, 1969) provides an excellent format for deepening understandings of these concepts. Using this model helps students differentiate between characteristics that define the concept and those that are merely associated with it. The Frayer Model also provides a visual way of distinguishing between items that represent the concept and items that are lacking some key characteristic of the concept.

Using the Strategy

The Frayer Model is a graphic organizer that contains four compartments for recording information related to a concept (see Frayer Model for Vegetable). A blank Frayer Model (see Appendix, page 158) could be given to students as a worksheet or displayed on a chalkboard or overhead transparency. It could also be used as a study guide for students as they read. Using the strategy involves the following steps:

1 Carefully analyze the concept you will be teaching to your students. Create a list of characteristics or attributes of the concept. For example, if the concept is *reptile*, the essential characteristics would include animal, cold-blooded, and vertebrate. If the concept is *vegetable*, essential characteristics would include nutritious food, found in non-woody plants, and contains vitamins and minerals.

2 Introduce the concept to students and have them generate examples. An effective method is to have students form cooperative groups and brainstorm as many examples as possible. List examples on the chalkboard or overhead transparency. Encourage students to add to the list or to challenge examples already offered. Start a second list of common characteristics or attributes. Ask students to identify the key characteristics of a concept. Questions likely to emerge for the vegetable example might be, What makes a vegetable a vegetable? What do all vegetables have in common?

3 Students are ready to read a selection about the concept. Distribute blank Frayer Models (see Appendix, page 158) to be used as an exercise while reading. Highlight the information to be entered in each section: essential characteristics, nonessential characteristics, examples, and nonexamples. Note that students will be reading to confirm or reject the information generated from the class. You may wish to have students work in pairs as they read and complete the grid.

When the students have completed their reading, go back to the original list generated by the students. On another Frayer Model, place examples and characteristics that students were able to confirm by the reading. Some items from their list may need to be placed in the nonessential and nonexamples sections. Students should also be encouraged to record the new information they learned from the reading in the appropriate section on the model. Further study may be needed to place some examples.

Students will likely pose additional questions: How are vegetables different from

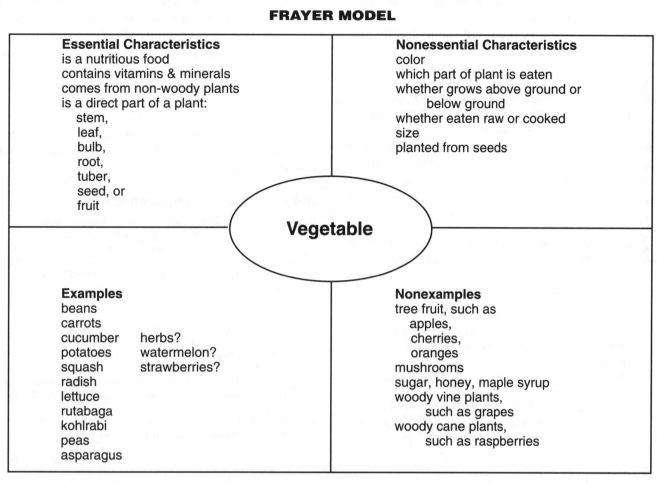

Essential Characteristics	Nonessential Characteristics

is a nutritious food
contains vitamins & minerals
comes from non-woody plants
is a direct part of a plant:
    stem,
    leaf,
    bulb,
    root,
    tuber,
    seed, or
    fruit
	color
	which part of plant is eaten
	whether grows above ground or
	    below ground
	whether eaten raw or cooked
	size
	planted from seeds

Examples
beans
carrots
cucumber   herbs?
potatoes   watermelon?
squash   strawberries?
radish
lettuce
rutabaga
kohlrabi
peas
asparagus
	Nonexamples
	tree fruit, such as
	    apples,
	    cherries,
	    oranges
	mushrooms
	sugar, honey, maple syrup
	woody vine plants,
	    such as grapes
	woody cane plants,
	    such as raspberries

The center oval contains: **Vegetable**

(Buehl, 1995; adapted from Frayer, Frederick, & Klausmeier, 1969)

fruits? Can certain edible weeds be counted as vegetables? How about mushrooms? Why are watermelons and strawberries referred to as fruit when they fit the definition of a vegetable? Do herbs have nutritional value? Can wheat be eaten as a vegetable in the same way as corn, or does it need to processed first?

4 After students practice using the Frayer Model, incorporate variations of this strategy into instruction. The Concept Attainment Strategy (Joyce & Weil, 1986) uses an inquiry process to introduce new concepts. Generate pairs of examples and nonexamples that exhibit major defining characteristics or attributes of a new concept. For example, a math teacher developing the concept *equation* might present the following pairs:

Example	Nonexample
5 + 3 = 8	3 + 7
3x − 2y = 7z	5x + 2y -3z
144 ÷ 6x = 12	27 ÷ 3 > 5

Present a pair to students and ask them to determine the characteristic that differentiates the two lists. For example, students might note that all equations have equal signs. Note that initial determinations should be considered hypotheses that will be subject to revision as the process goes on and students analyze more pairs.

Provide additional examples and nonexamples including some that might add more specific defining characteristics. This allows students to test their hypotheses and refine their understanding of the new concept. For example, if they encounter a nonexample such as 20 + 53 = 72, they will realize that there is more to the definition than merely the presence of equal signs. Nonexamples such as x + 3y ≠ 105 and 22 − y < 30 underscore that not all mathematical expressions are necessarily equations. Furthermore, a nonexample such as 12 ÷ 4 ≤ 3 shows students that an expression could be true but may not be an equation. Ask students to revise the list of characteristics or attributes of the equation concept. They now might observe that equations must have two sides, that the two sides must result in the same value, and that an equal sign must be between the two sides.

5 To further establish the concept, assign students to work in pairs to generate their own examples and nonexamples of the concept. To initiate this phase of the strategy, provide students with a list of several possible examples and additional nonexamples. After they are labeled, have each pair of students continue locating or creating their own examples and nonexamples. These are then shared with the entire class and students receive feedback on their choices.

6 Ask students to write a description of the equation concept that includes all the key or defining characteristics such as,

> An equation has two sides separated by an equal sign. The numbers on each side must end up equaling the same value. It doesn't matter whether you add, subtract, multiply, or divide on either side, as long as both sides result in the same value.

When completed, the Frayer Model provides students with organized information that can easily be used for writing tasks and as a graphically organized study guide.

Advantages

- Students go beyond mere definitions to flesh out deeper and more complex understandings of concepts.

- Students are guided into differentiating between characteristics that define a concept and those that may be sometimes associated with it.

- Students are involved in a process of discovery that allows them to build a concept by encountering progressively more sophisticated examples and nonexamples.

The Frayer Model can be used as a strategy for lessons in all subject areas. It works especially well in teaching science concepts.

References and Suggested Reading

Buehl, D. (1995). *Classroom strategies for interactive learning*. Madison, WI: Wisconsin State Reading Association.

Frayer, D., Frederick, W., & Klausmeier, H. (1969). *A schema for testing the level of cognitive mastery* (Working Paper No. 16). Madison, WI: Wisconsin Research and Development Center.

Joyce, B., & Weil, M. (1986). *Models of teaching*. Englewood Cliffs, NJ: Prentice-Hall.

Marzano, R., Pickering, D., Arredondo, D., Blackburn, G., Brandt, R., & Moffett, C. (1992). *Dimensions of learning teacher's manual*. Alexandria, VA: Association for Supervision and Curriculum Development.

Peters, C. (1979). The effect of systematic restructuring of material upon the comprehension process. *Reading Research Quarterly, 11*, 87–110.

Thelen, J. (1982). Preparing students for content grading assignments. *Journal of Reading, 25*, 544–549.

Guided Imagery

You are in the dark, forbidding forests of 18th-century North America. There is danger in the air as you march along. You remain in formation, even though you sense that an ambush is forming around you. You hear nothing but the tramping feet of your fellow soldiers. Yet, as you glance about, you think you see a glimpse of movement through the dense underbrush. Suddenly a war cry rips through the air from the thick foliage to the left of you. The Hurons!

This scene describes an episode from the evocative 1992 motion picture *Last of the Mohicans*. Sitting in the theater, moviegoers found it nearly impossible not to feel as though they personally were experiencing the French and Indian War—the tension, fear, and excitement of an impending conflict. Our imaginations placed us on the screen next to the characters and helped us identify with their lives and the historical events portrayed in the film.

As teachers, we know that showing a movie helps students to get a feeling for what they read. But effective readers also are able to generate images for themselves as they read. Guided Imagery (Gambrell, Kapinus, & Wilson, 1987) is a strategy that helps trigger visualization for students as they read and learn. For many students, textbooks are an endless parade of terms and facts. Helping students visualize what they are reading brings the material to life and makes it more meaningful. Guided Imagery can be used either to prepare students for a reading or to deepen their understanding after they have read. For example, although most students in a social studies class could readily visualize many of the hardships experienced by the pioneers traveling west across the U.S. Great Plains, Guided Imagery could help introduce the textbook passage. However, students in a science class would first need to read a passage on photosynthesis to acquire some basic knowledge before they could successfully visualize the process inside a plant.

Using the Strategy

Guided Imagery is a strategy that capitalizes on students' active imaginations. Activities such as role playing, pretending, and daydreaming are natural elements of children's play. Using this strategy involves the following steps:

1 To warm up students to using imagery, tell them you are going to suggest things for them to see in their minds. Have each student work with a partner. Suggest an image and have the students describe to their partners what they are seeing with their mind's eye. You might suggest images such as a storm, building, animal, food, relative, or sporting event. Allow students a few moments to elaborate on the image they are forming in their minds before sharing it with their partner.

2 Have students preview the reading selection. Emphasize that they should give special attention to pictures, drawings, or graphics that are included with the text. This is especially important for science or social studies texts, which typically feature a number of visual elements that enhance information. As students notice these visual elements, they begin to see what the material is about. You also may wish to use other sources for pictures that will stimulate the students' imaginations (see You Ought to Be in Pictures, page 149). For example, before biology students tackle the dense prose of their textbook, a science teacher can take them through a short, guided imagery exercise on fungi (see Guided Imagery for Science, page 60). After students imagine the fungi, they are directed to a photograph in their textbook to see how close their imaginations were to the actual item.

3 Tell the students to close their eyes, take several deep breaths, and relax. Introduce the exercise by giving them some background on the situation they will be visualizing. Encourage them to make use of all their senses as they imagine—sight, sound, physical sensations, and emotions. Suggest an image to students one sentence

STRATEGY INDEX
Cognitive Processes
Activating/Focusing
Selecting/Organizing
Integrating/Applying
Text Frames
Cause/Effect
Concept/Definition
Problem/Solution
Compare/Contrast
Proposition/Support
Goal/Action/Outcome
Student Activities
Developing Vocabulary
Brainstorming of Ideas
Learning Cooperatively
Promoting Discussion
Interactive Reading
Encouraging Writing
Graphic Representation
Building Study Skills

at a time, and pause for several seconds after each sentence to allow them time to process what you are saying and to visualize the picture. To prepare students for a reading about the rigors of farming in the Great Plains during the 1880s, begin with the following:

> Imagine being a homesteader on the Great Plains in the late 19th century. You are alone, and you see the prairie much the way it was before the settlers came (see Guided Imagery for Social Studies).

To prepare students for a Guided Imagery exercise on photosynthesis, you might say,

> Think about things you would find in a factory: machines, workers, raw materials, and energy source. Imagine that you can shrink to a size so small that you can walk through the pore of a leaf. You are now in a photosynthesis factory.

Continue with suggestions to help students visualize the process of photosynthesis in a plant. (See Lazear, 1991, for an excellent example of Guided Imagery for photosynthesis.)

4 Ask students to share their reflections about what they were imagining during the exercise. What did they notice with their imaginations? Do they have any questions about what they were attempting to visualize? This would be an excellent opportunity to have students write about what they visualized, as a way of summarizing their insights about the situation.

GUIDED IMAGERY FOR SCIENCE
Fungi

Imagine the air moving through the room. As the air slowly circulates, notice that on these air currents are carried thousands of microscopic, round, bead-like spores.

They are so small you have to look very closely to spot them. These spores are looking for an opportunity to grow. They are like tiny little seeds, searching for a food source that will enable them to grow and live. If they locate a food source with enough moisture, they can grow.

As you watch them drift by, notice that loaf of bread on the counter. The plastic bread bag has been left unopened.

The drifting spores get closer and closer. Some of them begin to land on a slice of bread.

Watch carefully as tiny little strings of cells began to grow from a spore. More and more cells grow out, farther and farther from the spore.

Soon there are so many of them that you see a tangled mass of little strings; these are growing denser and denser as they feed off the bread. You see some of them with little hooks that attach to the bread fibers. They continue to wind outward and outward.

You can start to see a velvety fuzz appearing on the surface of the bread. What colors are you seeing now?

GUIDED IMAGERY FOR SOCIAL STUDIES
The Great Plains

Imagine that you are in Nebraska. It is summer, 1887, and you are standing in the midst of rolling prairie for as far as you can see in all directions.

Look around and see that no trees, buildings, or other human beings are in sight.

Notice the wind gently swaying the 2-foot tall prairie grasses back and forth.

Feel the 90-degree heat from the hot noon sun as it beats down upon you.

Breathe in the dust and pollen from the grasses around you and imagine wiping the grimy sweat from your forehead.

Notice the tired ox standing next to your single-bladed steel plow.

See yourself trudging over to the plow and placing your hands on its rough wooden handles.

Watch the hard-packed deep black prairie soil turn over from your plow blade as you struggle along behind the ox.

Feel the blisters on your hands as they grip the plow handles.

Imagine the strain in your back muscles and in your arms and legs as the plow jerks you along.

Labor your way over a small hill, and in the distance notice the small hut made with thick squares of prairie sod.

Leave the plow and slowly make your way closer to the hut, noticing it in greater and greater detail.

Bend your head as you enter the dark, dank sod hut, and slowly pace around on the hard dirt floor.

5 As students gain practice in visualizing, have them create their own Guided Imagery exercises in cooperative groups or with partners, taking turns describing what they visualized as they read parts of the text.

Advantages

- Students are stimulated to generate their own images when they read.
- Students create vivid mental images of ideas and concepts that help them remember information longer.
- Students who are visual learners become more actively involved with their reading, which is especially true for low achieving students.
- Students find imagery techniques motivational, and they become more personally engaged with the material.

This strategy is appropriate for students from elementary through high school levels and can be effectively used with materials in all content areas.

References

Gambrell, L., Kapinus, B., & Wilson, R. (1987). Using mental imagery and summarization to achieve independence in comprehension. *Journal of Reading, 30*, 638–642.

Lazear, D. (1991). *Seven ways of teaching: The artistry of teaching with multiple intelligences*. Palatine, IL: Skylight.

History Change Frame

The Vikings emanated from the Scandinavian peninsula at the end of 800 A.D. and regularly plundered the inhabitants of northern Europe over the course of the next century. With their high-prowed, shallow-draft vessels, the Vikings created the perfect attack ship, which allowed them to sail long distances under a variety of oceanic conditions. But not only did they pillage monasteries and communities in the British Isles and France, they also became permanent settlers. The Vikings created the duchy of Normandy, for example, which eventually evolved into the country of France.

For many students, history lessons like this one seem to be a never-ending series of facts: names, dates, places, events. What is the point? Students can begin to make more sense of history if they are able to use facts to help them understand the important changes people have experienced, but changes tend to create problems that people have to confront. Learning about these changes helps us to understand better who we are and what we have to deal with today.

Teaching students to read history textbooks with a problem/solution frame of mind enables them to cue into the major changes discussed in a chapter. The History Change Frame (Buehl, 1992, 1995) is a prereading strategy that helps students avoid getting bogged down in the details of what they are reading. The History Change Frame focuses student attention on groups of people who are trying to solve problems brought about by change.

Using the Strategy

The Change Frame is an excellent strategy to use with students in history class when introducing a history textbook or readings. Using the strategy involves the following steps:

1 Select several time periods to be covered in class. In a brainstorming exercise, ask students who they expect will be featured in a reading for each time period. Emphasize that they should think of groups of people, not individuals: What groups of people would you expect to read about in a chapter on the American Revolution? The settling of the American West? The Vietnam War? As students consider what they know about each of these time periods, their responses might include angry colonists and the British;

pioneers, cowboys, and Native Americans; and protesters, the U.S. Army, and communist guerrillas.

2 Introduce the History Change Frame on an overhead transparency (see page 63). In your discussion, note that history tends to focus on people who must try to solve problems that are caused by change. Factual details in a chapter are presented to help readers understand the problems and the actions taken to solve these problems. Highlight the categories of change that are commonly featured in history texts (see Changes in History, page 63). Cue students to notice change dynamics within a section or chapter:

- **Population**—increases or decreases in a geographical area or changes in composition with regard to factors like age distribution or ethnic identity.
- **Technology**—new inventions or other innovations that affect the way things are done in a society.
- **Environmental**—changes in the physical geography of an area or in weather patterns.
- **Economic**—changes in how people make a daily living and in their standard of living.
- **Political**—changes in type of government, the nature of the leaders, elections, laws, court decisions, treaties, and wars.
- **Beliefs**—changes in or opposition to what people believe, including religious beliefs, ideas and views, and values.

3 Assign students a chapter to read. Have them survey the chapter to deter-

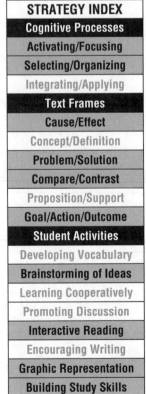

STRATEGY INDEX
Cognitive Processes
Activating/Focusing
Selecting/Organizing
Integrating/Applying
Text Frames
Cause/Effect
Concept/Definition
Problem/Solution
Compare/Contrast
Proposition/Support
Goal/Action/Outcome
Student Activities
Developing Vocabulary
Brainstorming of Ideas
Learning Cooperatively
Promoting Discussion
Interactive Reading
Encouraging Writing
Graphic Representation
Building Study Skills

HISTORY CHANGE FRAME

Who?
(Groups of
people)

take action

effects on

Problems?
What problems did
they face?

Solutions?
(What did
they do about
problem?)

cause

Changes?
(How were
things
changing?)

(Adapted from Buehl, 1995)

mine the groups focused on in the material. Model this process by thinking aloud as you examine the title, headings and subheadings, chapter objectives, advance organizers, primary source excerpts, pictures, and graphics. Determine with students who the players are in the chapter. Who is featured? Do not accept individual names during this phase, but ask students to generalize groups of people who will be involved in the action.

4 Ask students to continue surveying the chapter, looking for clues about problems the groups of people might be encountering: What problems did the pioneers face in the old West? The native inhabitants? What problems concerned women in the Progressive Age? Black Americans? Muckrakers? In some cases, the groups in the chapter may be causing problems that others must deal with: What problems came about because of the Robber Barons in the 1870s and 1880s?

CHANGES IN HISTORY

Categories

- Population
- Technology
- Environmental
- Economic
- Political
- Beliefs

5 As students read, have them work with a partner to fill in a blank History Change Frame Graphic Organizer (see Appendix, page 159). Have them select information from the text that describes the changes that are causing problems for each group of people. Ask students to identify actions taken by groups to solve their problems. For example, changes that affected Native Americans in the latter half of the 19th century included population (the demographic shift resulting from a huge influx of settlers of European ancestry), geographical (ranching and farming altered the prairie and the buffalo were depleted), technological (the railroad and more advanced weapons), economic (mining of gold and other minerals), and political (the passage of the Homestead Act, which promised affordable land to settlers). Conflict also resulted from the drastically divergent world views and beliefs of Native Americans and settlers.

6 Discuss with students how changes affect people in different ways. For example, both the building of the Transcontinental Railroad and the passing of the Homestead Act affected three groups of people in the American West: How did the railroad cause different problems for Native Americans, cattle ranchers, and prairie farmers? How about the Homestead Act? Students come to realize that the affects of changes vary depending on which group of people is considered. Sometimes a change benefits one group and causes problems for another (see History Change Frame for the American West, page 64). For example, the railroad clearly benefited ranchers but spelled ruin for Native Americans. The Homestead Act opened the floodgates to farmers heading west, but was resisted by both cattle ranchers and Native Americans.

Advantages

- Students are provided with a visual overview that helps them sort through a wealth of infor-

HISTORY CHANGE FRAME FOR THE AMERICAN WEST

Group *Native Americans*	Group *Cattle Ranchers*	Group *Prairie Farmers*
What problems did they face? • Less land to live on • Disapperance of Buffalo • Conflicts with settlers • Many were killed	**What problems did they face?** • End of the open range • Conflicts with Native Americans • Conflicts with farmers and sheep ranchers	**What problems did they face?** • Conflicts with Native Americans • Conflicts with cattle ranchers • Hardships of the prairie
What changes caused these problems? • Population—Increased numbers of settlers coming West • Economic—Discovery of gold and other metals • Political—Homestead Act • Technological—The railroad	**What changes caused these problems?** • Population—More settlers who wanted to farm and fence off the prairie • Political—Homestead Act • Technological—The railroad	**What changes caused these problems?** • Political—Homestead Act • Environmental—Harsh weather • Technological—The railroad • Economic—Recessions
What did they do to solve the problems? • Fought the settlers and soldiers • Agreed to treaties • Left reservations • Changed their way of life	**What did they do to solve the problems?** • Got help from Army against Native Americans • Range wars • Accepted fenced prairie	**What did they do to solve the problems?** • Got help from Army against Native Americans • Fenced in the prairie • Adapted to conditions: harsh weather, new machines

(Adapted from Buehl, 1995)

mation and recognize important points of a reading selection.

- Students come to see that the information included in a history chapter is not a series of randomly selected facts.
- Students see how the information fits together, and have a construct for making sense of what they read. The problem/solution text frame enables students to see patterns in history and to develop a coherent understanding of what history is and why it is studied.

The History Change Frame provides an excellent blueprint for writing assignments and other follow-up activities. Relevant information is clearly organized to allow relationships to be established and comparisons to be made. This strategy is appropriate for elementary through high school level students.

References

Buehl, D. (1992). A frame of mind for reading history. *The Exchange. Newsletter of the International Reading Association Secondary Reading Special Interest Group, 5*(1), 4–5.

Buehl, D. (1995). *Classroom strategies for interactive learning.* Schofield, WI: Wisconsin Reading Association.

History Memory Bubbles

Napoleon invaded Russia. The Marshall Plan helped Europe. The Sumerians wrote in cuneiform. George Washington stopped the Whiskey Rebellion. W.E.B. Du Bois was a founder of the National Association for the Advancement of Colored People. Charles I was executed during the English Civil War. The Mormons settled in Utah.

Facts—students reading history textbooks encounter a dizzying and seemingly endless array of factual information. For many, learning about history soon defaults to short-term memorization of isolated facts. The larger context of historical themes and ideas remains murky at best, and after the test is over, information is promptly jettisoned from their memories as the students begin anew with the next chapter.

In contrast, successful learners search for connections and relationships among information as they study. Instead of becoming engulfed by a torrent of disjointed facts, successful learners look for the "flow" of the information. In history textbooks, that flow tends to follow a problem/solution text frame.

The Strategy

History Memory Bubbles (Buehl, 1998) are a form of concept mapping that emphasizes problem/solution relationships in history. Using this strategy involves the following steps:

1 Emphasize to students that history does not consist of isolated facts, but instead tells stories of various groups of people who cope with problems and changes. Have students analyze key terms or facts in terms of their connection to a problem/solution text frame: What is the item? What does it have to do with problems discussed in the chapter? What does it have to do with solving these problems? What does it have to do with changes highlighted in this chapter?

2 Have students identify key terms or facts from a history selection that they have read. For example, the following terms are central to corrupt politics in the post–Civil War era in the United States: *Gilded Age*, *Tweed Ring*, *political patronage*, *graft*, and *Civil Service Act*. Ask students to concentrate solely on in-

formation that focuses attention on key themes and ideas, not on supportive detail (see Chapter 3 about Fact Pyramids). Students typically would approach learning these historical facts by scanning the chapter to locate and memorize minimal details associated with each term: *The Gilded Age* is a book by Mark Twain. The Tweed Ring was a group of dishonest elected officials in New York City. Political patronage was the practice of exchanging political jobs for political support.

3 Place a transparency of a blank History Memory Bubble on the overhead projector (see Appendix, page 160), and model this process using a key term such as *Tweed Ring* (see History Memory Bubbles, Tweed Ring, page 66). In addition to identifying the term, ask students to consider the problems connected to this term and list them on the Memory Bubble under Problems: bribes, election fraud, robbing the city treasury, and exchanging jobs and contracts for votes. The Tweed Ring caused reformers to emerge who prosecuted these crimes, which connects this concept to solutions to the problems: Civil Service reform mandated awarding of jobs based on merit.

4 Have students work with a partner to create Memory Bubbles for the remainder of the targeted terms. When they finish, invite volunteers to share their Memory Bubbles with the entire class. As part of this process, students will discover that corresponding information may not be available to fill all four bubbles for every term or fact. After practicing using this strategy, students can be asked to create Memory Bubbles independently as they learn new material. They will begin to perceive interlinking relationships among key

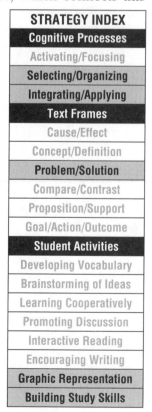

STRATEGY INDEX
Cognitive Processes
Activating/Focusing
Selecting/Organizing
Integrating/Applying
Text Frames
Cause/Effect
Concept/Definition
Problem/Solution
Compare/Contrast
Proposition/Support
Goal/Action/Outcome
Student Activities
Developing Vocabulary
Brainstorming of Ideas
Learning Cooperatively
Promoting Discussion
Interactive Reading
Encouraging Writing
Graphic Representation
Building Study Skills

HISTORY MEMORY BUBBLES

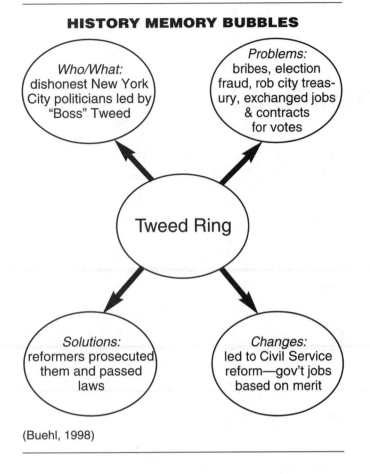

(Buehl, 1998)

terms as they flesh out several Memory Bubbles for a unit of study.

Advantages

- Students see connections that guide them toward remembering information in the context of larger issues and ideas.
- Students are engaged in establishing the significance of key factual material encountered in history textbooks.
- Students examine history terms as concepts that involve a number of connecting variables rather than memorize a single isolated fact about an important term.

History Memory Bubbles may be assigned as a homework activity and for study preparation for chapter exams.

Reference

Buehl, D. (1998). Memory bubbles: They help put information into context. *WEAC News and Views, 33*(7), 13.

Inquiry Charts

The Etruscans: The Etruscans invaded Italy about 600 B.C. They settled in an area by the Tiber River they called Rome. The Etruscans were farmers and they also traded with cities like Carthage. They built roads and cultivated the land. The Gauls defeated the Etruscans and sacked Rome in 390 B.C.

Teachers will have no trouble spotting the generic, rote, encyclopedically derived report unfolding in this example. Unfortunately, much student research results in uninspired, litany-of-fact writing. But what about the interesting stuff? What questions might arise about the ancient Etruscans that more research might answer? What was life like in an Etruscan community? What did they believe? And what impact did these people have on the succeeding Roman civilization? Inquiry Charts (I-Charts) (Hoffman, 1992) help emphasize to students that research is more than a mere collecting of isolated bits of information.

Using the Strategy

The Inquiry Chart is a strategy that helps students generate meaningful questions on which to focus their research and organize their writing. I-Charts are suitable for a whole-class, small-group, or individual inquiry. Using this strategy involves the following steps:

1 Select a topic familiar to students and solicit possible questions to explore. Ask the class to choose three or four of the most interesting questions, which will provide direction for student inquiry.

2 Introduce the I-Chart by modeling use of the chart to organize information on either a large sheet of paper or on a section of the chalkboard. You also may provide students with individual, blank I-Charts (see Appendix, page 161). Record the chosen questions in the boxes along the top. For example, a music teacher wants her musicians to become more knowledgeable about jazz before students began rehearsing a jazz piece for performance (see I-Chart for Jazz). After an array of questions has been generated, the class chooses four on which to center their inquiry: Who invented jazz? What kinds of music is jazz related to? Who were some famous jazz musicians? How has jazz influenced other music?

3 Brainstorm any preexisting knowledge about the topic. Ask students to offer what they know and have them indicate which question on the chart this information might answer. Knowledge not germane to the questions can be placed in the column labeled Other Interesting Facts. This process uncovers any misconceptions about a topic that will be confronted as students learn more.

Music students know that jazz is associated with African American culture and that New Orleans (Louisiana) is regarded as a founding city. They may offer that rock music is related to jazz and comment that instruments such as the saxophone, used with performers such as Bruce Springsteen, are often regarded as jazz-type instruments. Because of the recent centennial of Duke Ellington's birth some students may recall his name, although others might put forth Kenny G. as an example of a jazz musician. Their awareness of jazz clubs, which does not fit under the target questions, is recorded in the Other Interesting Facts column.

4 Provide access to a variety of materials, including newspaper and magazine articles, for students to consult to answer their target questions. Have students work in cooperative groups, with each group consulting a different source. The target questions will guide students as they decide which material in a source is useful and which is extraneous. Have each group record their information on sticky notes, one fact per note, which are affixed to the chart paper or chalkboard under the appropriate question. Color-coded sticky notes make it easier to identify the source from which the information was taken. As notes are added to the I-Chart, it becomes clear

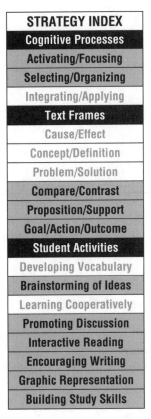

STRATEGY INDEX

Cognitive Processes
Activating/Focusing
Selecting/Organizing
Integrating/Applying

Text Frames
Cause/Effect
Concept/Definition
Problem/Solution
Compare/Contrast
Proposition/Support
Goal/Action/Outcome

Student Activities
Developing Vocabulary
Brainstorming of Ideas
Learning Cooperatively
Promoting Discussion
Interactive Reading
Encouraging Writing
Graphic Representation
Building Study Skills

I-CHART FOR JAZZ

Topic: Jazz	Q1: Who invented jazz?	Q2: What kinds of music is jazz related to?	Q3:Who were some famous jazz musicians	Q4: How has jazz influenced other music?	Other Interesting Facts	New Questions
What We Know:	African Americans New Orleans	Rock music	Duke Ellington Kenny G.	Rock—Bruce Springsteen has instruments like saxophone	There are jazz clubs in New Orleans.	
Source: Book—*The Story of Jazz*						
Source: *Smithsonian Magazine*— "Our Jazz Heritage"						
Source: *Groves Music Dictionary*— "Jazz"						
Summaries						

(Adapted from Hoffman, 1992)

whether enough information has been discovered and whether each question has been answered adequately.

As students consult sources on jazz, they discover a variety of facts and information that address their questions: Blues, a music with which they are less familiar, is a precursor of jazz, as are work songs and gospel songs. Ragtime is an early form of jazz. These facts are entered in the Question 2 column on the I-Chart. Students place information according to the specific source in which they found it, although some information is contained in all sources, which is also indicated on the I-Chart. Students are surprised to learn that classical music has been influenced by jazz, and they record information about George Gershwin and Leonard Bernstein in the Question 4 column. As they read about jazz compact disc clubs and jazz radio stations, a new question emerges from their research: How popular is jazz today?

5 Ask students to synthesize information from each question into a summary. Sometimes contradictory material is uncovered, which also needs to be acknowledged. Summarization provides a transition from inquiry to writing, as students decide on main idea statements for each question and organize pertinent details.

6 Students are ready to write about their topic, and they proceed to discuss each question and the information that relates to it. Each vertical column may comprise a paragraph or, with more sophisticated inquiry, a section of a written discussion of the topic. Students also may wish to respond to one or two additional questions that occurred to them as they delved into their sources, which can be added to either the Other Interesting Facts or New Questions columns.

Advantages

- As students become more independent, they can develop individual I-Charts that focus their inquiry and organize their notes.
- Student writing is less likely to be a rambling compendium of facts and is more likely to be centered on the significant questions that they had a role in developing.
- Students receive guided practice in synthesizing and summarizing information.

• Students use multiple sources that provide a variety of information as a basis for an inquiry project rather than answering identical questions based on a single source.

Reference

Hoffman, J. (1992). Critical reading/thinking across the curriculum: Using I-charts to support learning. *Language Arts, 69*, 121–127.

Interactive Reading Guides

Go to the big oak tree in the center of the park. Walk 20 paces in the direction the lowest limb is pointing. Go to the large speckled rock. Under the rock...

We all probably have participated in a treasure hunt. We were given a series of instructions or clues that led to several locations. At times we had to pause and think about a clue, and it helped to collaborate with others. If we followed all the instructions carefully, we would discover the spot that contained the treasure—the whole point of the hunt.

Getting the point of a reading assignment, however, is a difficult task for many students. They are confounded by the large amount of information they encounter in textbooks and find it difficult to differentiate key ideas from supporting detail. Students could benefit from a few clues to direct them through the text. Interactive Reading Guides make it possible for students to learn from text materials that may be too difficult for independent reading.

Using the Strategy

The Interactive Reading Guide (Wood, 1988) is an excellent strategy to assist students in productive reading of text materials. A variation of the study guide, Interactive Reading Guides involve students in working with partners or small groups to find the essential ideas in their reading. Using the strategy involves the following steps:

1 Preview students' reading assignment to determine major information to be learned and to locate possible pitfalls for understanding. Be especially concerned with the difficulties that struggling readers might have with the material. Notice salient features of the text that students might overlook such as pictures, charts, and graphs. Determine any mismatch between students and text. Does the author assume knowledge that some students might lack? Does the author introduce ideas and vocabulary without sufficient explanation or examples? Does the author use language or sentence style that may be difficult for some students?

2 Construct an Interactive Reading Guide for students to complete with partners or in cooperative groups. Design the guide to help students decide where to focus their attention during reading and to support their learning when the material might prove challenging. Pose questions that compel students to think carefully about the material and to make meaningful connections and draw conclusions. This will motivate students to problem-solve with one another in order to ascertain appropriate responses.

3 Divide the passage into segments—those to be read orally by individuals to their group, those to be read silently by each student, and those less important to be skimmed. Use the guide to provide additional background information or encourage students to brainstorm what they already know about the topic.

For a biology class, a department of natural resources publication detailing water conditions in streams may be too difficult for students to read independently. Instead, the teacher divides the reading among the cooperative groups, with each group reading one segment of the material (see Jigsaw, page 73). Each group is given a separate Interactive Reading Guide so that each group becomes expert on a particular segment about water: clarity, acidity, temperature, and amount of dissolved oxygen available in water (see Interactive Reading Guide for Biology). The Interactive Reading Guide helps students manage an otherwise formidable task. Later, students can analyze a local stream for four crucial water variables that affect fish, using the guides to remind them of the key information needed for their analysis.

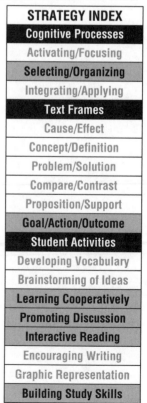

STRATEGY INDEX

Cognitive Processes
Activating/Focusing
Selecting/Organizing
Integrating/Applying
Text Frames
Cause/Effect
Concept/Definition
Problem/Solution
Compare/Contrast
Proposition/Support
Goal/Action/Outcome
Student Activities
Developing Vocabulary
Brainstorming of Ideas
Learning Cooperatively
Promoting Discussion
Interactive Reading
Encouraging Writing
Graphic Representation
Building Study Skills

INTERACTIVE READING GUIDE FOR BIOLOGY

Water Clarity and Sediments (pages 11–12)

1. Look at the drawing of the fish at the top of the page. Two things are mentioned as "stream trouble-makers." What are these two things?

2. A key word in your reading is "clarity." <u>Student A</u>: Read aloud paragraph 1 to your group. <u>Group</u>: Decide what "water clarity" means and write it below: If you were a fish, what would be the best type of water, according to paragraph 1?

3. Paragraph 2 talks about the color of a stream. <u>Group</u>: Silently skim this paragraph and find two things that can change the color of water in a stream.

4. Paragraph 3 is the main point of your article. <u>Student B</u>: Read paragraph 3 aloud to your group. <u>Group</u>: Decide what effects algae and sediments have on water.

5. Paragraph 4 describes algae. <u>Group</u>: Silently read the paragraph and look for the following information on algae:
   • What kinds of streams are most likely to have algae?
   • What exactly is algae?
   • What color is water that has a lot of algae?

6. <u>Student C</u>: Read paragraph 5 aloud to your group. <u>Group</u>: Tell what kinds of things could be "sediment" in a stream.

7. <u>Group</u>: Read paragraph 6 silently and look for ways sediment gets into streams. Discuss what these ways are and write them here.

8. <u>Group</u>: Silently skim paragraphs 7, 8, and 9. If you were a fish, which source of sediment sounds the worst to you?

9. Sediment and algae make water cloudy, which cause trouble for fish. The next paragraphs tell five reasons why. <u>Student A</u>: Silently read paragraphs 10 and 11. <u>Student B</u>: Silently read paragraphs 12 and 13. <u>Student C</u>: Silently read paragraph 14. Share the five reasons why cloudy water is bad for fish and write them below in your own words.

Developed by Doug Buehl & S. Krauskopf, 1998, Madison East High School, Madison, WI, USA.

INTERACTIVE READING GUIDE FOR HISTORY

Section A: Introduction to Ellis Island (pages 1–2)

1. <u>Class</u>: Listen and follow along in the article as I read this passage to you. Then based on what you remember respond to the questions below. If you need to, you can locate information from the article:
   • Ellis Island is located in what city?
   • What famous national landmark can be seen from Ellis Island?
   • List four reasons why immigrants came to the United States that were mentioned.

Section B: Early Immigration to the United States (pages 2–3)

1. <u>Partners</u>: Read paragraph 1 silently and decide on an answer to the following question:
   • Who were the first immigrants to the United States?

2. <u>Partner X</u>: Read aloud paragraph 2. <u>Partner Y</u>: Listen and decide how to answer the following questions:
   • Were the early immigrants to the United States regarded as a good thing?
   • Why or why not?

3. <u>Partner Y</u>: Read aloud paragraph 3. <u>Partner X</u>: Listen and decide how to answer the following questions:
   • Did the government keep very close track of immigrants in the early days?
   • What clues in the article helped you figure this out?

4. <u>Partners</u>: Read paragraphs 4, 5, & 6 silently. List four things that attracted people to the United States.

5. <u>Partner X</u>: Read paragraphs 7 & 8 out loud. <u>Partner Y</u>: Listen and decide how to answer:
   • What are some of the nationalities of the new immigrants?
   • What was the attitude of many Americans to the new immigrants?

Developed by Doug Buehl & P. McDonald, 1999, Madison East High School, Madison, WI, USA.

For a history class, an Interactive Reading Guide helps students navigate a challenging article on immigration to supplement a history textbook (see Interactive Reading Guide for History). After orally reading the first section to the entire class, students can confer with partners over the next couple of class periods as they read the material and complete the guide.

 Have each group use the completed guides as an outline to report their information to the whole class.

Advantages

- Students are conditioned to read materials at different rates for varying purposes, reading some sections carefully and skimming others.

- Students use partners as resources for tackling challenging reading assignments and discussing the material while they read.

- Struggling readers are especially supported by the use of Interactive Reading Guides.

Completed Interactive Reading Guides serve as organized notes for classroom discussions and follow-up activities, and also make excellent study guides for examinations.

Reference

Wood, K. (1988). Guiding students through informational text. *The Reading Teacher, 41*(9), 912–920.

Jigsaw

Think about the potluck dinners you have attended over the years. A potluck meal is a traditional way of feeding a large group of people. Everyone brings a dish, either a favorite recipe or a new recipe, to round out the meal. People tend to choose dishes that they feel especially confident preparing—some offer salads or desserts, while others create main dish specialties. Potluck is an especially efficient way to organize a meal because no one individual has sole responsibility for all the work, but a wide range of possibilities are offered and shared by everyone.

The potluck concept can be applied in imaginative ways to meet the needs of a wide range of student interests and abilities. A similar concept, the Jigsaw strategy (Aronson et al., 1978), involves students in reading different selections and then sharing what they have learned with a group or whole class. Reading tasks can be distributed among group members so that some students might receive more challenging materials than less skilled students. The Jigsaw strategy can be used in a number of ways in the classroom, for example:

- Students could be jigsawed to read different sections of a textbook chapter, different short stories that follow a similar theme, or stories by the same author.

- Students could investigate different areas of emphasis within a topic of instruction such as the impact of ozone depletion on plants, weather, bodies of water, and incidence of skin cancer; or in history class, investigate New Deal initiatives that focused on public relief, agricultural programs, public works projects, or industrial policies.

- Students could be jigsawed for independent research projects, each group responsible for tackling one area of study within a general topic.

Using the Strategy

This strategy is adaptable to a wide variety of curricular settings, all of which involve the following steps:

1 Identify a range of materials related to significant topics addressed in a lesson. Consider the skills of the students who will be involved in the exercise, and if necessary, collect selections of varying text difficulty and sophistication. For middle school students studying weather, a teacher could collect different sources about hurricanes: (a) a textbook excerpt that details atmospheric conditions that create hurricanes, (b) a magazine article that describes geographic areas subject to hurricanes and the resulting economic consequences, (c) an encyclopedia segment that provides a historical perspective of significant hurricanes, (d) a short book chapter that describes precautionary measures and preparations for hurricanes, and (e) a newspaper account that features a personal narrative of experiences and damages inflicted by a specific hurricane. (Each article could be color coded with colored dot stickers, to facilitate communication and grouping.)

2 Organize students into cooperative groups of four to six, depending on the number of selections available to be assigned. Each group member is responsible for reading one selection. Depending on the nature of the group, either assign selections or allow students to self-select.

3 Ask students to read selections independently. For photocopied selections, encourage them to underline important information to share with their group; for materials that cannot be marked, use sticky notes. Ask students to jot down notes or to follow a graphic notetaking outline for extracting important concepts from their reading (see Structured Notetaking, page 138).

4 Regroup students according to those assigned the same selection so

STRATEGY INDEX
Cognitive Processes
Activating/Focusing
Selecting/Organizing
Integrating/Applying
Text Frames
Cause/Effect
Concept/Definition
Problem/Solution
Compare/Contrast
Proposition/Support
Goal/Action/Outcome
Student Activities
Developing Vocabulary
Brainstorming of Ideas
Learning Cooperatively
Promoting Discussion
Interactive Reading
Encouraging Writing
Graphic Representation
Building Study Skills

that they can compare notes and discuss important concepts and information. (To minimize confusion, ask students to group by assigned color codes.) Have group members examine information gathered by each member, which they will merge into a coherent summary of key points, a concept map, a graphic outline, or a highlighted set of notes. Collect these from each group at the end of the class period and photocopy them so that all members of the class will have a personal copy the next day.

5 Direct students to return to their original group and have each group member share pertinent information from each selection, referring to the color-coded photocopied materials created before. The rest of the group is accountable for learning the new information, which will be assessed during the evaluation of this unit of study.

Advantages

- Students encounter a wider breadth of material than might be possible if each individual independently read all available sources.
- Students may elect to learn from materials more appropriate to their abilities and specific interests.
- Students receive support from class members in learning from their reading.
- Students gain practice in synthesizing important information from what they read as they assume the teacher role with group members.

Reference

Aronson, E., Stephen, C., Sikes, J., Blaney, N., & Snapp, M. (1978). *The jigsaw classroom*. Beverly Hills, CA: Sage.

K-W-L Plus
(Know/Want to Know/Learned)

Say you are planning a trip to a foreign country. As you prepare an itinerary, you consider what you already know about the country. As you sort through various travel guides, articles, maps, and brochures, you plot activities and designate places to visit. At this point you probably think to yourself, What don't I know that I would like to find more about? After you have immersed yourself in resources, you take stock of what you have learned about the destination and act on this knowledge by constructing an itinerary that matches your desires and priorities.

This scenario represents a very purposeful and pragmatic reading event. A persistent challenge for teachers is to encourage students to adopt a similar attitude in their classrooms—to be active thinkers while they read. Active readers make predictions about what they will be reading. Before they start, active readers consider what they already know about a story or topic. Then as they read they confirm whether their predictions were correct. Active readers have an idea of what to look for, and when they are done they evaluate what they have learned or experienced.

Many students are not active readers and are confused about what they should be thinking as they read. The K-W-L Plus strategy (Carr & Ogle, 1987) is a technique that helps students activate what they already know before they begin a reading assignment. Using this strategy with students will help them make predictions about what they will be reading through the generation of questions they would like to have answered. The strategy also helps students to organize what they have learned when they are finished reading.

Using the Strategy

K-W-L (Know/Want to Know/Learned) (Ogle, 1986) involves the use of a three-column graphic organizer that becomes the students' study guide as they read (see K-W-L for Rattlesnakes, page 86). The graphic organizer can be used as a worksheet or displayed on a chalkboard or an overhead transparency. Using the strategy involves the following steps:

1 Write the main topic of a story or selection at the top of the K-W-L grid. Ask students to contribute what they know or think they know about the topic.

Record these contributions in the first column K—What We Know. Students preparing to read a story about Eskimos might contribute the following: *live in the far north, ice and snow, igloos, warm clothes made from sealskins,* and *sled dogs.* A selection about rattlesnakes might elicit *poisonous, fangs, diamondbacks, live in deserts,* and *shake rattles as warning.*

2 Record students' questions as this information is shared in the middle column W—What We Want to Know: Are all rattlesnakes poisonous? Will you die if you are bitten? Do rattlesnakes always rattle before they strike? Ask students for other questions they would like answered about rattlesnakes, for instance, Do they live in our area? What do they look like?

3 Guide students in categorizing their knowledge and questions, which are recorded in a list titled Categories of Information We Expect to Use. Categories for rattlesnakes might include where they live (location), what they do (abilities), how they look (description), and their effects on people (people).

4 Ask students to read the story or selection to look for information that answers their questions or expands their understanding of the topic.

5 When the students have completed their reading, focus their attention on the third column L—What We Have Learned. Ask students to offer new information they discovered in the reading and record this on the grid. Ask what category this new information fits under (for rattlesnakes: location, abilities, description, or people) and indicate the appropriate code letter. New categories may also emerge. Experienced students may complete this step independ-

STRATEGY INDEX
Cognitive Processes
Activating/Focusing
Selecting/Organizing
Integrating/Applying
Text Frames
Cause/Effect
Concept/Definition
Problem/Solution
Compare/Contrast
Proposition/Support
Goal/Action/Outcome
Student Activities
Developing Vocabulary
Brainstorming of Ideas
Learning Cooperatively
Promoting Discussion
Interactive Reading
Encouraging Writing
Graphic Representation
Building Study Skills

K-W-L FOR RATTLESNAKES

K (Know)	W (Want to Know)	L (Learned)
• They have sharp fangs.	• What do they look like?	A—all are poisonous
• They are poisonous.	• Are all rattlesnakes poisonous?	A—often warn before biting
• They live in deserts.	• Will you die if you get bitten by a rattlesnake?	D—member of the pit viper family
• They shake their rattles before striking.	• Do all rattlesnakes rattle before biting?	L—28 varieties found from Canada to South America
• Diamondbacks are a type.	• Do any live in our area?	L—most found in deserts
• They live in holes.	• What medicine stops the poison?	L—some found in Midwest
• They eat mice.		D—rattle is set of horny pieces joined together
		P—bite can be fatal to small children
		P—some bites can kill adults
		A—young snakes are born live rather than from eggs

Categories of Information We Expect to Use:
1. Where they live (L—Location)
2. What they do (A—Abilities)
3. How they look (D—Description)
4. How they affect people (P—People)

(Buehl, 1995; adapted from Ogle, 1986)

ently by filling in new information on a K-W-L worksheet, but many students will need guidance and direction in organizing this information.

6 When the K-W-L grid is complete, create a concept map that brings together all the information under each category, designed by either the whole class or by individual students (see Concept Map for Rattlesnakes). In this way, the information is organized for student writing assignments or other projects. Questions from the W (Want to Know) column that are not answered by the reading provide the basis for independent projects and research.

Advantages

- K-W-L provides teachers with an inventory of students' background knowledge about a topic.
- Students have a structure for making predictions about what they will be reading.

- Students develop self-questioning skills and learn to read actively to answer their questions about a topic.
- Students are guided into meaningful organization of new information.
- Student misconceptions about topic are revealed and addressed during instruction.

K-W-L Plus can be used as a strategy for lessons in social studies, science, math, and other subject areas.

References

Buehl, D. (1995). *Classroom strategies for interactive learning.* Madison, WI: Wisconsin State Reading Association.

Carr, E.M., & Ogle D. (1987). K-W-L Plus: A strategy for comprehension and summarization. *Journal of Reading, 28,* 626–631.

Ogle, D. (1986). K-W-L: A teaching model that develops active reading of expository text. *The Reading Teacher, 39,* 564–570.

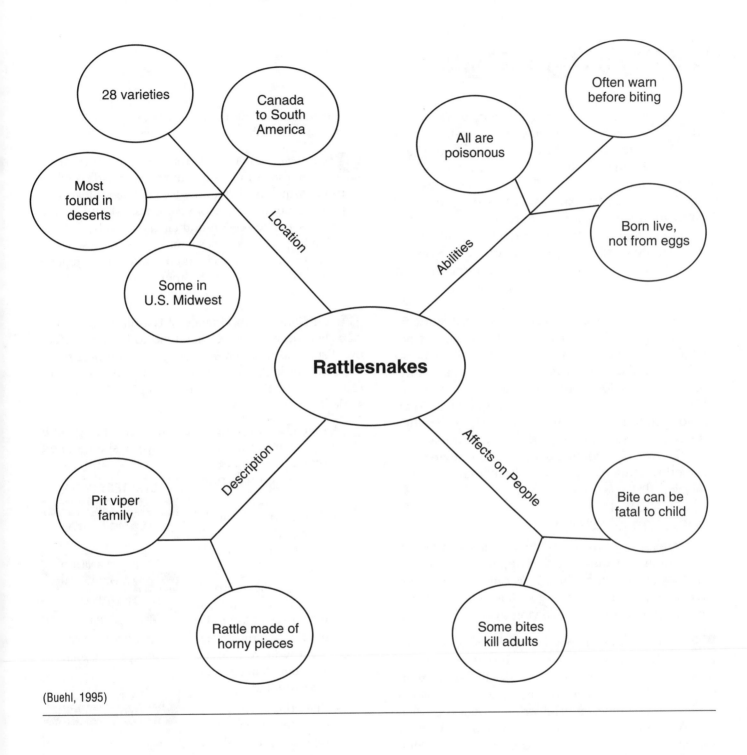

(Buehl, 1995)

Learning Logs

"What did you learn in school today?" This timeless greeting by parents to their children after another day in the classroom asks to share in their children's newly developed insights and explorations into knowledge. But the responses frequently received by parents to this daily query—half-hearted shrugs and vague replies—are not encouraging. Students find it difficult to summarize meaningfully what they are learning, and parents often are left with the impression that their children cannot communicate what they are learning in the classroom.

One reason for this occurrence is that students have had insufficient practice in reformulating what they learn into their own language. They become so immersed in the vocabulary and factual detail of their classes that they lose sight of the need to translate all of this into their own personal understandings. They are so preoccupied with the work of school that they lose sight of actual learning. Integrating Learning Logs into the classroom routine is an excellent strategy for prompting students to think about their learning (Fulwiler, 1980).

Using the Strategy

Learning Logs involve students in informal reflective writing and stimulate thinking about what and how they are learning. These Logs can become a journal component of a class notebook assignment. Using the strategy involves the following steps:

1 Discuss with students how verbalizing thoughts through writing is an essential part of truly understanding a concept or a process. (Reflective writing may be a new process for many students.) Model the concept by reflecting and writing about your own experience; for example, share a journal entry about something you are currently engaged in such as computer applications:

> I am still unclear about the process of pasting graphics, such as a photograph, into a Web page. Sometimes it works fine, but sometimes the picture takes up way too much memory and I don't know what to do to make it smaller. Consequently, the Web page takes forever to come up. The manual is a little confusing on this

process, so maybe I need to talk to Ken (a fellow teacher) about the problems I am having.

2 Emphasize to students that Learning Logs are a mechanism for recording thoughts and ideas while learning, which is also a time for evaluating learning. Depending on the nature of your class, ask students to reserve a separate section of their class notebook for a Learning Log. In some cases it may make more sense to follow a thematic approach and have students integrate their reflections along with other homework and assignments recorded in their notebooks.

3 Highlight the importance of Learning Logs in the classroom, because they tend to be most effective if students do them frequently—two or three times a week. Students may be given 2 to 10 minutes to record entries. Establish the following guidelines with students:

- that Learning Logs are informal writing—the recording of reflections—not polished, edited writing, and that the focus is more on thinking and less on writing form;

- that Learning Logs be kept and organized in the class notebook;

- that class notebooks will be collected periodically, read, and perhaps responded to by the teacher, thus creating a written dialogue between teacher and students; and

- that the process is nonthreatening and allows for students' self-expression.

4 Use Learning Logs as an integral part of the routine for learning in your classroom. You might have students write an entry to

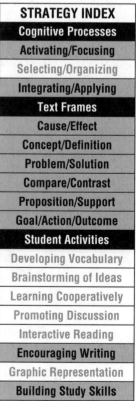

STRATEGY INDEX
Cognitive Processes
Activating/Focusing
Selecting/Organizing
Integrating/Applying
Text Frames
Cause/Effect
Concept/Definition
Problem/Solution
Compare/Contrast
Proposition/Support
Goal/Action/Outcome
Student Activities
Developing Vocabulary
Brainstorming of Ideas
Learning Cooperatively
Promoting Discussion
Interactive Reading
Encouraging Writing
Graphic Representation
Building Study Skills

prepare for learning new material. For example, before a group of fifth graders reads a science passage on glaciers, ask them to write about some of the things they already know about this topic:

> Glaciers are made of ice. I know we had them in Wisconsin, because of a camping trip our family took. We hiked along hills the glacier made. All the Wisconsin glaciers must have melted, but I don't know why.

Reflective writing is also appropriate after students have read a selection; for example, an entry by a ninth grader reading a U.S. history passage on the Progressive Era:

> I was especially upset that the Progressives were doing these reforms and they were ignoring African Americans. I agree that they did a lot of good things like the child labor laws, but they mostly left racism alone, I didn't know that the NAACP was started then, but I can see that the NAACP were the Progressives who wanted to fight racism.

Learning Logs can be used to evaluate how learning is proceeding. For example, high school seniors working on a research project might be asked to comment on the various stages involved in putting their project together. One entry about using the *Readers Guide to Periodical Literature* might note:

> I started by using the Reader's Guide program on the library computers. I wanted to find information on how visualization techniques can help tennis players. But I couldn't find enough listings for visualization and tennis, sports, or athletics. I also tried relaxation and stress as key words but I wasn't finding the right sources. After 2 days I was ready to quit, but then I picked up some ideas from the book *Inner Tennis*, and I was able to locate some more magazine articles. I had no idea it would be this frustrating!

5 Learning Logs have a number of applications in the classroom (Santa & Havens, 1991). This strategy can be especially useful as an introductory exercise to initiate class or cooperative-group discussions. Learning Logs provide students with the opportunity to explore their thinking before being called on to communicate their ideas to others. Other applications include:

- reflecting on a unit of study to prepare for exams;
- predicting results of experiments or situations;
- expressing personal opinions related to what is being studied;
- explaining why something happened;
- summarizing understandings of a previous lesson;
- clarifying points of confusion and raising questions about material that is not yet clearly understood;
- recording observations, such as during a science experiment or the viewing of a video; and
- comparing how ideas have changed after learning, or how misconceptions have been corrected.

Advantages

- Students are encouraged to reflect on their learning and they receive practice in using writing to internalize what they are studying.
- Students write for themselves as an audience, which personalizes their learning.
- Students receive regular prompts to express their learning in their own words.
- Teachers are provided with direct feedback and insight into how their students are understanding their curriculum and what difficulties are being encountered.

This strategy can be effectively used in all subject areas and is appropriate for elementary through high school age students.

References

Fulwiler, T. (1980). Journals across the disciplines. *The English Journal, 69*(9), 14–19.

Santa C., & Havens, L. (1991). Learning through writing. In C. Santa and D. Alvermann (Eds.), *Science learning: Processes and applications* Newark, DE: International Reading Association.

Magnet Summaries

Consider for a moment the many pieces of federal legislation that are considered by the U.S. Congress each year on a variety of public issues. One example is the Clinton adminstration's proposal for universal health care in the United States. This proposal was packaged in a large document filled with information relating to health-care providers, insurance companies, managed competition, costs of services and pharmaceuticals, core benefits, and other aspects of health care. What sense could be made out of such a formidable body of information? How could we cut to the essence of the program for the average citizen?

Mostly, we rely on summarization—the distillations by various experts, analysts, and writers, and ourselves—which renders a bulk of information manageable for understanding. As adults, both on the job and in other aspects of daily life, we are bombarded by information that needs to be summarized in order to be understood. Summarization skills also are critical for students, many of whom find it difficult to reduce information to essential ideas in order to learn it. Lack of summarization skills results in many of our students not being able to "see the forest for the trees" as they read. The Magnet Summary (Buehl, 1993) is a strategy that helps students rise above the details and construct meaningful summaries in their own words.

Using the Strategy

Magnet Summaries involve the identification of key terms or concepts—magnet words—from a reading, which students use to organize important information into a summary. Using this strategy consists of the following steps:

1 Introduce the idea of magnet words to students by inquiring what effect a magnet has on metal. Just as magnets attract metal, magnet words attract information. To illustrate, ask students to read a short portion of their text assignment, looking for a key term or concept to which the details in the passage seem to connect. After students finish reading, solicit from them possible magnet words, commenting that most will come from information in the passage. Note that magnet words frequently appear in titles, headings, or may be highlighted in bold or italic print but caution

students that not all words in bold or italic are necessarily magnet words.

2 Write the magnet word on the chalkboard or overhead transparency. Ask students to recall important details from the passage that are connected to the magnet word. As you write these details around the magnet word, have students follow the same procedure on an index card. Allow them a second look at the passage so they can include any important details they may have missed.

Ninth-grade students studying a U.S. history section on the westward movement of settlers may decide on the magnet word *Homestead Act*. The key details surrounding this concept might include *160 acres*, and *must farm land for 5 years*.

3 Ask students to complete the reading of the entire passage. Distribute three or four additional index cards to each student for recording magnet words from the remaining material. For younger students, indicate that they should identify a magnet word for each paragraph or section following a heading. In cooperative groups, have students decide on the best magnet words for the remaining cards. Have them generate the important details for each magnet word. When the groups are finished, each student will have four or five cards, each with a magnet word and key related information (see Magnet Summaries for History).

4 Model for students how the information on one card can be organized and combined into a sentence that sums up the passage of text. The magnet word should occupy a central place in the sentence. Omit any unimportant details from the sentence.

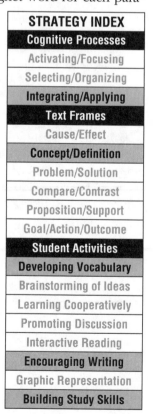

STRATEGY INDEX

Cognitive Processes
Activating/Focusing
Selecting/Organizing
Integrating/Applying
Text Frames
Cause/Effect
Concept/Definition
Problem/Solution
Compare/Contrast
Proposition/Support
Goal/Action/Outcome
Student Activities
Developing Vocabulary
Brainstorming of Ideas
Learning Cooperatively
Promoting Discussion
Interactive Reading
Encouraging Writing
Graphic Representation
Building Study Skills

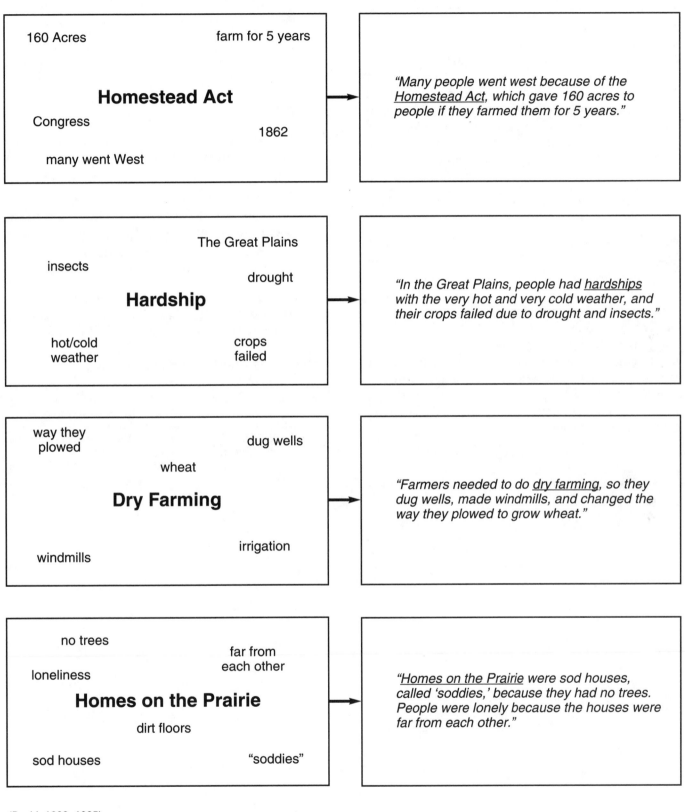

160 Acres   farm for 5 years

Homestead Act

Congress   1862

many went West

"Many people went west because of the *Homestead Act*, which gave 160 acres to people if they farmed them for 5 years."

The Great Plains

insects   drought

Hardship

hot/cold weather   crops failed

"In the Great Plains, people had *hardships* with the very hot and very cold weather, and their crops failed due to drought and insects."

---

way they plowed   dug wells

wheat

Dry Farming

windmills   irrigation

"Farmers needed to do *dry farming*, so they dug wells, made windmills, and changed the way they plowed to grow wheat."

---

no trees   far from each other

loneliness

Homes on the Prairie

dirt floors

sod houses   "soddies"

"*Homes on the Prairie* were sod houses, called 'soddies,' because they had no trees. People were lonely because the houses were far from each other."

(Buehl, 1993, 1995)

5 Have students return to their cooperative groups to construct sentences that summarize each of their remaining cards. Urge students to combine information in one sentence, although it may be necessary to construct two sentences for a particular card. They may decide to omit some details if they judge them to be of secondary importance. Have students work their sentences on scratch paper first. Then instruct them to write the final version of each sentence on the back of the appropriate card and underline the magnet words. For example, the card for the Homestead Act might be summarized as follows:

> Many people went west because of the Homestead Act, which gave 160 acres to people if they farmed them for 5 years.

6 Direct students to arrange the sentences in the order they wish their summary to read. At this point, the sentences will need to be altered so they flow smoothly from one to the other. Model inserting connectives and other language that integrates the sentences into a summary. At this point students should also judge whether all important ideas are included, and whether anything further can be deleted. Students can then test their summaries by listening to how they sound when they are read aloud. The following example is a Magnet Summary for a history passage on life in the Great Plains in the 1880s:

> Many people moved west because of the Homestead Act, which gave them 160 acres if they farmed this land for 5 years. But in the Great Plains, people had hardships from the very hot and very cold weather, and their crops failed due to drought and insects. Therefore farmers needed to do dry farming, so they dug wells, made windmills, and changed the way they plowed to grow wheat. The farmers' homes on the prairie were sod houses, called "soddies," because there were no trees. The people were lonely because the houses were far from each other.

Advantages

- Students gain practice in translating key concepts into their own words.

- Students flesh out their understandings of key vocabulary and ideas.

- Students learn to identify main ideas and relate significant information to these ideas.

- Students are actively involved in constructing a meaningful synthesis of what they have read.

This strategy is appropriate for students from elementary level through high school level and can be successfully used with materials in all content areas.

References and Suggested Reading

Buehl, D. (1993). Magnetized: Students are drawn to technique that identifies key words. *WEAC News & Views, 29*(4), 13.

Buehl, D. (1995). *Classroom strategies for interactive learning.* Madison, WI: Wisconsin State Reading Association.

Hayes, D. (1989). Helping students GRASP the knack of writing summaries. *Journal of Reading, 33*, 96–101.

Vacca, R., & Vacca, J. (1999). *Content area reading* (6th ed.). New York: Longman.

Math Reading Keys

An angle is the union of two rays that have the same endpoint. The sides of angles are the two rays; the vertex is the common endpoint of the rays. Angles may be formed by segments, as in polygons, but the sides of the angle are still considered to be rays. (Adapted from Scott, Foresman, 1991)

Um...let's see here. An angle is formed when two rays (straight lines) come together and touch. The parts of the angle are the rays (the sides) and the vertex (point where they touch). Figures like polygons (a square for example) have angles because lines (segments) touch here too. We know that segments and rays are both straight lines, but why does the example state that segments (lines with beginnings and ends) are the same as rays (lines that continue to infinity)?

Increasingly, mathematics textbooks and assessments require students to use reading as a means to learn and demonstrate knowledge. But as the geometry example illustrates, text found in math textbooks presents special challenges for students. Math language is very precise and compact—each sentence conveys a heavy load of conceptual information. Presumably, textbook authors know a lot about math and often assume that readers have more previous knowledge than they actually do. In addition, many students have the mind-set that math is only the manipulation of numbers. They glide over math text in an attempt to jump right into solving problems and rely on the teacher to clear up misunderstandings. Therefore, students must take a different approach to reading math compared with social studies, science, or literature.

Using the Strategy

Math Reading Keys, strategies that help students key into the unique features of math text, will help them learn more effectively from their reading. Using these strategies involves the following steps:

1 Have students establish the identity of the math textbook author(s). Emphasize that university professors and math experts use vocabulary unfamiliar to students or expect students to know more than they actually do. Students need to approach math text with careful deliberation. Especially significant questions for

math are, What does the author assume that I already know? and What previous math concepts does this author expect me to remember? (See Questioning the Author, page 112.)

2 Model how to read through a challenging section of text. Reproduce a few pages from a textbook on an overhead transparency and have students follow in their textbooks as you think aloud. Highlight *knowledge gaps*—spots where the author thinks that readers have sufficient knowledge and therefore need no further explanation. For example, a passage on decimal notation in a pre-algebra text states,

> The decimal system of writing numbers is based on the number 10. The digits we use in the decimal system are 0, 1, 2, 3, 4, 5, 6, 7, 8, 9. Numbers written in the decimal system are said to be in decimal notation. In our system, the smallest 10 whole numbers are written with only a single digit. (Adapted from Scott, Foresman, 1995)

Your think-aloud on this passage might unfold as follows:

Decimal system—I know about decimals. Decimal points are used for a part of a number, like .4, .59, or .823. But the author doesn't talk about decimal points here. The author must think I know what whole numbers and digits are, because he doesn't define them. He gives examples (0, 1, 2,...) for digits, and I remember that from before. I'm not clear about the statement: based on the number 10. Does that mean like four tenths, or five tenths? This part on decimal notation is not clear. I better go over that again or ask for clarification.

3 Point out how your think-aloud followed the steps in the Math Reading Keys bookmark (see exam-

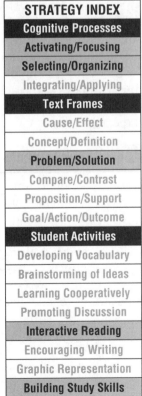

STRATEGY INDEX
Cognitive Processes
Activating/Focusing
Selecting/Organizing
Integrating/Applying
Text Frames
Cause/Effect
Concept/Definition
Problem/Solution
Compare/Contrast
Proposition/Support
Goal/Action/Outcome
Student Activities
Developing Vocabulary
Brainstorming of Ideas
Learning Cooperatively
Promoting Discussion
Interactive Reading
Encouraging Writing
Graphic Representation
Building Study Skills

MATH READING KEYS BOOKMARK

1. Read carefully to make sure each sentence makes sense.
2. Summarize what you read in your own words.
3. When you encounter tough words, think of easier words that mean that same thing and substitute.
4. Discuss with a partner what you read
   a. to make sure you understand, and
   b. to clear up things you don't understand.
5. Look for
   a. things the author assumes you already know, and
   b. things you have learned in math before.
6. Read with a pencil
   a. to work any examples provided, and
   b. reread each section after working the examples.
7. Write and store your own definitions for key terms in a notebook.

(Buehl, 1998)

TRANSLATING MATH TERMS INTO ENGLISH
Decimal Notation

The way we write numbers, using 0, 1, 2, 3, 4, 5, 6, 7, 8, 9. Each place in the number is a power of ten.

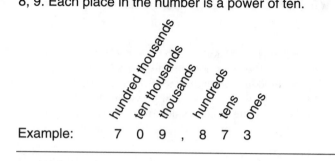

Example: 7   0   9   ,   8   7   3

---

ple). Use an analogy such as reading the operating manual for a piece of equipment or reading instructions for assembling an item. Often these documents are frustrating to read, so it is tempting to discard them and figure out what to do on your own, running the risk of making an important or costly error. Instead, it may be necessary to read the material several times, consult with another person, or eventually translate the confusing instructions into something you can understand.

4 Pair students with partners to read together portions of math text during class time. Typically, such reading is assigned as independent work, and many students skip it and attempt to solve problems by following examples in the text. As students follow the math keys and reach points of confusion, they can check with their peers or, as a final resort, consult with the teacher.

5 Encourage students to compile their own definitions of key terms in a notebook or on index cards. Students often discover that terms not clearly defined in a chapter are equally unclear in the book's glossary. For example, the book definition of *decimal notation*—a notation in which 10 digits are used to write numbers, with each place in the number standing for a power of 10—can be defined in a more student friendly way (see Translating Math Terms Into English). Urge students to treat difficult math language the same way as they would a foreign language. For example, once they translate a sentence from Spanish into English, it makes more sense. They must also get into the habit of translating math into English so that it, too, is personally meaningful.

6 Have students create a classroom dictionary of key math terms. Have students work with partners to write student friendly definitions that can be voted on by the entire class. The definitions for each term voted as the easiest to understand are penned on index cards and placed in a file box on the teacher's desk as the official classroom dictionary.

Advantages

- Students are encouraged to consider how effectively an author has communicated information and to problem-solve when things are not clear.

- Students learn to translate text into more personal and understandable language, and to make connections to prior knowledge.

- Students learn strategies that can aid them in understanding conceptually dense text.

References and Suggested Reading

Beck, I.L., McKeown, M.G., Hamilton, R.L., & Kucan, L. (1997). *Questioning the author: An approach for enhancing student engagement with text.* Newark, DE: International Reading Association.

Buehl, D. (1998). Making math make sense: Tactics help kids understand math language. *WEAC News and Views, 34*(3), 17.

Other Works Cited

Scott, Foresman. (1991). *Geometry* (University of Chicago, School Mathematics Project, 106). Glenview, IL: Author.

Scott, Foresman. (1995). *Transition mathematics* (University of Chicago, School Mathematics Project, 106). Glenview, IL: Author.

Mind Mapping

Drive down Leonardo Street for about 10 blocks until you come to the second set of lights. Turn left onto Raphael and go about 3 blocks until you see a Supermart. Continue another 1/2 block and take the first right. You are now on Botticelli Boulevard, which winds through a subdivision and then along a heavily wooded park. When you come to the railroad intersection, go about 1/4 mile until you see the Lutheran Church. Take a sharp left on Van Gogh and....

What we really need here is a map! Maps are visual representations designed to guide us to our destinations. They allow us to perceive how the necessary information is connected within the context of the larger picture. They let us see where we are going and alert us to important signposts along the way. Likewise, students find that visual representations—maps—displaying major concepts and their relationships can make journeys through textbook chapters more navigable. Buzan (1983) describes visual representations or graphic organizers that demonstrate connections among key concepts and ideas as Mind Maps.

Using the Strategy

Mind Maps are structured outlines that can effectively introduce new material to students (Barron, 1969). Tierney, Readence, and Dishner (1990) describe the following steps for using this strategy as a preview for learning:

1 Analyze a passage that students will read in terms of the important ideas and concepts to be learned. Next, identify key facts and vocabulary from the reading necessary for understanding these concepts. Ignore any difficult terms in the text not essential to learning the central ideas. This way students won't get sidetracked by terms that are only of secondary importance when they read. For example, as you peruse a chapter on glaciers in an earth science textbook, determine the following central concepts: (1) glaciers are moving masses of ice; (2) glaciers have had great impact on the features of the Earth; and (3) glaciers have periodically covered much of the land surface of the Earth. Key vocabulary for this chapter might be: *ice front; erosion; lateral, ground,* and *end moraines; till; drumlin; esker, kame, kettle;* and *ice age.*

2 Organize key concepts and vocabulary into a mind map that shows relationships and connections among the terms (see Mind Map for Glaciers, page 86). Include visual elements such as arrows, boxes, circles, pictorial representations, or other creative touches to make the Mind Map more vivid and memorable. In addition to specific vocabulary featured in the reading, integrate into the map relevant terms that the students already know. These familiar "landmarks" will help students recognize how the material fits into their current background knowledge of the subject. In the glacier example, add well-known glacial features such as the many lakes of northern Minnesota and Wisconsin, and references to global warming that students could relate to this concept.

3 Present the map to the class to prepare them for learning new material. Show an overhead transparency of the Mind Map to the entire class or provide students with individual copies to discuss as a small-group activity. Encourage students to speculate on the meanings of new vocabulary words and the nature of the relationships among concepts. Stimulate discussions with open-ended questions such as, What can you tell me by looking at this overview?

One effective method to encourage investigation of the Mind Map is the Expert/Novice strategy (see Paired Reviews, page 88). Have students work as partners, with one student designated as the Expert, the other as the Novice. When both have had ample opportunity to examine the map, the Expert is to describe what the topic is

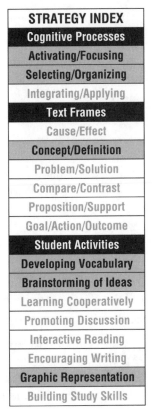

STRATEGY INDEX
Cognitive Processes
Activating/Focusing
Selecting/Organizing
Integrating/Applying
Text Frames
Cause/Effect
Concept/Definition
Problem/Solution
Compare/Contrast
Proposition/Support
Goal/Action/Outcome
Student Activities
Developing Vocabulary
Brainstorming of Ideas
Learning Cooperatively
Promoting Discussion
Interactive Reading
Encouraging Writing
Graphic Representation
Building Study Skills

MIND MAP FOR GLACIERS

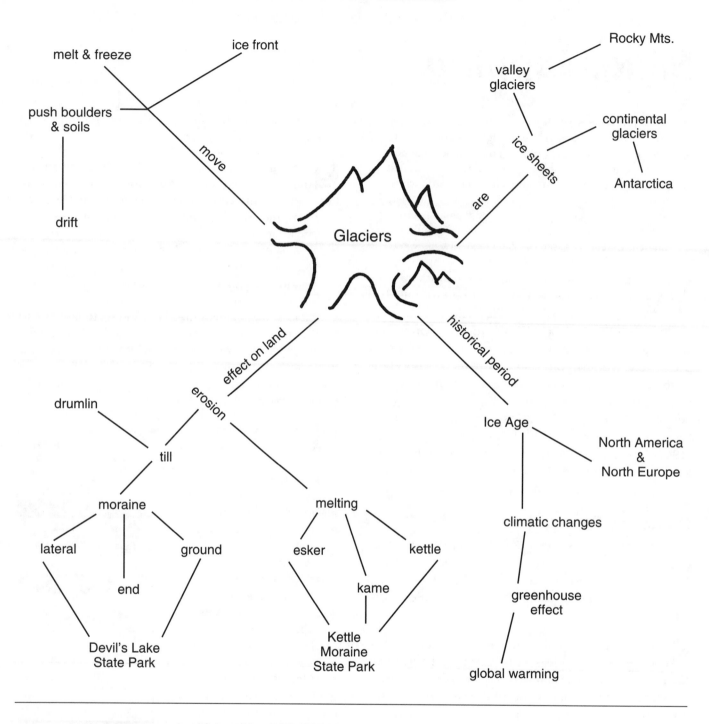

about by systematically going through the Mind Map, and the Novice is to point out any elements that remain confusing.

4 Recommend to students that they have their Mind Maps available to consult while reading the new selection. To prompt the use of these Mind Maps as guides, ask them to add new words, both from the text and from their experiences as they make connections while reading. After reading, have students return to their small groups to incorporate into the maps any additional important ideas and terms.

5 After students have practice with Mind Mapping, they can use the strategy in a variety of ways:

- Students can add illustrations to represent key terms, and color code each off-shoot of information from the central concept with highlighter pens.
- Students can create their own Mind Maps using a list of important concepts and terms. This is especially effective in helping students to see relationships within material they have just read and can be done both individually and in small groups.
- Students can select their own list of important concepts and terms from a passage and create a Mind Map that represents their understanding of the relationships. In addition, they can add to the map information from their background knowledge.
- Students can be assigned to map a chapter and present the overview to fellow students to introduce a new reading.

Mind Maps are an increasingly popular strategy that helps students to see the whole picture as they learn.

Advantages

- Students encounter and discuss new vocabulary before reading a challenging passage.
- Students have a visual outline of major ideas and relationships between important information to guide them as they read.
- Students are encouraged to consider how their prior knowledge fits into the new material they will study.

Mind maps can be created for use in all content areas and are appropriate for elementary through high school levels.

References

Barron, R. (1969). The use of vocabulary as an advance organizer. In H. Herber & P. Sanders, *Research in reading in the content areas: First year report* (pp. 29–39). Syracuse, NY: Syracuse University.

Buzan T. (1983). Use both sides of your brain (Rev. ed.). New York: E.P. Dutton.

Tierney, R., Readence, J., & Dishner, E. (1990). *Reading strategies and practices: A compendium* (3rd ed.). Boston: Allyn & Bacon.

Paired Reviews

"Time Out!" In the midst of a frantically paced basketball game, a player's hands signal a *T*. At a crucial juncture during a football game, a coach wants the clock stopped. Often during athletic competitions, coaches and players periodically need to pause the proceedings to take stock of events and plot adjustments necessary for a successful outcome.

Students, too, can benefit from a time out or pause. At times during the flow of learning new information and ideas, students need to signal time out so they can collect their thoughts and reflect on what they are learning. Like athletes, students may need to catch up with what is going on, raise questions, clear up confusions, and set their minds for what will happen next.

Mature learners know that understanding is not a one-step process. Often, we need to revisit what is being learned to make sure we "have it." Therefore, a pause for a second look clears up uncertainties and helps to mentally reconstruct material so that it makes sense. Reflecting, clarifying, and paraphrasing are automatic responses during learning.

However, many students cling to the habit of reading new material only once, whether they truly understand it or not. They may become preoccupied with completing an assignment rather than pondering the meaning of a passage. As a result, students' reading becomes a race to get done and close the book, retaining only a vague notion of what was read. Classroom strategies that encourage review and reflection help students to better understand and remember what they are learning.

Paired Review strategies enhance clarifying and paraphrasing skills and establish regular patterns of brief interruptions, which allow students to process what they are learning.

Using the Strategies

Steps for using four Paired Review strategies—the Three-Minute Pause (McTighe, in Marzano et al., 1992), Paired Verbal Fluency (Costa, 1997), Think/Pair/Share (McTighe & Lyman, 1988), and Reflect/Reflect/Reflect (Costa, 1997)—are outlined as follows:

Three-Minute Pause

During the Three-Minute Pause, students will engage in three modes of thinking: (1) summarizing what they have learned, (2) identifying interesting aspects or what they already know, and (3) raising questions about what they find confusing or do not understand. Using this strategy involves the following steps:

1 Introduce the Three-Minute Pause by asking students to imagine working at a computer, perhaps writing a story or essay. After an hour, students quickly stand and turn off their computers. Many students will gasp and ask incredulously, "Without saving?" Some will blurt out that an hour's worth of work is gone forever. Some may offer instances when they neglected to save and irrevocably lost work they had labored over and subsequently had to redo. Recount personal instances when you were lax in saving and lost your work. Computer manuals recommend that you save frequently so that unexpected problems do not wipe out your work.

Extend the analogy to classroom learning. If you do not pause every few minutes to think about what you are hearing, viewing, or reading, then you are not saving or retaining the information. New information may be stored in memory banks for a limited period, but a lot of it will be heard, seen, or experienced and then forgotten soon after. By pausing every 10 or 15 minutes to think through new material, emphasize that you are in effect beginning to save it in your memory.

2 Have students choose partners or "learning buddies" for a lesson or unit. Each pair decides who is Partner A and Partner B. When a Three-Minute Pause

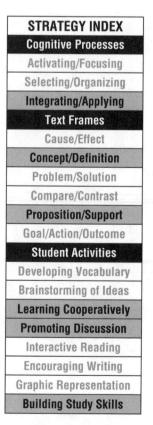

STRATEGY INDEX
Cognitive Processes
Activating/Focusing
Selecting/Organizing
Integrating/Applying
Text Frames
Cause/Effect
Concept/Definition
Problem/Solution
Compare/Contrast
Proposition/Support
Goal/Action/Outcome
Student Activities
Developing Vocabulary
Brainstorming of Ideas
Learning Cooperatively
Promoting Discussion
Interactive Reading
Encouraging Writing
Graphic Representation
Building Study Skills

is called, either A or B is selected to summarize, question, and identify interesting information for his or her partner. Use a stopwatch to time the pause, which will accentuate the urgency of moving directly to task in order to complete the duties within a specific time period. For example, in a history class viewing a film portraying the background of the U.S. Civil Rights movement, pause the film after 10 or 15 minutes.

3 During the pause, Partner A summarizes key points and Partner B comments on both familiar and confusing material. At the next pause, reverse these roles.

Paired Verbal Fluency

Paired Verbal Fluency is a similar strategy that provides students with practice in "summing up" what has been read or learned. Students take turns reviewing with a partner what they learned from a reading, a video, a class presentation, or a discussion. Using this strategy involves the following steps:

1 Pair students as Partner A and B. Partner A begins by recounting something memorable or interesting in the reading and talks steadily for 60 seconds, while Partner B listens. After 60 seconds, tell the partners, "Switch," and change roles. Partner B cannot repeat anything recalled by A.

2 When Partner B has talked for 60 seconds, tell the partners to switch again. Now, Partner A has 40 seconds to continue the review. Again, stipulate that nothing stated by either partner can be repeated. Announce another switch in which Partner B gets a 40-second turn.

3 Follow the same pattern, allowing each partner 20 seconds to recap. This strategy is a fast-paced way for students to summarize their learning. The no-repeat rule forces partners to dig deeper into the information and to listen carefully during the review rather than mentally rehearsing what to say during a summary. Time periods can be adjusted to fit the needs of the students, and when the activity is completed, confusions or questions that surfaced during the review can be addressed. Allowing students access to their notes or textbook during the review is optional.

Think/Pair/Share

This strategy is an extended version of the pause strategy. Using this strategy involves the following steps:

1 Provide students with a specific question or issue to consider, allowing them a short "wait time" to ponder their thinking individually.

2 Have students discuss the topic in pairs.

3 Ask students to share their thoughts in a whole-class discussion. Cue students to move from phase to phase of this process. In addition to discussion, ask students to engage in other types of thinking during the pair phase: reaching a consensus on an issue, problem solving, or arguing an opposing position.

4 As another variation of Think/Pair/Share, have one partner assume the role of Expert as though she were explaining new content to a Novice. The Expert must talk about material so that a person unknowledgeable or unfamiliar with the information can understand it. Unfamiliar concepts and vocabulary must be translated in order to make sense to the Novice. The Novice asks clarifying questions and repeats what is understood about the content to the Expert, who verifies whether the novice has understood correctly and clears up any misunderstandings.

As students become more independent, have them practice the Expert role with people outside of class. For example, a student studying chemistry might explain the day's concepts to a parent. The challenge is to translate the technical language of chemistry into layman's terms. If a parent understands, the student knows that she has successfully paraphrased it.

Reflect/Reflect/Reflect

As students become more comfortable retelling what they learned, engage them in Reflect/Reflect/Reflect, a more sophisticated strategy for paraphrasing and clarifying. The strategy involves dividing students into groups of three. Each member of the triad, Partner A, B, and C, takes a turn assuming the roles of Authority, Reporter, and Observer. To help students understand the roles, ask them to imagine a news program in which a reporter interacts with an authority about a topic (or show a short film clip of such an interaction). Ask students to notice how the Authority presents information and personal thoughts about the topic; the Reporter at times summarizes the Authority's words and asks clarifying questions, or delves into the Authority's attitudes and emotions; and the Observer takes stock of what the Authority is saying and what the Reporter is summarizing and clarifying. At times the Observer may want to declaim at the screen, "But what about...?" or "That's not exactly right!" This strategy involves the following steps (see the Reflect/Reflect/Reflect Outline):

REFLECT/REFLECT/REFLECT OUTLINE

Step 1. Partner A—Authority—presents information and personal thoughts about information.

Partner B—Reporter—summarizes information presented by Authority (I heard you say...).

Partner C—Observer—comments on presentation and summary (Was anything missed or incorrectly stated?).

Step 2. Switch Roles

Partner B—Authority—presents information and personal thoughts about information.

Partner C—Reporter—summarizes information presented by Authority (I heard you say...) and asks questions to clarify or get more information.

Partner A—Observer—comments on presentation and summary (Was anything missed or incorrectly stated? Is anything still unclear?).

Step 3. Switch Roles

Partner C—Authority—presents information and personal thoughts about information.

Partner A—Reporter—summarizes information presented by Authority (I heard you say...) and asks questions to clarify or get more information and notes emotions (You seem to feel...).

Partner B—Observer—comments on presentation and summary (Was anything missed or incorrectly stated? Is anything still unclear?).

1 Allow the Authority about 2 minutes to talk about a part of the material that was interesting, familiar, confusing, or perhaps difficult to learn. Assign the Reporter the task of paraphrasing what the Authority says. Ask the Observer to comment on the accuracy of the paraphrasing and whether any important information was omitted.

2 Students read the next passage. Each partner switches to a different role and proceeds as he or she did in Step 1. But this time, the Reporter must not only paraphrase the Authority's remarks, but must clarify them by asking questions. The Observer evaluates the paraphrasing and comments on whether questions were clarified.

3 Again, students read the next portion of text. Partners now assume the third role, with the Authority continuing as before. This time the Reporter does three things: paraphrases, asks questions to clarify, and identifies emotions exhibited by the Authority, such as excitement, frustration, confusion, or disagreement. This step interjects empathy with a fellow learner into the interaction. The Observer completes the activity as before, commenting on the paraphrasing, clarifying, and empathizing.

Advantages

- Students internalize the importance of reflecting on and personalizing their learning.

- Students are reminded that merely hearing, viewing, or reading is not enough; they also must pause periodically and think about what they are experiencing.

- Students must verbalize their learning both to others and to themselves.

- Students are encouraged to use classmates to help construct personal meanings from important content, as well as clarify and remember new information.

These strategies also can be used for eliciting student knowledge about a topic before introducing a new lesson.

References

Costa, A. (1997). *Teaching for intelligent behavior.* Davis, CA: Search Models Unlimited.

Marzano, R., Pickering, D., Arredondo, D., Blackburn, G., Brandt, R., & Moffett, C. (1992). *Dimensions of learning teacher's manual.* Alexandria, VA: Association of Supervision and Curriculum Development.

McTighe, J., & Lyman, F. (1988). Cueing thinking in the classroom: The promise of theory-embedded tools. *Educational Leadership, 45*(7), 18–24.

Point-of-View Study Guides

"Excuse me, but what do you think about...?" We live in an age when people's points-of-view are being solicited almost continuously. Public opinion polls, radio call-in shows, newspaper sound-off columns, man-in-the-street interviews, telephone surveys—all are attempts to find out what we think.

The Point-of-View Study Guide (Wood, 1988) is a strategy that capitalizes on this interest in examining the perspectives of others. Students read a selection, not as themselves, but as if they were a character involved in the events being described. The process of reading becomes more personalized as students integrate information related to a role into their understanding of the text. The Point-of-View Study Guide follows an interview format and encourages students to respond in their own words to the ideas and information in the reading.

Using the Strategy

Point-of-View Study Guides can be constructed for a wide variety of material, including literature, social studies, and science selections. Using this strategy involves the following steps:

1 Identify an appropriate role or character from a selection that students have already read. Model the strategy for students by assuming this role yourself. Ask students to interview you by having them generate meaningful questions that could be answered by information in the text. For example, following the reading of a textbook passage about explorers to the New World, you could be interviewed as a Native American of that time. Or following a selection on endangered species, you could be interviewed as a whale. Slip into a character during your modeling, showing how your reading of the material is affected by the perspective you bring. Demonstrate that your attitudes might diverge from the point-of-view of the author in the textbook or novel. Students will notice that you are connected to the material more emotionally than they are, because you are talking about things that affect you and that you really care about.

2 Choose a role or character from a new selection. Create a series of interview questions that will help students focus on the important elements of the text. Distribute these questions as the study guide for the selection. Students reading the novel *Bridge to Terabithia*, by Katherine Paterson, could be asked to comment on events at the end of the book from the perspective of Leslie, the girl who had died. Students reading a history passage on immigration could be asked to read from the perspective of a specific immigrant (see Point-of-View Study Guide for Social Studies). Students reading a biology selection on roots could answer interview questions from the perspective of a taproot (see Point-of-View Study Guide for Science).

3 As students read, have them look for information that will enable them to respond to interview questions. Interview responses should be written in the first person and should elaborate on material from the reading. The responses should read as dialogue, not as typical answers to questions in the text. For example, the following is a student response to a question asked of an Italian immigrant regarding the difficulties of life in the United States:

> We have not been accepted by many Americans. We have encountered prejudice because of our different languages and customs. We also have had to work in jobs with long hours and low wages, and some of us have experienced acts of violence. Some of us are accused of being anarchists or socialists, and are treated as if we are a threat to the government.

An even more intriguing use of Point-of-View Study Guides involves assigning groups of students different characters with different sets of questions relevant to each role. For example, in addition to being interviewed as an Italian immigrant, students might assume the role of a native-born factory worker,

STRATEGY INDEX
Cognitive Processes
Activating/Focusing
Selecting/Organizing
Integrating/Applying
Text Frames
Cause/Effect
Concept/Definition
Problem/Solution
Compare/Contrast
Proposition/Support
Goal/Action/Outcome
Student Activities
Developing Vocabulary
Brainstorming of Ideas
Learning Cooperatively
Promoting Discussion
Interactive Reading
Encouraging Writing
Graphic Representation
Building Study Skills

POINT-OF-VIEW STUDY GUIDE FOR SOCIAL STUDIES
Chapter 5: The Age of Industry

You are about to be interviewed as if you were a person living in the United States in the mid- to late 1800s. Respond to the following interview questions as if you were an Italian immigrant.

1. During what time period did most of your fellow Italian immigrants come to the United States?
2. What made you decide to leave Italy?
3. When you landed in New York, you met immigrants from many other countries. What countries were they from and what were some of their reasons for coming to the United States?
4. What types of employment did you have to choose from when you came to the United States?
5. Why do some immigrants object to the process of assimilation?
6. Have you encountered any difficulties being an immigrant in the United States? What kinds of problems have you and your fellow immigrants experienced?
7. As an immigrant, what are your feelings toward legislation to limit immigration? Would you support or oppose such legislation?

POINT-OF-VIEW STUDY GUIDE FOR SCIENCE
Chapter 23: Roots and Stems

You are about to be interviewed as if you were a part of a plant. Respond to the following questions as if you were a taproot.

1. What plant are you a taproot for? What other plants have taproots?
2. We notice that some plants have fibrous root systems. How are you different from these roots?
3. Not to get personal, but all you roots seem rather hairy. Why do you roots have those hairy growths?
4. Could you take a couple of moments and describe how you grow?
5. Roots must need to be tough for growing through the soil. What enables you to push through the soil?

---

an African American sharecropper, a U.S. Senator, or a New York City social activist. After reading, have each group conduct their interview for the entire class. The multiplicity of viewpoints will significantly enhance students' understanding of and insight into the material.

4 As the students become familiar with Point-of-View Study Guides, have them create their own interview questions. Assign a role, and have students work in pairs. Have one student read the selection as the character, and have their partner read as the interviewer. The interviewer's task is to formulate questions to be posed to the character. Following the reading, have students participate in a mock interview, or have them answer the questions as a writing exercise.

Advantages

- Students become more personally engaged in the reading, which helps bring material to life.

- Students gain practice in translating the language of text into their own words and are involved in a more in-depth processing of the material.

- Students are encouraged to draw from their own experiences to understand events in text and are asked to elaborate on information in a meaningful way.

- Students develop sensitivity to different perspectives of events and ideas.

This strategy can be used effectively with materials in all content areas and is especially effective with social studies and literature.

Reference and Suggested Reading

Wood, K. (1988). Guiding students through informational text. *The Reading Teacher, 41*, 912–920.

Wood, K.D., Lapp, D., & Flood, J. (1992). *Guiding readers through text: A review of study guides*. Newark, DE: International Reading Association.

Other Work Cited

Paterson, K. (1978). *Bridge to Terabithia*. New York: HarperCollins.

Possible Sentences

In the days before e-mail and fax machines, when the telegram was the best way to contact someone quickly, key words were used to communicate the gist of a message. If you had received a telegram that contained only the following words: *Hepatitis A, outbreak, gourmet restaurants, Chicago, epidemic, health inspector, quarantine, incubation period, viral*, and *liver*, do you think you could piece together the probable meaning? In all likelihood, you would draw from your background experiences and knowledge to construct a prediction for the entire message:

> There is an outbreak of Hepatitis A in Chicago, Illinois. Health inspectors have quarantined some gourmet restaurants associated with the outbreak. Hepatitis A has an incubation period before it appears and is a viral disease that affects the liver.

Possible Sentences (Moore & Moore, 1986) is a strategy that helps students process the key vocabulary of a passage before they begin reading. It encourages students to make predictions about the probable meaning of a passage based on what they know or can anticipate about a number of key word or terms. Then when students begin reading, they have already previewed the major ideas of the text. Their reading becomes an exercise in discovering the accuracy of their predictions about key terms.

Using the Strategy

Possible Sentences can be implemented with a wide variety of materials. Using this strategy involves the following steps:

1 Identify 10 to 15 key concepts or terms in material students will be reading. Include terms that will be familiar, as well as those that may be obstacles in their reading. List these on the board or on an overhead transparency. For example, the key terms from a social studies textbook passage on ancient Greece might include *Hellenic Age, architecture, Parthenon, Plato, philosophy, theater, democracy*, and *The Republic*.

2 Ask students to select at least two terms and write them in a sentence that could possibly appear in the reading. You are essentially asking them to predict how the terms might be used in the passage. Elicit a

sentence from the class and write it exactly as given on the chalkboard. Underline key words. Ask for a second sentence that uses different terms. Continue until all the words from the list are represented in sentences on the board. For terms that are unfamiliar, encourage students to guess at a probable meaning and to construct possible sentences. For example, from a passage on the ancient Greeks, students might know that the Parthenon was a temple with many statues, and that the ancient Greeks did a lot with architecture, philosophy, and the arts. They may not know about Plato and Aristotle, so they would offer guesses based on the key terms (see Possible Sentences for Social Studies).

3 Have students read the passage and check the accuracy of the possible sentences. They should evaluate each possible sentence in terms of whether it is true (the text backs up their prediction), false (the text presents a different use of the term), or don't know (the statement can be neither proved nor disproved based on the text). For example, some possible sentences in the ancient Greece example are directly contradicted by the text: Aristotle was the Father of Biology, and *The Republic* is a work by Plato (not the name of the Greek government). Other possible sentences were not clearly dealt with in the text. Many of Aristotle's activities were detailed, but any connection with Greek theater was not mentioned. Tragedies were discussed as a form of theater, but the book did not mention whether this time in history was also a time of tragedy.

4 After students have read the passage and evaluated their possible sentences, work with them to

STRATEGY INDEX
Cognitive Processes
Activating/Focusing
Selecting/Organizing
Integrating/Applying
Text Frames
Cause/Effect
Concept/Definition
Problem/Solution
Compare/Contrast
Proposition/Support
Goal/Action/Outcome
Student Activities
Developing Vocabulary
Brainstorming of Ideas
Learning Cooperatively
Promoting Discussion
Interactive Reading
Encouraging Writing
Graphic Representation
Building Study Skills

POSSIBLE SENTENCES FOR SOCIAL STUDIES
Chapter 4: Greek Culture

Key Terms

Hellenic Age	Plato
architecture	philosophy
Parthenon	The Republic
democracy	theater
tragedies	Aristotle
the arts	statues
temple	Father of Biology

Possible Sentences

DK 1. The <u>Hellenic Age</u> was a time of many <u>tragedies</u>.

T 2. The ancient Greeks did a lot with <u>architecture</u>, <u>philosophy</u>, and <u>the arts</u>.

T 3. The <u>Parthenon</u> was a <u>temple</u> with many <u>statues</u>.

F 4. The Greeks had a <u>democracy</u> and their government was called <u>The Republic</u>.

F 5. <u>Plato</u> was called the <u>Father of Biology</u>.

DK 6. Greek <u>theater</u> performed plays by <u>Aristotle</u>.

Key:

T = True based on the Reading.
F = False based on the Reading, needs to be rewritten.
DK = Don't Know; not mentioned in the Reading.

determine how the sentences could be changed to be more consistent with the reading. Have students locate relevant portions of text in order to defend their corrections. Students may find that some statements need to be expanded to two or three sentences in order to accurately reflect the text. Students may also generate entire new sentences to add to the original group. Possible Sentences for the passage on ancient Greece may be altered by the students to read as follows:

The Hellenic Age was a time of great achievement in architecture, philosophy, and the arts.

Greek theater featured tragedies and comedies.

The Parthenon was a temple with many statues. The Parthenon was an important example of Greek architecture.

The Greeks were the first people to develop a democracy.

Aristotle was called the Father of Biology.

Aristotle and Plato were famous for philosophy. Plato wrote *The Republic.*

Possible Sentences is an excellent strategy for students to complete in cooperative groups. As they become familiar with the process, students can generate, evaluate, and revise their own Possible Sentences as a cooperative group activity.

Advantages

- Students become acquainted with key terms and vocabulary from a passage before they begin to read.

- Students are engaged in actively predicting major ideas of material.

- Students are involved in a process that helps them to establish their purposes for reading.

- Students activate what they know about information before they read, and are able to share background knowledge with their classmates.

Reference and Suggested Reading

Moore, D., & Moore, S. (1986). Possible sentences. In E. Dishner, T. Bean, J. Readence, and D. Moore (Eds.), *Reading in the content areas: Improving classroom instruction* (2nd ed.). Dubuque, IA: Kendall-Hunt.

Readence, J., Moore, D., & Rickelman, R. (2000). *Prereading activities for content area reading and learning* (3rd ed.). Newark, DE: International Reading Association.

Power Notes

Say you are in the market for a new automobile. Your mind immediately begins to sort and categorize information relevant to your decision. As you consider vehicles you would like to own, the first mental sorting divides vehicles into "cars you can afford" and "cars you cannot afford." Next you might group the affordable cars into subcategories, perhaps, based on vehicle size or fuel efficiency. Finally, within these clusters, you might list the makes of vehicles that are potential purchases.

Classifying and subdividing information is a natural mental activity and an essential process in classroom learning. As a mature reader, you can "separate the wheat from the chaff." For example, as you peruse the daily newspaper, you delve into a complex article about the stock market that is full of market terms: *the Dow; drop of 32 Points; day traders; NASDAQ; corporate downsizing; Alan Greenspan; Microsoft antitrust; Internet overvaluing; the new economy.* As you read, however, you dwell less on specific details and organize your thinking around main ideas, such as causes of current U.S. economic shifts and the possible impact on consumers.

Many students struggle with perceiving integral relationships in their reading. As a result they have difficulty distinguishing attributes, examples, and details from main ideas. Power Notes (Santa, Havens, & Macumber, 1996) provides a systematic way to help students organize information for their reading, writing, and studying.

Using the Strategy

The Power Notes strategy is a streamlined form of outlining that is easy to introduce to students. Main ideas or categories are assigned a power 1 rating. Attributes, details, or examples are assigned power 2, 3, or 4 ratings. Using the strategy involves the following steps:

1 Start by modeling Power Notes using categories familiar to students. Point out how the powers relate to each other: Power 1 is a main idea: Fruit. Power 2s are examples or elaborations of power 1: bananas, peaches, grapes, pears, and apples. Power 3s are examples or elaboration of a power 2 (apples): varieties such as Macintosh, Yellow Delicious, and Granny Smith. For power 4s, students might offer characteristics, such as *red-skinned, great for pies,* and *keeps a long time.*

2 Illustrate how the powers relate to one another by creating on the chalkboard or overhead transparency the following example:

    1. Football Penalties
        2. On Offense
            3. Holding
            3. Clipping
        2. On Defense
            3. Off Sides
            3. Pass Interference
            3. Grabbing Face Mask
        2. On Special Teams

3 Provide students with practice using Power Notes to categorize information and relationships found in factual material. Select a number of power 1, 2, and 3 terms from a unit of study. Write them on separate index cards. Distribute sets of cards to students working in cooperative groups. As students group the cards, have them determine what power each term represents and then arrange the cards according to powers and corresponding relationships. For example, cards for a U.S. history unit, Age of Reform, would include a power 1, *reformers*; power 2s, *populists, unions,* and *progressives*; and power 3s, *NAACP, Farmer's Alliance,* and others. Students might arrange the cards as follows:

STRATEGY INDEX
Cognitive Processes
Activating/Focusing
Selecting/Organizing
Integrating/Applying
Text Frames
Cause/Effect
Concept/Definition
Problem/Solution
Compare/Contrast
Proposition/Support
Goal/Action/Outcome
Student Activities
Developing Vocabulary
Brainstorming of Ideas
Learning Cooperatively
Promoting Discussion
Interactive Reading
Encouraging Writing
Graphic Representation
Building Study Skills

1. Reformers
   2. Populists
      3. National Grange
      3. Farmer's Alliance
      3. Populist Party
   2. Unions
      3. The Knights of Labor
      3. American Federation of Labor
      3. IWW
   2. Progressives
      3. Muckrakers
      3. NAACP
      3. Progressive Party

This activity is an excellent review exercise. As an additional study technique, provide students with blank cards so they can add power 4 information to power 3 cards or integrate other items in the outline.

4 To help students organize their writing, have them use a simple 1–2–2–2 outline to construct a well-organized paragraph:

1. Healthy Methods to Lose Weight
   2. Set Realistic Goals
   2. Eat Fewer Calories
   2. Develop Regular Exercise Program

You should follow healthy methods if you want to lose weight. First, you should set realistic weight-loss goals. Next, you should plan a diet that involves eating few-

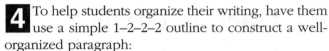

CONCEPT MAP FOR THE RED CROSS

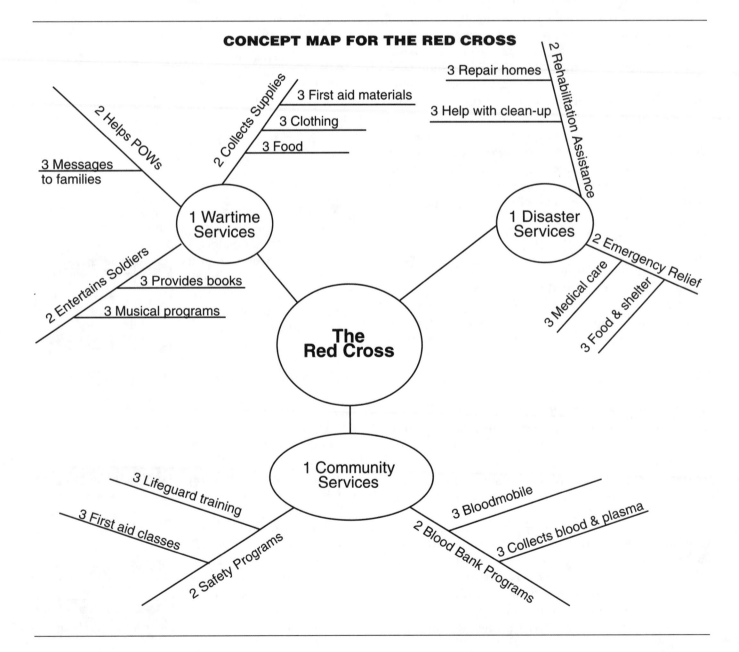

er calories. Finally, you should develop a regular program of exercise in addition to your diet.

Students can further elaborate each point by adding power 3 and 4 details to their outline. Power Notes gives students a means to analyze their writing in terms of structure and development of ideas.

Power Notes and Concept Maps

After students understand the concept of Power Notes, the strategy can be expanded to enhance comprehension and learning. Power Notes work well with concept mapping activities (see Mind Mapping, page 85). Concept Maps, visual webs of information that illustrate important relationships within material, are sometimes constructed by students without a sense of superordinate and subordinate information. The maps may be only a mishmash of facts. Combining Power Notes and Concept Maps involves the following steps:

1 Model Concept Mapping using Power Notes with students. Reserve the center of the map for the topic being developed. Stress that only power 1 ideas can emanate from the center. Each power 1 idea is further defined with power 2s, and power 3s elaborate on the power 2s on the map (see Concept Map for the Red Cross). For example, students reading an article about the Red Cross determine three power 1s: wartime services, disaster services, and community services. Each category is developed with power 2 and 3 details. The completed map is a strong visual representation of key information with corresponding relationships clearly defined.

2 Have students work with partners to create Concept Maps from a new selection. One option is to provide transparency film that can be displayed on an overhead projector, giving students the option of sharing their maps with the entire class.

Power Notes and Pattern Puzzles

A second application of Power Notes is the Pattern Puzzle strategy (Santa, Havens, & Macumber, 1996). Pattern Puzzles prompt students to notice topic sentences, transition words, and paragraph structure as they read. This activity also models how to write well-organized paragraphs and essays. Using this strategy involves the following steps:

1 Choose a well-organized paragraph and segment it into individual sentences. Separate the sentences on slips of paper, each containing one sentence. Have students work within cooperative groups to arrange the sentences into a paragraph that reads smoothly and makes sense. To accomplish this task, students will

---

PATTERN PUZZLE FOR BIOLOGY

1 Bacteria are extremely small.

  2 A typical bacterium is about 2μm long.

  2 Yet each bacterium is a complete organism.

    3 Packaged into each cell are all the nucleic acids, enzymes, and other substances necessary to carry out the cell's life processes.

1 Many bacteria form a protective structure called an *endospore*.

  2 An endospore consists of a thick wall surrounding the nuclear material and a small amount of cytoplasm.

  2 Endospores can withstand boiling water, drying out, or other extreme conditions.

    3 When the environment becomes favorable, cells emerge from the endospores and begin normal growth.

  2 Many disease-causing bacteria form endospores.

    3 Therefore, methods to kill spores are important in food preservation and in medicine.

      4 Endospores are usually killed by exposing them to pressurized steam at 121°C for 10 to 15 minutes—a procedure called *sterilization*.

(Adapted from McLaren et al., 1991)

---

have to attend to the power 1, 2, 3, or 4 information in the sentence, and they will also have to be sensitive to transition language that helps ideas flow from sentence to sentence. (See Pattern Puzzle for Biology.)

2 Pattern Puzzles can be used in a variety of ways. For example, have students assemble a paragraph that represents a sequence or series of steps, such as the directions for conducting an experiment, so that they carefully analyze why order is important in the procedure. Math word problems or poetry are also excellent sources for developing Pattern Puzzle activities. As part of the process, students may discover that multiple solutions are possible for arranging sentences into paragraphs. In some cases, students may find their configurations of sentences from a passage preferable to those in the original text.

Advantages

- Students become aware of text structure as they read and write.
- Power Notes offer an easy-to-understand strategy for classifying information.
- Students learn to read actively and to prioritize main ideas from supportive details as they study.

- Students are prompted to look for relationships within material they are studying.
- Power relationships can guide students in taking coherent notes from textbooks or classroom presentations.
- Power Notes can be integrated into a number of other strategies to help students perceive how information is interconnected.

Reference

Santa, C., Havens, L., & Macumber, E. (1996). *Creating independence through student-owned strategies*. Dubuque, IA: Kendall/Hunt.

Other Work Cited

McLaren, J., Rotundo, L., & Gurley-Dilger, L. (1991). *Heath biology. Lexington, MA: D.C. Heath*.

Problematic Situations

How did the Egyptians build the pyramids? What did people use for medicines before there were commercial drugs? What would happen if you put too much yeast in a bread recipe? What would you expect the countryside to look like after a glacier has melted? How did Stone-age hunters kill large animals, such as woolly mammoths? What would you do if someone threatened to beat you up after school?

Children are never at a loss for questions, and from a young age many of these queries focus on "how" or "what." Tapping into this natural curiosity is an excellent way to prepare students for reading material that deals with problems and solutions. Problematic Situations (Vacca & Vacca, 1999) is a strategy that presents students with a circumstance that is subsequently developed or explained in a reading selection.

Before reading the passage, students first brainstorm possible solutions to or results of the problematic situation. This process activates what students may already know about the situation and helps them focus attention on key elements of the text as they read. Problematic Situations also increases motivation for reading, as students want to find out whether their solutions will be confirmed by the author.

Using the Strategy

Problematic Situations can be used to prepare students for any type of reading material that deals with a problem/solution relationship. Using this strategy involves the following steps:

1 Examine a reading assignment and develop a problematic situation for students to consider. Provide students with enough relevant information about the situation so that they are able to identify key ideas in the passage as they read. It is especially important that the context of the problem be clearly defined. The following problematic solution is created from the short story "The Most Dangerous Game" by Richard Connell:

A man is trapped on a small island covered with jungle vegetation. He has a 3-hour start on someone who is trying to kill him. The killer is well armed, but the man has only a knife. The killer will be pursuing the man with trained hunting dogs. What can this man do to try to save himself?

2 Pose the Problematic Situation to the students in cooperative groups. Have them generate possible results or solutions. Have each group record responses as they are discussed. Have them discuss each response and explain why each is appropriate or would be successful. For example, students read a passage on nutrition and how different nutrients affect the body and are given the following problematic situation:

You are the conditioning coach for a national Olympics team. Two athletes come to you for advice about what foods they should be eating to stay in the best performing condition. One is a 180-pound sprinter, the other is a huge 275-pound heavyweight wrestler. What training suggestions would you give each athlete?

Students might list foods like the following for the sprinter: steak, potatoes, vegetables, pasta, milk. Their reasoning might be that the sprinter needs to be strong but also fast, and will burn up a lot of energy on the field. The students realize that the wrestler is in danger of eating himself out of the competition. He needs to watch his weight, so they decide he should eat more vegetables, salads, and fruits and avoid fatty foods such as pizza or french fries.

3 Have each group decide on the most promising result or solution. As part of the deliberations, have groups develop justifications for their decision. For example, students discussing possible solutions for *The Most Dangerous Game* problematic situation will consider planning various ambushes and setting a variety of traps as the most conceivable and likely choices. Some solu-

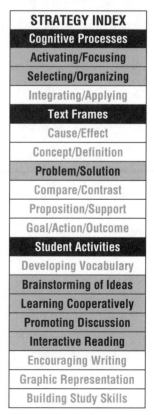

STRATEGY INDEX

Cognitive Processes
Activating/Focusing
Selecting/Organizing
Integrating/Applying

Text Frames
Cause/Effect
Concept/Definition
Problem/Solution
Compare/Contrast
Proposition/Support
Goal/Action/Outcome

Student Activities
Developing Vocabulary
Brainstorming of Ideas
Learning Cooperatively
Promoting Discussion
Interactive Reading
Encouraging Writing
Graphic Representation
Building Study Skills

tions will be too improbable or take too much time to devise. Have groups present their solutions to the entire class for discussion.

Another example is a selection about the Pilgrims and their religious beliefs. Students decide what course of action might work best for the following problematic solution:

> A group of very religious people is living in a country where they cannot worship freely. They feel that the laws of the country and the government discriminate against them. Other people in this country attack their beliefs and this religious group feels persecuted. What can they do to solve their problem?

4 Have students test their solutions by reading the selection further. Instruct students to add to or modify solutions as they gain more information from the text. Students reading the nutrition selection may realize that the 275-pound wrestler also could eat lean meats as part of his diet but watch how many carbohydrates he consumes. Students reading *The Most Dangerous Game* may discover that the hunted man, Rainsford, unsuccessfully tries some of their ideas as he struggles to outwit his adversary. Students reading about the Pilgrims may discover that the Pilgrims attempted several of the students' solutions before embarking to the New World to create a new society.

5 Have students compare predictions with information provided in the text. Revisit the original problematic situation and solicit any revisions, additions, or

further comments students may have now that they have read the selection. Open a discussion to consider whether some of the students' solutions might be better than those of the author.

Advantages

- Problematic Situations help students to successfully analyze material that deals with *how* or *what* relationships.
- Students have an opportunity to take stock of background knowledge that relates to ideas in a reading.
- Students' curiosity is piqued, and they are more motivated to tackle a reading that will answer their questions.
- Students anticipate the problem-solving frame of mind that they will need to assume when reading.
- Students consciously connect new information to their questions about problematic situations.

Reference

Vacca, R., & Vacca, J. (1999). *Content area reading* (6th ed.). New York: Longman.

Other Work Cited

Connell, R. (1924). *The most dangerous game*.

Proposition/Support Outlines

Imagine you are reading the latest George Will column in *Newsweek* magazine; an editorial in the newspaper; or a review of a recent movie, new book, or local restaurant. The text of each of these items features a style of writing that offers a proposition that is discussed and supported. The propositions vary: Jesse Ventura is a controversial but highly effective politician. The proposed school bond referendum should be passed. *Mission Impossible 2* is an entertaining movie sequel that does not measure up to the original film. The food served at La Ritz is expensive but outstanding.

These statements cover a broad range of topics, but your frame of mind while reading this style of writing remains the same. You ask yourself, What proposition is being offered, and is the support for the proposition convincing?

Proposition/Support Outlines (Buehl, 1992) help students become critical readers of material that presents viewpoints, opinions, debatable assertions, theories, or hypotheses. Proposition/support writing places a special premium on analytical-thinking abilities, which many students find especially challenging. It is no accident that many questions that students face on SAT and ACT college entrance tests target an author's point of view and supporting argumentation. Proposition/Support Outlines supply students with a framework for analyzing the types of justification an author uses to support a conclusion or generalization.

Using the Strategy

Proposition/Support Outlines work in a variety of contexts; they are especially useful with issues-related text, and with language arts and social studies materials. Using this strategy involves the following steps:

1 Initiate a discussion with students about the differences between facts and opinions. Brainstorm with students definitions of each and generate a list of examples. "The Earth's rain forests are shrinking" is a fact statement. "The loss of rain forests will lead to an environmental disaster" is an opinion—in this case a hypothesis—that may or may not be supported by facts. Emphasize that fact statements can be proven right or wrong, opinion statements cannot. Clearly, some opinion statements are more defensible than others because they are well supported by known facts. Opinions that have little basis in fact are termed *unfounded*.

2 Introduce the term *proposition*—a statement that can be argued as true. Provide students with several possible propositions:

> The United States needs more national parks.
>
> Drug testing is necessary for Olympic athletes.
>
> Cats make the best pets.
>
> The neighborhood park needs new playground equipment.
>
> Today's movies are too violent.

Divide students into cooperative groups and assign each group the task of generating several arguments that could support one of these propositions. Introduce a blank Proposition/Support Outline on an overhead transparency (see Appendix, page 162), and model with students how various supports for a proposition can be categorized in five ways—as facts, statistics, examples, expert authority, or logic and reasoning.

3 Assign students a selection that adheres to a proposition/support text frame and have them complete the outline as they analyze the author's arguments. Select for students a text that features a clear proposition. Initially, it may be desirable to have students work in pairs to identify the proposition and to share how clues in the text were used to determine it. For example, students in a social studies class read an article detailing how the loss of the world's rain forests portends global environmental disaster. After ascertaining this proposition, they complete the out-

STRATEGY INDEX
Cognitive Processes
Activating/Focusing
Selecting/Organizing
Integrating/Applying
Text Frames
Cause/Effect
Concept/Definition
Problem/Solution
Compare/Contrast
Proposition/Support
Goal/Action/Outcome
Student Activities
Developing Vocabulary
Brainstorming of Ideas
Learning Cooperatively
Promoting Discussion
Interactive Reading
Encouraging Writing
Graphic Representation
Building Study Skills

line in order to categorize arguments supporting the global-catastrophe scenario. In this case, the rain forest article contained information and arguments reflected in all five support categories (see Proposition/Support Outline for Rain Forests).

4 Analyze with students the type of support presented. How convincing is it? Does the author rely solely on logic, reasoning, and examples, neglecting to use statistics or other facts? Is only a single expert authority cited? How reliable are the statistics? (For example, public survey results are statistics but are volatile and change frequently.) Do the examples seem to be typical or atypical? Has important counteracting information been omitted from the discussion?

PROPOSITION/SUPPORT OUTLINE FOR RAIN FORESTS

Proposition: The loss of rain forests will lead to an environmental disaster.

Support:

1. Facts

- Rain forests use carbon dioxide.
- There is increased carbon dioxide in the earth's atmosphere.
- The rain forests contain many endangered plant and animal species.
- Deforestation leads to widespread soil erosion in many areas.
- The burning of fossil fuels puts carbon dioxide into the environment.

2. Statistics

- The 1990s were the "hottest" decade in the last 100 years.
- One acre of rain forest disappears every second.
- Four million acres (larger than the state of Connecticut) disappear every year.
- Fifty to 100 species are destroyed with each acre of forest cleared.
- If present trends continue, half the rain forests of Honduras and Nicaragua will disappear by year 2000.

3. Examples

- India has almost no remaining rain forest.
- Current plans target eliminating much of the Congo's rain forest.
- Run-off from deforestation in Indonesia threatens their coral reefs and diminishes the fish population.
- Cutting of rain forests in Bangladesh and the Philippines has led to killer floods.

4. Expert Authority

- Computers predict doubling of carbon dioxide in the 21st century, raising temperatures by 3 to 9 degrees.
- National Center for Atmospheric Research believes increased carbon dioxide will lead to the Greenhouse Effect and global warming.
- Environmentalist leader Al Gore calls the Greenhouse Effect our most serious threat ever.

5. Logic and Reasoning

- Warmer temperatures will harm crops and increase energy costs.
- More people will starve because of less food and increased population growth.
- The polar glaciers will melt and raise the sea level, flooding coastlines.
- Many species useful to humans will disappear.
- More sections of the world will become uninhabitable deserts due to soil loss, erosion, overgrazing, and overcultivation.

(Buehl, 1992, 1995)

As the Rain Forest outline is discussed, students will make a judgment about the case presented by the author—whether to accept or reject the author's proposition.

As students become confident using Proposition/Support Outlines, they will find them applicable in a variety of classroom contexts.

5 Have students read to investigate several possible propositions from a textbook passage. For example, students in a history class may be asked to read a passage on the Mexican War to locate support for the proposition: Santa Anna was looking out for the best interests of the Mexican people. Other students could be asked to defend this proposition based on information in the text: The Americans had good reasons for wishing to expand their borders to the southwest. Such an exercise prompts an organized classroom debate on the various propositions. But instead of students merely offering their personal opinions, they have preorganized, pertinent information and arguments on which to base their debatable assertions.

The Proposition/Support Outline is also an excellent guide for independent research, as it provides students with a framework for scrutinizing reference materials for relevant information and arguments. For example, students assigned the task of writing a position paper on a topic will find the strategy to be an excellent prompt for examining sources and organizing writing.

Advantages

- The outlines provide students with practice in developing critical reading skills as they become adept at noticing author viewpoint.
- Students learn to identify propositional writing and analyze supporting arguments.
- Completed outlines help focus class discussions or debates, and they provide structure for writing assignments such as advocacy papers or independent research.

References and Suggested Reading

Buehl, D. (1992). Outline helps students analyze credibility of author's premise. *WEAC News & Views, 28*(1), 8.

Buehl, D. (1995). *Classroom strategies for interactive learning.* Madison, WI: Wisconsin State Reading Association.

Cook, D. (Ed.). (1989). *Strategic learning in the content areas.* Madison, WI: Department of Public Instruction.

Santa, C., Havens, L., & Macumber, E. (1996). *Creating independence through student-owned strategies.* Dubuque, IA: Kendall/Hunt.

Pyramid Diagram

Visualize the following setting: a corporate meeting room of a major company with a table surrounded by executives, each responsible for delivering a report. What follows is a parade of statistics, an array of colorful charts and computer graphics, and a pile of data. But what sense is to be made from all this information? Clearly, the point of the meeting is to understand the implications of the information so that important decisions can be made.

As a critical part of their daily reading demands, students also need to sort through information to draw conclusions and make generalizations. Yet national studies of reading achievement consistently indicate that students have much more difficulty making inferences than identifying facts. The Pyramid Diagram (Solon, 1980) is a strategy that guides students in selecting appropriate information from a reading to be analyzed and possible implications considered.

Using the Strategy

The Pyramid Diagram engages students in both reading and writing activities. Using this strategy involves the following steps:

1 Provide students with a focusing question that will help them select relevant information from a reading. For example, a focusing question for students reading a selection about Benjamin Franklin might be, What were Ben Franklin's accomplishments during his life? A focusing question for students reading a passage on hurricanes might be, What are the problems caused by hurricanes?

2 Distribute index cards to the students and have them read a selection. As they read, they should record on the cards information that deals with the focusing question. One piece of information is recorded on each card. Students looking for Franklin's achievements might write, "invented the lightning rod" on one card, and "was ambassador to France" on a second card. Students continue making cards until they finish reading the passage.

3 Model the process of categorizing the selected information from the reading by soliciting student responses from their cards. Write each response on a

5 × 8 index card and line the cards along the chalkboard tray in the order given. Next, ask students if any of the cards can be grouped together. Allow discussion and recognize disagreements as students determine how the cards might be categorized. Move the cards to reflect the class consensus, thus forming the *foundation layer* of the pyramid diagram (see Pyramid Diagram for Benjamin Franklin).

4 Ask students to brainstorm category headings for each grouping of cards. Again, allow discussion and help the class reach a consensus. Write the headings selected for each group on new cards and tape them to the pyramid as a second layer above the corresponding categories. For example, students might decide on *statesman*, *politician*, or *leader* for cards detailing Franklin's roles as delegate to the Constitutional Convention and diplomat to France. Several of Franklin's other accomplishments could fall under the category *inventor*, *writer*, and *scientist* after they consider the information on the other cards.

5 Draw on the chalkboard two rectangles representing the top two layers of the pyramid. Ask students to determine an appropriate title for the pyramid. The title should reflect the overall topic area of the selection and is placed in the top rectangle. *Benjamin Franklin* or *Franklin's Accomplishments* might be offered as potential titles for the social studies example. Then, using the title, category labels, and details from the reading, have each student write a one-sentence statement that summarizes the information represented in the pyramid. For example, after constructing a Ben Franklin pyramid, students might conclude:

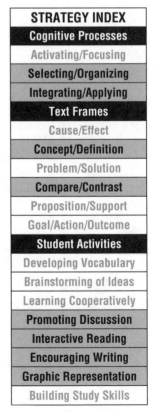

STRATEGY INDEX
Cognitive Processes
Activating/Focusing
Selecting/Organizing
Integrating/Applying
Text Frames
Cause/Effect
Concept/Definition
Problem/Solution
Compare/Contrast
Proposition/Support
Goal/Action/Outcome
Student Activities
Developing Vocabulary
Brainstorming of Ideas
Learning Cooperatively
Promoting Discussion
Interactive Reading
Encouraging Writing
Graphic Representation
Building Study Skills

PYRAMID DIAGRAM FOR BENJAMIN FRANKLIN

Benjamin Franklin							
Ben Franklin's accomplishments in writing, science, and government show that he was a man of many talents and interests.							
Writer		Inventor		Scientist		Statesman	
Published *Poor Richard's Almanack*	Wrote his autobiography	Invented the lightning rod	Devised the Franklin stove	Conducted experiments on electricity	Studied weather patterns	Delegate to the Constitutional Convention	Diplomat to France during the Revolutionary War

(Buehl, 1995; adapted from Solon, 1980)

Ben Franklin's accomplishments in writing, science, and government show that he was a man of many talents and interests.

6 Students now write a one-paragraph conclusion that addresses the focusing question. The second layer of the pyramid provides them with a topic sentence. The third layer suggests subsequent sentences that will expand on the topic sentence. The bottom layer identifies appropriate details that may be used to illustrate each of these examples:

> Benjamin Franklin's accomplishments in writing, science, and government show that he was a man of many talents and interests. Franklin was a well-known writer who published the popular *Poor Richard's Almanack* and wrote his autobiography. As an inventor, he is responsible for inventing the lightning rod and Franklin stove. He also was a scientist who conducted experiments on electricity and studied weather patterns. Finally, Franklin was an important statesman who served as a delegate to the Constitutional Convention and as a diplomat to France during the Revolutionary War.

Once students have become comfortable with using pyramid diagrams, these steps may be accomplished in cooperative groups. Students first read the selection and complete their cards and then meet to construct the rest of the pyramid as a group. Students could then write their one-paragraph conclusions as individuals or as a group.

Advantages

- Students construct a visual representation of how important details are used to draw conclusions and make observations.

- Students are directive in their reading so that they actively search for appropriate information from a selection.

- Students gain practice in writing well-organized summaries of text.

This strategy can be adapted for use from elementary through secondary levels, and is appropriate for all content areas.

References and Suggested Reading

Buehl, D. (1995). *Classroom strategies for interactive learning.* Madison, WI: Wisconsin State Reading Association.

Kinkead, D., Thompson, R., Wright, C., & Gutierrez, C. (1992). Pyramiding: Reading and writing to learn social studies. *The Exchange. Newsletter of the International Reading Association Secondary Reading Interest Group, 5*(2), 3.

Solon, C. (1980). The pyramid diagram: A college study skills tool. *Journal of Reading, 23,* 594–597.

Question-Answer Relationships

"I can't find the answer to this question!" The irritated tone of voice signals a growing frustration from a student struggling to complete an assignment. Indeed, from a student viewpoint, finding answers to questions seems to occupy most of the time spent in schoolwork.

Understanding how the question-answer relationship works is a critical component of learning. Many students are unaware of the different levels of thinking that questions may elicit. As a result, they follow a literal approach to answering questions—seeking direct statements from the text to answer questions—and feel betrayed or even give up when this strategy does not work. Other students pay only cursory attention to their reading; instead, they rely solely on what they already know to obtain answers, regardless of what is in the text. For them, answering questions becomes an exercise in using common sense rather than a thoughtful consideration of new information encountered in print.

Raphael (1982, 1986) offers a powerful strategy for helping students to analyze and understand questions. Her Question-Answer Relationships (QARs) divide questions into two categories: those that have answers supplied by an author (*in-the-book* QARs), and those that have answers that need to be developed based on the reader's ideas and experiences (*in-my-head* QARs). Question-Answer Relationships help students to recognize the kind of thinking they need to engage in when they respond to questions.

Using the Strategy

Teaching students to use Question-Answer Relationships involves ongoing classroom discourse about what various questions require from a reader. Using the strategy involves the following steps:

1 Introduce QARs with a simple example that clearly distinguishes between in-the-book and in-my-head QARs. Use a history passage to illustrate these differences (see QAR for Lewis and Clark). Ask a question that refers to something directly stated in the Lewis and Clark passage such as, What river did Lewis and Clark follow in the spring of 1804? As students provide the answer (the Missouri River), have them locate the place in the text that provides the informa-

tion for the answer. Then ask a question that requires background information in addition to the text in order to answer. An in-my-head question could be, Why was communicating with the Native Americans a difficult process for Lewis and Clark? To answer, students must draw from their background knowledge—that different languages were spoken by European settlers and Native Americans.

2 Discuss with students how some answers can be found explicitly in the text and others require additional information based on what the reader already knows. Students are now ready for a more sophisticated analysis of Question-Answer Relationships. Again, using the sample passage, point out that some in-the-book questions require more thinking than others. For example, the question, How long did it take Lewis and Clark to complete their explorations? requires students to put information together from more than one part of the passage. The answer, about 2½ years, can be obtained only after putting two pieces of information together—the dates mentioned in the first and last sentences.

Share with students that there are two types of in-the-book QARs: *right-there questions* (the river they followed), and *putting-it-together questions* (the length of their trip). Both answers are in the text, but putting-it-together questions involve constructing answers using several pieces of information. Putting-it-together questions mandate the examination of more than one sentence in order to connect facts and draw conclusions. Another way to describe the two in-the-book QARs is right-there questions are already preassembled, waiting for you to find them; and putting-it-together questions have all the necessary pieces in the text but the reader has to

STRATEGY INDEX
Cognitive Processes
Activating/Focusing
Selecting/Organizing
Integrating/Applying
Text Frames
Cause/Effect
Concept/Definition
Problem/Solution
Compare/Contrast
Proposition/Support
Goal/Action/Outcome
Student Activities
Developing Vocabulary
Brainstorming of Ideas
Learning Cooperatively
Promoting Discussion
Interactive Reading
Encouraging Writing
Graphic Representation
Building Study Skills

QAR FOR LEWIS AND CLARK

Lewis and Clark followed the Missouri River for several hundred miles as they moved westward in the spring of 1804. Along with their goal of mapping the new territory, the two explorers were also instructed to keep careful records of their journey. As they traveled, the explorers gained a great deal of information through the difficult process of trying to communicate with the Native Americans they met. Their journals were filled with words, such as *skunk, hickory, squash, raccoon,* and *opossum,* which are Native American terms for plants and animals. After their return in September 1806, Lewis and Clark reported to President Jefferson and their journals were eventually published.

Right there:

1. What river did Lewis and Clark follow in the spring of 1804?
2. What was the goal of Lewis and Clark's journey?

Putting it together:

3. How long did it take Lewis and Clark to complete their explorations?
4. Why did the explorers keep journals during their travels?

Author and me:

5. Who sent Lewis and Clark on their expedition?
6. Why was trying to communicate with the Native Americans a difficult process for Lewis and Clark?

On my own:

7. Why did Lewis and Clark use Native American terms for many of the plants and animals they encountered?
8. How do you think the Native Americans felt about the Lewis and Clark expedition?

---

locate each piece and assemble the pieces to create the answer (see Where's the Answer?).

3 Demonstrate that in-my-head QARs also can be of two types: *author-and-me* and *on-my-own.* The question in the example concerning the explorers' dif-

ficulty communicating with the Native Americans can be answered using clues from the author (e.g., noticing that Native American terms appeared in the journals) and general background knowledge (e.g., realizing that these peoples spoke different languages). This question is an author-and-me QAR, because answers are constructed partly from hints in the text and partly from the reader's personal knowledge base. Another example is, Who sent Lewis and Clark on their expedition? The article does not directly address this question, but an answer is implied. According to the text, the explorers reported to President Jefferson when they returned. Student experiences may tell them that people who complete a mission usually report what happened to whomever sent them on that mission. Therefore, students would infer that Jefferson recruited this expedition.

The second type of in-my-head QAR—on-my-own—relies almost solely on the reader's personal knowledge. A question such as, Why did Lewis and Clark use Native American terms for many of the plants and animals they encountered? cannot be answered based on the information in the passage. Students will have to hypothesize answers based on what they know. Students might offer that because North America contained many plants and animals unfamiliar to European settlers, it was natural for them to adopt Native American terms.

On-my-own QARs often can be answered without reading the passage, which may lead to a variety of plausible responses. An on-my-own question such as, How do you think the Native Americans reacted to the Lewis and Clark expedition? could lead to important discussions regarding the changing dynamic in the American West, but very little in the passage would contribute to this discussion.

4 Provide students with opportunities for classifying questions according to these four categories. Emphasize that recognizing the question type is an essential first step toward deciding an appropriate answer. Ask students to work in pairs or small groups

---

WHERE'S THE ANSWER?

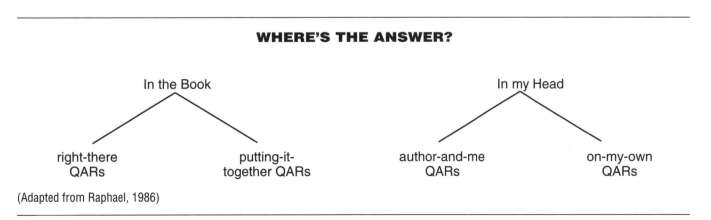

(Adapted from Raphael, 1986)

---

to label questions as well as answer them. This activity can be an effective way to foster classroom discussions about how an answer can be determined and develop the ability to handle questions that require inferential thinking and reacting to several parts of a passage—the putting-it-together and author-and-me QARs.

5 As students become comfortable with identifying types of questions, have them write examples of their own in lieu of responding to your questions. These student-generated questions can be exchanged with classmates, who then answer and classify the student-produced questions.

Advantages

- Students begin to perceive that a variety of strategies are needed to answer questions.

- Students are guided in understanding that valuable responses to reading can range from the literal identification of basic information to very open-ended discussions that have no set, correct answer.

- Students are prompted to constantly tap into their own knowledge base as they encounter new information in reading.

- Teachers have a framework for analyzing comprehension gaps due to lack of adequate background knowledge rather than from an inability to answer in-the-book QARs.

This strategy can be used with students from elementary through high school levels. In addition, students preparing for the comprehension passages on ACT and SAT college entrance tests will find this an insightful strategy.

References

Raphael, T.E. (1982). Question-answering strategies for children. *The Reading Teacher, 36*, 186–190.

Raphael, T. (1986). Teaching question answer relationships, revisited. *The Reading Teacher, 39*, 516–522.

Question Dissection

- Discuss three ways in which President Roosevelt's New Deal changed the role of the federal government in the United States.
- In *Of Mice and Men* by John Steinbeck, should George have taken Lenny's life at the end of the book? Justify your answer by citing specific incidents from the novel.
- Identify the various stages of the water cycle and describe what happens at each of these stages.

The dreaded essay question—that looming empty space on the test page, waiting malevolently for evidence that you actually can discuss what you have learned. More forbidding and less sporting, perhaps, than the "games of chance" that students prefer on tests: multiple choice, matching eliminations, or 50/50 shots on true and false. Some students will take a quick glance at what the question seems to be about, and then quickly and incoherently unload whatever stray facts come to mind. Others will ponder painfully; start, stop, and start again, and as their tortured writing unfolds to discover that a disproportionate amount of testing time has been diverted to this task. Sadly, a number of students will merely leave the space blank, resigned to forfeiting the points on their exam score.

Of course, a few individuals will proceed with confidence. For most students, however, the essay question is the most challenging test item, and with the inclusion of more written responses on state and national assessments, students face increasing demands to exhibit their thinking through writing. Essay-exam writing should be treated like any other skill that students need to develop. Teachers cannot expect students to know automatically how to create appropriate responses to essay questions. Question Dissection (Williams, 1986) is a strategy that will help students to analyze questions and to better understand how to approach writing essay answers.

Using the Strategy

In Question Dissection, students analyze essay questions by verbalizing to themselves exactly what is being asked. They take stock of what they know and determine how to organize that knowledge into an ap-

propriate answer. Using the strategy involves the following steps:

1 Brainstorm with students about what makes essay questions difficult. Have them work with partners for a few minutes to jot down problems and frustrations experienced when writing essay answers: essay answers take more work, students aren't sure what to write, they have trouble getting started, the questions take a great deal of time during the test, and essay questions require a lot of thinking. Some students will express concern about the ability to express themselves through writing.

Ask students about the ways in which essay items require a different kind of thinking than for objective items:

- Students usually have to produce information from their memories with few prompts or perhaps none at all.
- Students are asked to *use* information rather than merely recall what they have learned as they formulate their answers.
- Students are asked to clarify their understandings of a concept, to draw conclusions, to make generalizations, and to perceive connections between facts.
- Students have a greater opportunity to express their personal understandings of important material.

In summary, essay items ask students to demonstrate their thinking as well as display their knowledge.

STRATEGY INDEX
Cognitive Processes
Activating/Focusing
Selecting/Organizing
Integrating/Applying
Text Frames
Cause/Effect
Concept/Definition
Problem/Solution
Compare/Contrast
Proposition/Support
Goal/Action/Outcome
Student Activities
Developing Vocabulary
Brainstorming of Ideas
Learning Cooperatively
Promoting Discussion
Interactive Reading
Encouraging Writing
Graphic Representation
Building Study Skills

2 Introduce the protocol for Question Dissection (QD). Emphasize that essay questions can contain clues about how to structure an acceptable answer, which students often overlook. The QD protocol leads students through a rapid step-by-step analysis of an essay question:

- **Test Verbs** are verbs used to introduce an essay question, which imply or give clues to the style or format of the answer. *Discuss, compare, contrast, describe, explain, criticize, evaluate,* and *summarize* are commonly used test verbs.

- **Topic** is the knowledge domain that is being tested and suggests the segment of learning that needs to be recalled and showcased for the question.

- **List** is the listing or elaboration of types of information that every essay question requires: causes, reasons, ways in which something is influenced, steps or instructions, etc. Identifying a list helps to narrow the focus within a topic.

- **Number** specifies or implies that a number of things should be included in your answer: a single reason, cause, or method; a specific number (3 reasons, 2 causes); or multiple items (many causes, or some ways).

- **Order** is a particular order of information asked for in the answer. Some questions allow information to be listed in any order (flexible), while others require a specific sequence.

- **First Sentence** is the recasting or reconstruction of the essay question so that it becomes the first sentence of your answer. This provides momentum to begin writing and helps with structuring an organized response to the question.

Students will need a great deal of modeling of the Question Dissection strategy so that it becomes an automatic response to tackling essay questions. To model the protocol, use an essay question that relates to material that students are currently studying (see Question Dissection for Civil Rights). When the protocol is first used with an exam, include a prompt box (see QD Protocol Box) so that students can fill in information quickly for the first five steps of the protocol before starting to write their answer.

3 Familiarize students with the variety of question types that will be encountered on essay tests. Typically, students do not know the questions on essay exams ahead of time and may not have any fore-knowledge of topics about which they will be asked to write. Initially, as you prepare students, provide them with an essay question in advance of the test. Use this opportunity to analyze the kinds of thinking suggested by different test verbs (see Chapter 2):

QUESTION DISSECTION
FOR CIVIL RIGHTS

Evaluate the effectiveness of three tactics used by the civil rights movement in the United States to improve conditions for African Americans in the 1950s and 1960s.

1. Test Verb—What is the test verb that you must use to organize your answer? *Evaluate*

2. Topic—In what topic area are you asked to demonstrate your knowledge? *civil rights movement*

3. List—What things are you asked to list and talk about in your answer? *tactics used to improve conditions*

4. Number—How many things are you asked to list in your answer?
   - single or multiple? *multiple*
   - set number or open number? *set number: 3*

5. Order—In what order do you need to list information in your answer?
   - flexible or sequence? *flexible*

6. First Sentence—Rewrite the test question so it is the first sentence of your essay.

   Three tactics used by the civil rights movement to improve conditions for African Americans in the 1950s and 1960s were.... The first tactic was effective in the following ways....

QUESTION DISSECTION
PROTOCOL BOX

1. Test Verb?

2. Topic?

3. List?

4. Number?
   - single or multiple?
   - set number or open number?

5. Order?
   - flexible or sequence?

6. First Sentence—Rewrite the test question.

(Buehl, 2000; adapted from Williams, 1986)

- Identify Similarities and Differences—show how things are alike or not alike (*compare, contrast, distinguish*).
- Outline a Cause/Effect Relationship—tell how or why something happens or happened (*explain, relate, interpret, discuss*).
- Support an Argument—use information to back up statements or ideas (*criticize, evaluate, defend, justify, prove*).
- Organize Details and Examples—use language to help us visualize something (*describe, illustrate, define*).

4 Introduce strategies that guide students in organizing knowledge into a coherent essay answer. Model for students how to "fact pack" their responses to a target question. What information, what terms and details, should be cited in a complete answer? A word-association web is an excellent stimulus for generating those key terms for an essay answer. For example, students in a world history class might be given the following essay question: Contrast the lives of the nobles with the peasants during feudalism.

As students work with partners to brainstorm terms for the topic of feudalism, their word-association web might feature: *fief, castle, allegiance, protection, knight, vassal, thatched hut, farmer, France, rent, artisan, famine, jousting, chivalry* (see LINK, page 32). Once a web is complete, students have prompts for answering the question and a visual reminder of information that should be integrated into their essay. As they consider the test verb (*contrast*), they can begin to do a quick sort of terms that are characteristic of the nobles and peasants. Starting to write begins to look like a less forbidding enterprise.

5 Additional strategies can help students continue to improve their preparation and organization. Have students predict the topic areas that may be featured in an essay question for the next test, and have them work with partners to write possible essay questions.

Student-generated questions may actually be placed on the exam. Another preparation technique is to allow students to use notes for the essay portion of an exam. For example, the topic of an essay question is provided in advance, and students are permitted to bring to the test all the notes they can write on a 4×6 index card. This fact packing encourages them to seach for key terms and ideas ahead of time, and provides a focus to their study.

Another strategy is to supply the test verb for the essay question, so students can brainstorm possible questions about the topic that might include that verb (see Template Frames, page 141). Allocating instructional time for writing successful essays will lead students to a more directive and positive attitude toward essay responses on tests.

Advantages

- Students begin to learn the terminology of essay exams and perceive how distinctions among test verbs influence the nature of the expected essay.
- Students receive guidance in how to improve expository writing skills.
- Students are encouraged to see connections in material rather than approaching study as mere memorization of facts.
- Students are engaged in upper level thinking processes, such as supporting arguments or recognizing cause/effect relationships.

References

Buehl, D. (2000). Breaking it down: Understanding the question leads to a better answer. *WEAC News and Views, 35*(6), 14.

Williams, D. (1986, May). Unlocking the question. In H. Carr (Chair), *Using research to support teacher change and student progress in the content areas.* Paper presented at the 31st Annual Convention of the International Reading Association, Philadelphia, Pennsylvania.

Questioning the Author

Position the factory-applied nailing fin drip cap upright for installation. Ensure drip cap lip hangs over the head jamb extrusion. Note: Clad Safe-T-Plus model lacks drip cap attachment to head jamb nailing fin. Do not apply the nailing fin corner gaskets at this time....

The do-it-yourself nightmare! You are poised to undertake a project, and the enthusiasm you have kindled begins to fizzle as you are confronted with the inevitable set of incomprehensible directions and obscure illustrations. Who writes this stuff anyway?

Who indeed. Imagine for a moment the author who wrote these guidelines for installing a window (which is, believe it or not, what is being described!). Who does this writer think will be reading these instructions? What does the writer think readers will already know? What expectations does the writer apparently have about readers' ability to make sense of this document? What could the writer have done to make the writing more accessible? Is it any wonder that after reading directions such as these, many readers would toss the directions aside and try to "wing it" through their project?

Students also deal with textbook frustrations by throwing in the towel after their struggles. They tend to view textbooks as anonymous authorities, repositories of unassailable truth. It does not occur to most students that textbooks are written by actual people, who may not have been entirely successful in communicating their ideas. Some read their assignments only in a cursory way, trying to piece together answers to questions by skimming for details. Others bypass the book entirely, depending on the teacher and class interactions for their information. And some just give up, assuming that they are incapable of learning the material. Questioning the Author (Beck et al., 1997) is a strategy that can help students cope with challenging text materials.

Using the Strategy

Questioning the Author (QtA) conditions students to think about what the author is saying, not what the textbook states. Using the strategy involves the following steps:

1 Introduce to students the topic of authorship of text materials. Have them "personalize" the authors by identifying these individuals by name and locating any biographical information that provides insight into who they are. What perspective do they bring to the book: that of university professors, experts in the field, or classroom educators? Select a passage from the textbook and model examination of the authorship with students. What is not clear or not easy to understand? What do the authors expect students to know? What could the authors add or change to make a better written passage? Emphasize the fallibility of the authors: Authors have opinions and make decisions about what to put in their writing. And, although authors are very knowledgeable about the material, sometimes they may have trouble expressing their ideas in ways that students can understand.

Note that the intent of the modeling is not to condemn textbooks as poorly written, but to underscore the natural tension that occurs between readers and writers. Writers have a responsibility to clearly communicate their ideas to the audience they are targeting. Readers have a responsibility to size up what an author provides and what they must do to make sense of a text. (As mentioned in Chapter 1, some textbooks are more considerate to readers than others in the way they present information and ideas.)

2 Preview a section of the textbook that will be assigned for reading. Decide what is most important for students to understand from this material. In addition, identify any segments that may present difficulties for students. Choose places in the text where you will stop students and initiate discussion to clarify key points. Unlike most textbook les-

STRATEGY INDEX
Cognitive Processes
Activating/Focusing
Selecting/Organizing
Integrating/Applying
Text Frames
Cause/Effect
Concept/Definition
Problem/Solution
Compare/Contrast
Proposition/Support
Goal/Action/Outcome
Student Activities
Developing Vocabulary
Brainstorming of Ideas
Learning Cooperatively
Promoting Discussion
Interactive Reading
Encouraging Writing
Graphic Representation
Building Study Skills

sons that involve discussion before or after reading, a QtA activity has the teacher lead discussion *during* reading, at predetermined breaks in the text. Students might read a paragraph or two before a discussion break, or you might wish to follow a pivotal single sentence with discussion. For example, the following earth science passage is deceptively difficult:

> Earthquakes can occur for many reasons. The ground can shake from the eruption of a volcano, the collapse of a cavern, or even from the impact of a meteor. However, the major cause of earthquakes is the stress that builds up between two lithospheric plates. (Adapted from Namowitz & Spaulding, 1989)

The author assumes that students are aware of giant underground caverns, although why these should collapse and how often they do so is not explained. The author also assumes that students know about meteors and that these objects sometimes collide with the earth, which is implied in the paragraph, although the frequency with which this occurs also is not discussed. Finally, the author taps into assumed previous learning about volcanoes and lithospheric plates, which is an excellent place to pause the reading and clarify information with students.

3 Focus discussion during this pause on *author queries*, questions that are not asked specifically about the information but about the author's intentions: What is the author trying to say? What is the author's message? Did the author explain clearly? How does this connect with what the author has told us before? Why do you think the author tells us this now? (See QtA Queries.) Model for students how a proficient reader endeavors to make sense of sometimes confusing or inadequate text. Discuss what the author is trying to communicate; affirm key points offered by students, sometimes paraphrasing them; and turn student attention to the text for clarification of specific issues. Provide students with additional information to fill in any gaps in the text. The strength of QtA discussions is derived from the modeling of appropriate problem-solving questions that help readers think about their comprehension as they read.

4 As students become comfortable responding to QtA queries, ask them to generate their own for a section of the textbook. With a partner, ask them to lightly pencil in an asterisk in a few places in the text where they believe a reader should stop and ponder. Have them select one or more of the queries from the QtA Queries (listed on a classroom poster or on an individual copy, such as a bookmark), which a reader might ask at each of these junctures. For added practice, group two sets of partners together and have

---

QtA QUERIES

- What is the author trying to say?
- What is the author's message?
- What is the author talking about?
- Did the author explain clearly?
- Does this follow with what the author told us before?
- How does this connect with what the author told us before?
- What does the author assume that we already know?
- Does the author tell us why?
- Why do you think the author tells us this information now?

---

them pose their queries to one another. Questioning the Author makes the previously overlooked actions of the author more visible to students as they attempt to learn from textbooks.

Advantages

- Students are less likely to be frustrated by difficult text as they realize that part of the responsibility for a passage making sense belongs to the author.
- Students are taught to be metacognitive—readers who actively monitor their comprehension during reading.
- Students become deeply engaged with reading, as issues and problems are addressed while they learn, rather than afterward.
- Students learn to internalize a self-questioning process that proficient readers use to monitor and enhance their comprehension.

QtA discussions can be used to introduce selections that students will read independently, perhaps as homework. They are especially helpful when students may need some assistance coping with difficult but important segments of a chapter. QtA discussions are also valuable as a comprehension-building strategy for struggling readers. QtA lessons may be developed in all content areas and can be tailored for young students as well as adolescent learners.

Reference

Beck, I.L., McKeown, M.G., Hamilton, R.L., & Kucan, L. (1997). *Questioning the author: An approach for enhancing student engagement with text.* Newark, DE: International Reading Association.

Other Work Cited

Namowitz, S., & Spaulding, N. (1989). *Earth science.* Lexington, MA: D.C.Heath.

RAFT
(Role/Audience/Format/Topic)

Who do you imagine yourself to be as you read? As you drift through a novel, *The Great Gatsby*, for example, who are you? Do you identify with the tragic Jay Gatsby? Or the unhappy Daisy? Maybe Tom, the aggrieved but inadequate husband? Or the narrator, Nick Carraway, observing the unfolding story as an increasingly involved outsider? Or perhaps Daisy's friend, Jordan Baker? As you become engaged in the story and emotionally attached to the characters, you splice yourself into the action. You indulge yourself in the delicious experience of living other people's lives, vicariously, through print.

The ability to interject ourselves into our reading deepens our comprehension and broadens our learning as we begin to develop empathy for the situations of others and perceive perspectives that are not necessarily our own. Encouraging students to adopt this mental role-playing frame of mind can help them to improve their reading of classroom materials and to provide focus to writing assignments.

We know, in particular, that writing is an effective way to help students think about what they have read. But often teachers are frustrated with the quality of writing completed by students—writing that is too brief, lacking in detail, poorly organized, bereft of imagination, and carelessly thrown together. Students tend to view writing as a laborious task in which they have no personal investment. As a result, the purpose of using writing as a tool for learning is sometimes defeated.

The RAFT strategy (Santa, 1988) is a technique that attempts to address teacher concerns with student writing. RAFT is a method that works to infuse imagination, creativity, and motivation into a writing assignment. The strategy involves writing from a viewpoint other than that of a student, to an audience other than the teacher, and in a form other than a standard theme or written answers to questions.

Using the Strategy

RAFT is an acronym for

R—Role of the writer (Who are you?)

A—Audience for the writer (To whom are you writing?)

F—Format of the writing (What form will your writing assume?)

T—Topic to be addressed in the writing (What are you writing about?)

Using the strategy involves the following steps:

1 Analyze the important ideas or information that you want students to learn from reading a story, a textbook passage, or other classroom material. Consider how a writing assignment will help to consolidate this learning. How might writing help students remember the stages of the digestive system? Or understand the frustrations of the American colonists? Or empathize with the emotions of a character in a story? This establishes the topic for the writing.

2 Brainstorm possible roles students could assume in their writing (see Examples of RAFT Assignments). For example, students studying the colonial period in a U.S. history class could assume the role of a colonist upset with more British taxes. Students reading the book *James and the Giant Peach* in a language arts class could assume the role of James, who needs to tell somebody about how his malevolent aunts are treating him. Students in a science class could impersonate a french fry, describing the physical changes experienced during each stage of the digestive process.

Decide who the audience will be for this communication and determine the format for the writing. For example, the colonist could be writing in the form of a petition intended for other outraged colonists. James could be writing a letter to state adoption authorities complaining of his ill treatment. The french fry could be writing in the format of a travel journal, to be read by other french fries headed toward the digestive system.

STRATEGY INDEX
Cognitive Processes
Activating/Focusing
Selecting/Organizing
Integrating/Applying
Text Frames
Cause/Effect
Concept/Definition
Problem/Solution
Compare/Contrast
Proposition/Support
Goal/Action/Outcome
Student Activities
Developing Vocabulary
Brainstorming of Ideas
Learning Cooperatively
Promoting Discussion
Interactive Reading
Encouraging Writing
Graphic Representation
Building Study Skills

EXAMPLES OF RAFT ASSIGNMENTS

Role	Audience	Format	Topic
Newspaper Reporter	Readers in the 1870s	Obituary	Qualities of General Custer
Lawyer	U.S. Supreme Court	Appeal Speech	Dred Scott Decision
Abraham Lincoln	Dear Abby	Advice Column	Frustrations With His Generals
Oprah	Television Public	Talk Show	Women's Suffrage in Early 20th Century
Frontier Woman	Self	Diary	Hardships in West
Constituent	U.S. Senator	Letter	Need for Civil Rights Legislation in 1950s
Newswriter	Public	News Release	Ozone Layer Has Been Formed
Chemist	Chemical Company	Instructions	Dangerous Combinations to Avoid
Graham Cracker	Other Graham Crackers	Travel Guide	Journey Through the Digestive System
Plant	Sun	Thank You Note	Sun's Role in Plant's Growth
Scientist	Charles Darwin	Memo	Refute a Point in Evolution Theory
Square Root	Whole Number	Love Letter	Explain Relationship
Repeating Decimal	Set of Rational Numbers	Petition	Prove You Belong to This Set
Cook	Other Cooks	Recipe	Alcoholism
Julia Child	TV Audience	Script	How Yeast Works in Bread
Doctor's Association	Future Parents	Web Page	Need for Proper Prenatal Nutrition
Advertiser	TV Audience	Public Service Announcement	Importance of Fruit
Lungs	Cigarettes	Complaint	Effects of Smoking
Huck Finn	Jim	Telephone Conversation	What I Learned During the Trip
Joseph Stalin	George Orwell	Book Review	Reactions to *Animal Farm*
Comma	Ninth-Grade Students	Job Description	Use in Sentences
Trout	Self	Diary	Effects of Acid Rain on Lake
Mozart	Prospective Employer	Job Interview	Qualifications as a Composer

(Buehl, 1995)

3 After students complete the reading assignment, write RAFT on the chalkboard and list the role, audience, format, and topic for their writing. Assign all students the same role for the writing, or offer several different roles from which students can choose. For instance, after reading a passage on soil erosion, students could write from the perspective of a farmer, a fish in a nearby stream, a corn plant, or a worm in the topsoil. Students could be given the choice of several characters from a story to represent their role for writing.

Before students begin writing the RAFTs, help them develop a deeper understanding of their roles (Shearer, 1998). Some students will be confused and uncertain about how their role might react to the topic. Place students assuming the same role in a cooperative group, and have them brainstorm critical elements of that role. Suggest the following questions for the group to consider:

What perspective would my role have on the assigned topic?

Why do I care about this particular topic?

Where would I look to find out more about this perspective?

What information (or parts of the story) do I need to examine carefully for my role?

What should I be particularly concerned about within this topic?

What emotions might I be feeling as I think about this topic?

Is this a role that might lead me to be in favor or against something related to this topic?

Could a person in my role have a choice of several viewpoints on this topic? Which viewpoint might appeal to me the most?

How can I give my role some personality?

How can I ensure that what I say about the topic in my role is accurate?

To provide a visual framework for this brainstorming phase, provide each student with a three-column matrix, which will prompt them to write down pertinent thoughts as they probe their role in their groups (see Role Definition Matrix). The matrix can serve as a guide for their writing.

4 Make available sample formats for a specific RAFT project for students to use as they plan their writing. For example, if they are creating a television script, supply examples to help them visualize what to include in their versions. By consulting actual examples, students can rely on a measure of reality to give them ideas for how to proceed with their person-

ROLE DEFINITION MATRIX

Personality—Who am I and what are some aspects of my character?	*Attitude*—What are my feelings, beliefs, ideas, concerns?	*Information*—What do I know that I need to share in my writing?

al RAFTs. As students become comfortable with writing in the guise of various roles, they eventually can be expected to define their own RAFT assignments. Students can devise an appropriate role for a unit of study, designate a relevant audience, and consider possible formats for communicating their thoughts.

Advantages

- Students offer more thoughtful and often more extensive written responses as they demonstrate their learning.
- Students are actively involved in processing information rather than merely writing out answers to questions.
- Students are given a clear structure for their writing. They know what point of view to assume, and they are provided with an organizational scheme. Furthermore, the purpose of the writing is outlined clearly.

- Students are more motivated to undertake a writing assignment, because it attempts to involve them personally and allows for more creative responses to learning the material.
- Students are encouraged to examine material from perspectives other than their own and gain insights about concepts and ideas that may not have occurred to them during the initial reading of an assignment.

RAFT is a strategy adaptable to all content areas, including science, social studies, and math.

References

Santa, C. (1988). *Content reading including study systems.* Dubuque, IA: Kendall/Hunt.

Shearer, B. (1998, February). *Student directed and focused inquiry.* Paper presented at the Wisconsin State Reading Association Conference, Milwaukee, WI.

Read-Alouds

- A booklet of instructions to assemble and install a ceiling fan.
- Directions for completing sections of various federal income tax forms.
- An article on the brain that discusses the activities of neurotransmitters.
- A logic problem that stipulates conditions to be met for arriving at a solution.

What do these different examples of prose have in common? Each is an example of the technical writing that we may encounter daily, which often can be frustrating and hard to comprehend. Most likely, we will reread it in an attempt to get things straight and to ensure that we understand what is being communicated. In addition, most of us will automatically employ a strategy that we know will help us navigate difficult text—we will read the passage out loud. Reading aloud is a natural response to comprehension difficulties and is an excellent strategy that supports students when confronting challenging material in the classroom.

Using the Strategy

Although silent reading is grounded in oral language, sometimes it is necessary to vocalize in order to assist comprehension. Among the number of read-aloud strategies, one method—round robin oral reading—has significant disadvantages. As students wait for their turn to read, they may or may not pay attention to the reader. Some students will find the pace too slow-moving, especially if a reader is not fluent and is laboring over a passage. Struggling readers will view the task with apprehension—performing in front of an entire group exhibits their lack of skill in oral reading. There are, however, a number of read-aloud strategies that can be used successfully in the classroom.

Teacher Read-Aloud

Model fluent oral reading by regularly reading segments of class materials to students. There are a number of opportunities for teacher read-alouds in the curriculum:

1 Read aloud beginning sections of material that students will continue to read independently, which will "prime" them for the task and introduce important concepts or vocabulary.

2 Read aloud especially difficult passages to model problem-solving with demanding text. Read aloud from additional sources related to topics explored in the curriculum to pique student interest in personal investigations and to enhance understanding. Trelease (1989) offers the following guidelines for teacher read-alouds:

- read with expression, so that through your intonation, pauses, and phrasing students can "hear" the meaning of the passage;
- be careful not to rush through the passage, so that students have time to "absorb" while they listen; and
- encourage questions and discussion as you read, so that you can spark a dialogue with students about what you are reading.

Say Something Read-Aloud

Gaither (1997) recommends the "Say Something" strategy for paired oral reading.

1 Have each student work with a partner and read a passage about life during the Depression from a history textbook. Have one student read aloud the first paragraph while the partner follows along and listens. When the reader finishes, the listener must *say something* about what was read: comment on interesting material, make a prediction, raise a question, identify confusing information, or relate infor-

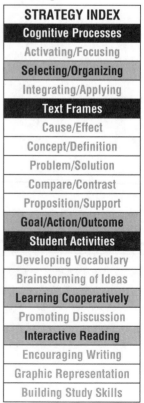

STRATEGY INDEX
Cognitive Processes
Activating/Focusing
Selecting/Organizing
Integrating/Applying
Text Frames
Cause/Effect
Concept/Definition
Problem/Solution
Compare/Contrast
Proposition/Support
Goal/Action/Outcome
Student Activities
Developing Vocabulary
Brainstorming of Ideas
Learning Cooperatively
Promoting Discussion
Interactive Reading
Encouraging Writing
Graphic Representation
Building Study Skills

mation from the paragraph to personal background experiences or knowledge.

2 Ask partners to switch roles and continue with the next paragraph. Unlike round robin reading—one student reading and the entire class listening—paired reading involves half the class reading while partners listen. Because all students are either reading aloud or listening and commenting, the sound level in the classroom accords a measure of privacy to individual readers, which is especially helpful to struggling readers who may need assistance from their partners as they read. The Say Something strategy provides a more interactive format for classroom read-alouds and allocates students more opportunity to practice oral reading fluency. The strategy stimulates conversation about a passage and encourages students to make connections as they read, and to work at clarifying information that is difficult or confusing.

Readers Theatre Read-Aloud

This strategy sometimes involves advance preparation by the teacher and readers so that students feel comfortable reading to the class.

1 Preview materials to identify passages that could be modified for read-alouds by a group of students. Some passages are appropriate for Readers Theatre with little editing, and a group of four or five students can take turns reading sentences. For example, a science passage on the life cycle of a moth is read by five students, with Student A reading the first sentence, Student B reading the second, and so on through the passage.

2 If necessary, rework any material to fit the Readers Theatre format. For example, have students read portions of a textbook chapter on life during the Depression, alternating female and male voices. Or change the language to first person from third person (*he* and *they* become *I* and *we*). Therefore, a descriptive passage becomes a personal narrative when delivered by the Readers Theatre group (see Readers Theatre for Social Studies and Readers Theatre for Biology).

3 Readers Theatre read-alouds need not be elaborate productions. However, allow students sufficient time to review their lines so that they can be read with polish for the entire class.

Advantages

- Read-alouds offer variation in the classroom routine of learning from text materials.

READERS THEATRE FOR SOCIAL STUDIES
The Triangle Fire

(Readers A & B—News Reporters; Readers C & D—Immigrant Workers; Reader E—Rose Schneiderman)

A Progressives also worked to improve workplace safety.

B Tragic events in March 1911 catapulted the need for such reforms onto the front pages of the nation's newspapers.

A Late in the afternoon on Saturday, March 25, some 500 employees,

B most of them young Jewish or Italian immigrant women,

A were completing their 6-day work week at New York City's Triangle Shirtwaist Company.

C Shortly before quitting time, as we rose from our crowded worktables and started to leave, a fire erupted in a rag bin.

D Within moments the entire eighth floor of the 10-story building was ablaze.

C Escape quickly became impossible—there were only two stairways, and most of the exit doors were locked.

D Leaping from high windows was our last, desperate way out.

C 60 of us workers took it—to our deaths.

D Through the night, weeping family members wandered among our crushed bodies on the sidewalk, looking for their loved ones.

C In all more than 140 of us perished in the Triangle fire.

D We were victims of a thoroughly unsafe workplace.

A Rose Schneiderman was a Women's Trade Union League organizer.

B She argued that only a strong working class movement could bring real change to the workplace.

E This is not the only time girls have been burned alive in the city. Each week I must learn of the untimely death of one of my sister workers. Every year thousands of us are maimed. The life of men and women is so cheap and property is so sacred. There are so many of us for one job it matters little if 143 of us are burned to death.

A But it did matter.

B The public outcry was so great that lawmakers were pressured to pass protective legislation.

A The New York legislature enacted the nation's strictest fire safety code.

(Adapted from Boyer & Stuckey, 1998.)

READERS THEATRE FOR BIOLOGY
Monerans

ABCDE We are Monerans!

B   Bacteria

A   Viruses

ABCDE Monerans!

C   Almost all of us have a cell wall.

D   The cell wall protects the cell and gives it shape.

C   Without a cell wall, most of us moneran cells would absorb water by osmosis.

ABCDE and explode!

E   Some of us have a layer outside our cell wall.

A   This layer is called the capsule.

B   It is a sticky material

A   that helps us cling to surfaces.

E   Those of us who are disease-causing often have a capsule, which may protect us from our host's immune system.

C   We Monerans are extremely small.

D   A typical bacterium,

C   me for example,

D   is about 2 micrometers long.

C   That's one millionth of a meter.

D   Yet each of us is a complete organism.

C   Packaged into my cell are all the nucleic acids, enzymes, and other substances necessary to carry out my cell's life processes.

E   Many monerans have long, thin structures called flagella that allow us to move around.

A   The flagella act like tiny propellers.

B   They rotate and move us in response to chemical stimuli.

E   Some of us also have many short, hairlike protein strands called pili.

A   These pili enable us to stick to a surface and obtain food.

C   Under harsh conditions, many of us bacteria form a protective structure called an endospore.

B   An endospore consists of a thick wall surrounding the nuclear material and a small amount of cytoplasm.

READERS THEATRE FOR BIOLOGY
(continued)
Monerans

A   Endospores can withstand boiling water,

D   drying out,

E   or other extreme conditions.

C   When the environment becomes favorable, we emerge from the endospores and begin normal growth.

B   Many of us are bacteria that cause disease from endospores.

A   Therefore, methods to kill spores are important in food preservation and in medicine.

C   If you want to kill me, you better expose me to pressurized steam at 121°C for 10 to 15 minutes.

E   This procedure is called *sterilization*.

(Adapted from McLaren, Rotundo, & Gurley-Dilger, 1991)

- Students practice oral fluency with material that may be better understood if it is heard as well as read.
- Students are involved in nonthreatening and supportive oral reading experiences.
- Read-alouds involve interaction between students and dialogue about what is being learned.

A wide range of content materials, both fiction and nonfiction, are appropriate for classroom read-alouds.

References

Gaither, P. (1997, May). *Caught in the act: Strategies to engage readers with informational text.* Paper presented at the 47th Annual Convention of the International Reading Association, Atlanta, GA.

Trelease, J. (1989). *The new read-aloud handbook.* New York: Penguin.

Other Works Cited

Boyer, P., & Stuckey, S. (1998). *The American nation in the 20th century.* Austin, TX: Holt, Rinehart, and Winston.

McLaren, J., Rotundo, L., & Gurley-Digler, L. (1991). Heath biology. Lexington, MA: D.C. Heath.

Save the Last Word for Me

Think back on various point-counterpoint news programs that you have watched. Sometimes you witness a verbal free-for-all, with a news correspondent desperately mediating between two or more individuals who have diverging viewpoints they are eager to express. Each wants to capture air time to tell you, the public, what "it really means." And each wants the last word.

Wouldn't it be refreshing if your students also wanted the last word about what they are learning in class? Instead, only a handful of students venture thoughts about what they found interesting in class reading assignments. The rest of the class is often hard-pressed to verbalize "what the reading really means" to them.

For many students, *reading* means taking a quick, superficial trip through a text for the sole purpose of answering assigned questions. Unfortunately, these students often never achieve more than a cursory, literal idea of what they have read. Classroom discussions that encourage students to think about their reading tend to sputter as a result, because students do not engage in reflective reading behavior.

Activities that stimulate students to reflect on what they read help to develop active and thoughtful readers. One effective strategy for developing readers who are thinkers is Save the Last Word for Me (Burke & Harste, described in Vaughan & Estes, 1986). Save the Last Word prompts students to actively engage with the text and provides a cooperative group format for the subsequent class discussion.

Using the Strategy

Save the Last Word for Me (see page 122) is an excellent strategy to use with material that may elicit differing opinions or multiple interpretations. This discussion format is controlled by the students rather than directed by the teacher. The small-group setting is more inviting to students who are reluctant to talk in front of an entire class, and in addition, gives them time to rehearse their comments by writing their thoughts on index cards. Using the strategy involves the following steps:

1 Assign a story, selection, or passage to be read. Have students locate five statements that they find interesting or would like to comment on—statements with which they agree or disagree or that contradict something they thought they knew. They could be statements that particularly surprised, excited, or intrigued them. When reading literature, students also could select revealing statements or actions made by characters in a story. Have students place a light pencil mark next to their five chosen statements.

2 Distribute five index cards to each student, a card for each selected statement. Have students write one statement on the front side of a card. On the reverse side, have them write comments about the statement. For example, a student reading a selection about wolves as an endangered species might select the following statement for the front of a card: "Wolves are sometimes illegally shot by ranchers who fear that their livestock will be attacked." On the reverse side, the student may write the following comment: "Ranchers ought to have a right to protect their animals from dangerous predators like wolves."

3 Divide the class into small groups of four or five members. All students in each group share one of their five statements with other group members. The first student reads a statement to the group and helps members locate the statement in the text. However, the student is not allowed to make any comments on the statement until the other members of the group give their reactions or responses. In effect, the student gets "the last word" in the discussion of the statement. For example, a student might share the following statement: "Wolves naturally try to avoid contact with humans." But the student does not discuss her comments— that people's fears of wolves

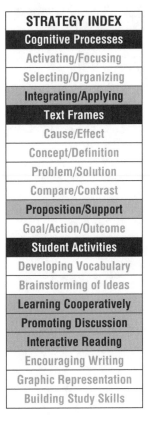

STRATEGY INDEX
Cognitive Processes
Activating/Focusing
Selecting/Organizing
Integrating/Applying
Text Frames
Cause/Effect
Concept/Definition
Problem/Solution
Compare/Contrast
Proposition/Support
Goal/Action/Outcome
Student Activities
Developing Vocabulary
Brainstorming of Ideas
Learning Cooperatively
Promoting Discussion
Interactive Reading
Encouraging Writing
Graphic Representation
Building Study Skills

are exaggerated, especially because of the way wolves are treated in fairy tales—until other group members have commented about the statement. The attitude during this phase is: Here is a statement that interested me. You tell me what you think, and then I will tell you what I think.

4 Have students continue the process until everyone in the group has shared one statement and has provided the "last word" in the discussion. Begin another round with students sharing another of their cards.

Advantages

- Students are given an opportunity to adopt a more reflective stance as they read.

- Students are encouraged to talk about things in the reading that they personally connect to, and they all have an opportunity to participate in the class discussion on the reading.

- Students are able to hear classmates' views before offering their own, which gives them the chance to adjust their comments and reflect on ideas before expressing them to others.

This strategy is adaptable to most subject areas and is appropriate for elementary through high school level students.

SAVE THE LAST WORD FOR ME

1. As you read, make a check mark (√) in pencil next to five statements that you
   - agree with,
   - disagree with,
   - have heard of before,
   - found interesting, or
   - want to say something about.

2. After you finish reading, write each statement on the front of a separate index card.

3. On the back of each card, write the comment you would like to share with your group about each statement.

4. When you meet in your group
   a. select a group member to go first;
   b. the selected member reads the statement from the front of one of his or her cards, but is not allowed to make any comment;
   c. all other group member talk about the statement and makes comments;
   d. when everyone is done commenting, the member who wrote the statement makes comments; and
   e. a second group member is selected, and the process is repeated until all cards are shared.

Reference

Vaughan, J., & Estes, T. (1986). *Reading and reasoning beyond the primary grades.* Boston: Allyn & Bacon.

Science Connection Overview

How does the world around us work? What is in a match head that makes it burst into flame when scratched? Where do rainbows come from? Why do cats purr? How does electricity move through wires? What does aspirin do to your body to make it feel better? Why does our hair turn gray as we become older? Questions—all part of the process of making sense of the world we live in and making sense of ourselves. We are born into this world observing the phenomena around us, and we spend a lifetime trying to understand it. Humans, as a species, seem determined "to know."

This natural curiosity about the workings of the world should form a strong foundation for student learning in science classrooms. Yet for many students, science does not necessarily appear to be connected to their questions about how things are. Instead, science looms as a formidable body of difficult technical information that intimidates and frustrates. For these students, reading science materials is like reading a foreign language. Consider the following biology example:

> Humans as well as most animals are vertebrates. Vertebrates are chordates that have a vertebral column. The first vertebrates evolved from the class of jawless fishes known as agnathans. Agnathans today include the lampreys, whose skeleton is composed mostly of cartilage. Lampreys have a notochord, which functions as their major support column. The gills of these creatures are contained in pouches that branch out from the pharynx. Many lampreys live as external parasites and cause great damage to the host populations of fish.

Whew! Students reading science materials may encounter an avalanche of unfamiliar words that have precise meanings in the language of science. Many of these new terms are seen only rarely outside a science context. Students soon become bogged down in this detailed information and lose sight of possible relationships between the science in their books and their understandings of the world around them.

The Science Connection Overview (Buehl, 1992) is a prereading strategy that guides students into making these connections.

Using the Strategy

The strategy involves previewing a science chapter or article before reading in order to link the content with something students already know or have experienced. Before students become immersed in the details of the reading, they are thus able to "see the big picture" of how this chapter will relate to some part of the world around them. Using this strategy involves the following steps:

1 Introduce the exercise by discussing with students how science helps them to understand some aspect of their lives or world. Select several examples of science material and elicit from the class how each can be connected to their lives; for example, a passage on cold and warm fronts and the resulting rain might connect to student questions about why rain occurs when it does or why it is often colder after it rains. For a chapter on microorganisms that live in water, students might connect by reflecting on why it is unsafe to drink lake or river water. For an article on endangered plants and animals, students might connect to news stories about the Amazon jungle or dolphins captured in tuna nets.

2 Distribute a blank Science Connection Overview (see Appendix, page 163) to students, and model how to use it using an overhead projector. Tell students to follow along as you skim a portion of a science text and think aloud about things mentioned in the text that you recognize or with which you are familiar. Ignore technical terms or information that seems unfamiliar. For example, modeling an overview of a biology chapter on fungi, you would pass over terms like *basidiomycota*, *multinucleate*, and *zygospore*. Instead

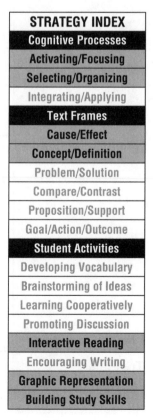

STRATEGY INDEX
Cognitive Processes
Activating/Focusing
Selecting/Organizing
Integrating/Applying
Text Frames
Cause/Effect
Concept/Definition
Problem/Solution
Compare/Contrast
Proposition/Support
Goal/Action/Outcome
Student Activities
Developing Vocabulary
Brainstorming of Ideas
Learning Cooperatively
Promoting Discussion
Interactive Reading
Encouraging Writing
Graphic Representation
Building Study Skills

you would focus on familiar terms, such as *mushrooms, bread mold, yeast,* and *Dutch Elm disease.*

3 Have students survey the remainder of the chapter. Have them work with partners to complete the What's Familiar section of the Connection Overview (see Science Connection Overview for Fungi).

Emphasize that only familiar, nontechnical information should be gleaned from their survey and skimming of the chapter. Encourage them to use the pictures and graphics in the chapter to assist them in making connections. For example, students doing an overview of the chapter on fungi would likely discover that even

---

SCIENCE CONNECTION OVERVIEW FOR FUNGI

What's Familiar?

> What's the Connection? Skim and survey the chapter for things that are familiar and that connect with your life or world. List them below:
> - *mushrooms*
> - *mold on spoiled food*
> - *spores*
> - *yeasts*
> - *plant rusts*
> - *fungi on rotting plants*
> - *lichens*
> - *penicillin*
> - *Dutch Elm disease*

What topics are covered?

> Read the Summary. What topic areas seem to be the most important?
> - *how they look or are structured*
> - *how they reproduce*
> - *how they feed and stay alive*

What questions do you have?

> Questions of Interest. What questions do you have about this material that may be answered in the chapter?
> - *Why do mushrooms grow in damp places?*
> - *Why does food get moldy when it spoils?*
> - *Why do they put yeast in bread doughs?*
> - *Why are some mushrooms poisonous?*
> - *How can you tell which mushrooms are poisonous and which are safe?*
> - *What do fungi eat?*
> - *Does the medicine penicillin come from a fungus?*

How is it organized?

> Chapter Organization: What categories of information are provided in this chapter?
> - *Structure of Fungi*
> - *Nutrition*
> - *Reproduction*
> - *Variety of Fungi:* molds   imperfect
>   yeasts
>   mushrooms
>   lichens

Translate

> Read and Translate: Use 3×5 cards for vocabulary.

(Buehl, 1992)

though the text contains a heavy load of terminology, there is much that connects to their lives and experiences. Most students would recognize many of the mushrooms, lichens, and molds featured in chapter photographs. They can begin to place where in their life's experiences this chapter would fit.

4 If the chapter has a summary, direct students to read it as the next phase of the overview. Ask them to identify key topics that seem to be the focus of the chapter. Although summaries are typically placed at the end of a chapter, students should develop the habit of consulting this study feature before becoming immersed in the new information. For example, the summary of the fungi chapter indicates that three general areas appear to be addressed: how fungi are structured, how they reproduce, and how they feed, which are entered in the What topics are covered? section of the overview.

5 Ask students to generate personal questions about the material. Working with partners, encourage them to think about what they know in this topic area and what they might want to find out. These are entered in the What questions do you have? section. Initially, you will need to model the kinds of questions that people normally have about science—questions typically not featured in textbooks, which instead tend to emphasize factual details. Instead, pose more general questions about the material that naturally inquis-itive people might raise. For example, questions generated about fungi might be: Why do mushrooms grow where they do? Why are some mushrooms poisonous? Why do they put yeast in bread? Why does food get moldy? Are there spores in the air in this room? What happens when you breathe them in? How can they get medicine from fungi?

6 Will students' questions receive answers in the reading? Have students complete the How is it organized? portion of the Connection Overview by outlining the chapter organization. Categories on information are usually signaled by headings or section titles. The fungi chapter was organized into four sections: structure, nutrition, reproduction, and variety. Students now have taken an aggressive and directive survey of the chapter. They have focused on making connections with the material rather than allowing themselves to become overwhelmed by a mass of challenging new vocabulary.

7 Ask students to read the first section of the chapter, having their Connection Overview available to remind them what the chapter is about as they encounter technical terminology and detailed information. As students read, have them use index cards to translate technical terms (see Card for Vocabulary). Technical terms usually are featured in easily identifiable ways within the text, and students are adept at locating the definitions and writing them down as an-

---

CARD FOR VOCABULARY

Front
of
Card

rhizoid
(rye bread)

Back
of
Card

little fibers that grow out of a bread mold

they are like roots and they hook the mold onto the bread or other food swers to questions; however, they may not comprehend what the terms mean. Encourage students to treat science vocabulary as they would foreign language vocabulary: by translating it into English. Have students use the index cards for the same purpose—to translate science terms into more understandable language.

8 Integrating memory clues on index cards is an especially effective technique for helping students become conversant with the new vocabulary (Levin, 1983). A memory clue helps students associate the word with its meaning or explanation (see Vocabulary Overview Guide, page 143). For example, the memory clue *rye bread* for the term *rhizoid* may trigger remembering that rhizoids are the little hooks that attach mold to rye bread. The clue is suggested by the pronunciation of the word, which triggers a connection between rhizoids and their later appearance on a slice of rye bread. Encourage students to use their imagination when developing these memory clues for different vocabulary.

Advantages

- Students make meaningful connections with the material before they are asked to process unfamiliar information.
- Students see how the information fits together and have a construct for making sense of what they read.
- Students are provided with a structure for translating difficult material into something that makes sense to them.

This strategy may be adapted for use with elementary through high school level students.

References

Buehl, D. (1992). The connection overview: A strategy for learning in science. *WSRA Journal, 36*(2), 21–30.

Levin, J. (1983). Pictorial strategies for school learning. In M. Pressley & J. Levin (Eds.), *Cognitive strategy research: Educational applications.* New York: Springer-Verlag.

Semantic Feature Analysis

You are plowing through a magazine article brimming with densely packed information about allergies—*allergic rhinitis, hay fever, antibistamines, pollen, hives, heredity, dust mites, immune system, and antibiotics*—what a load of technical vocabulary! A visual representation of the key terms would aid you in developing a strong conceptual understanding of this information. Then you could readily perceive what factors lead to which reactions and what treatments or preventative measures will combat which types of allergies. In all likelihood, you would then feel more comfortable conversing about allergies using the related terminology.

It is well established that vocabulary knowledge is a key predictor of how well a student will comprehend a given text. But developing vocabulary knowledge involves much more than learning dictionary definitions of words. Students need vocabulary instruction that helps them to broaden their understanding of concepts and to differentiate between related or similar words.

The Semantic Feature Analysis strategy (Johnson & Pearson, 1984) is a technique that guides students through analyzing vocabulary by identifying key characteristics and comparing these characteristics with other known concepts. Through the use of a matrix grid, students are able to code a number of key vocabulary or concepts in terms of several important qualities. When they have completed a semantic feature matrix, students have for reference a visual reminder of how various concepts are alike or different.

Using the Strategy

Anders and Bos (1986) recommend using the Semantic Feature Analysis strategy as a learning tool in content classrooms. Using the strategy involves the following steps:

1 Model Semantic Feature Analysis with your students by using a familiar category to illustrate the principles of the strategy. For example, place a blank Semantic Feature Analysis Grid (see Appendix, page 164) on an overhead transparency and choose a category, such as sports. For the vertical column, solicit various sports from the students, such as baseball, football, tennis, track, wrestling, golf, and boxing. Ask students to offer different features of sports that may or may not be present in a particular example, such as "is played with a ball," "is played as a team," "is done as an individual," "score is kept," "players wear protective apparel," and "has regular contact between opposing players." Write each of these features in one of the slots that appear along the upper horizontal section of the grid. Guide students with coding each attribute for each sport.

Students will have a visual display of how various sports compare and contrast, and may be surprised to see the similarities among them.

2 Select from your unit of instruction a category of concepts to be analyzed. Younger students will respond better to concrete concepts such as farm animals, vegetables, planets, or musical instruments. As students become more experienced, abstract categories such as forms of government, ecosystems, character traits, or geometric forms can be analyzed using this strategy. List several terms within this category in the left vertical column of the Semantic Feature grid (see Semantic Feature Analysis: Government Officials). The terms should be familiar to students. For example, terms within the category of farm animals might include *cow, dog, cat, chicken, pig,* and *horse.* Words within the category of people in government might include *president, senator, judge,* and *governor.* List three or four key features (traits, properties, or characteristics) that these terms may share. Features for farm animals may include *has fur, has feathers, can be house pet, makes food,* and *is used for meat.* Features for government officials may include "elective

STRATEGY INDEX
Cognitive Processes
Activating/Focusing
Selecting/Organizing
Integrating/Applying
Text Frames
Cause/Effect
Concept/Definition
Problem/Solution
Compare/Contrast
Proposition/Support
Goal/Action/Outcome
Student Activities
Developing Vocabulary
Brainstorming of Ideas
Learning Cooperatively
Promoting Discussion
Interactive Reading
Encouraging Writing
Graphic Representation
Building Study Skills

Category — People in Government / Features	is an elective office	is an appointive office	has term lengths	has limits on service	can be held by any legal voter	passes laws	vetoes laws	administers laws	declares laws unconstitutional	serves the entire United States	works within the United States
President of United States	+	-	+	+	-	-	+	+	-	+	+
Governor of Wisconsin	+	-	+	-	+	-	+	+	-	-	+
U.S. Senator	+	-	+	-	-	+	-	-	-	?	+
Secretary of Defense	-	+	-	-	+	-	-	+	-	+	+
Supreme Court Justice	-	+	-	-	+	-	-	-	+	+	+
Ambassador to England	-	+	-	-	+	-	-	?	-	+	-
State Legislative Member	+	-	+	-	+	+	-	-	-	-	+

(Buehl, 1995)

position," "passes laws," "has limits on service," and "serves the entire country."

3 Have students code each feature in terms of whether the targeted words typically possess that feature. A plus sign (+) is entered if the word exhibits that feature; a minus sign (-) is entered if the word does not exhibit that feature. A question mark (?) can be entered if students are not sure. For example, students completing a Semantic Features Analysis of the Governor of Wisconsin would place plus signs in features such as, "is an elective office," "has term length," "can be held by any legal voter," "vetoes laws," "administers laws," and "works within the U.S." An analysis of the role of a U.S. senator might lead to minus signs in features such as, "is an appointive office," "has limits on service," and "can be held by any legal voter." Students might place a question mark in the feature of "serves the entire U.S.," for it could be argued that a senator serves the state he or she represents but may also have a national perspective.

4 The Semantic Feature grid is now ready to accommodate more items within the selected category and more features to be analyzed. Ask students to offer additional terms and features to be included in the matrix. Other governmental officials suggested by students could be members of the cabinet, state legislature, or city council. Other features might focus on terms in office or jurisdiction of service. These additional elements are then coded with plus or minus signs or question marks.

5 Examine the grid and discuss similarities and differences between the terms for the category. Guide students in developing generalizations about how each word is unique from other related concepts. If two items have the same pattern of plus and minus signs, challenge students to identify a feature that will differentiate between the two.

In the government officials example, students can distinguish clearly the elective from nonelective positions and have a readily accessible information source to refer to and refine as they continue their learning in this topic area.

Advantages

- Students begin to analyze key vocabulary as concepts rather than as short definitions.
- Students become aware of relationships between words within a specific category, and they develop sensitivity for how these words are similar and different.

- Students can expand and refine a Semantic Feature grid during a unit of study. As new information is learned and new concepts are encountered, they can be added to the grid.

- Students are provided with an excellent summary of a unit and review for exams. The grid also presents students with organized information for writing assignments.

Semantic Feature Analysis is a strategy adaptable to all grade levels and all content areas, including science, social studies, and math.

References and Suggested Reading

Anders, P.L., & Bos, C.S. (1986). Semantic feature analysis: An interactive strategy for vocabulary development and text comprehension. *Journal of Reading, 29,* 610–616.

Buehl, D. (1995). *Classroom strategies for interactive learning.* Madison, WI: Wisconsin State Reading Association.

Johnson, D., & Pearson, P.D. (1984). *Teaching reading vocabulary* (2nd ed.). New York: Holt, Rinehart, & Winston.

Pittelman, S., Heimlich, J., Berglund, R., & French, M. (1991). *Semantic feature analysis: Classroom applications.* Newark, DE: International Reading Association.

SMART (Self-Monitoring Approach to Reading and Thinking)

What is it about proficient readers that sets them apart from students who struggle with reading? One major difference is that proficient readers carry on an internal monologue while they read. It is as though proficient readers operate with a split personality. One personality is hard at work with the task at hand—reading a textbook chapter, for instance. This is the personality concerned with cognitive activities such as selecting what is important in the chapter, organizing the information in conjunction with what is already known, and preparing to answer a series of questions about the material. It is this personality that gets most of the attention from teachers. We are able to observe a student at work and assess the results—the student we see sitting at a desk, interacting with print.

But it is the second personality that separates the proficient readers from the less effective readers. This personality works in the background, directing and evaluating all the cognitive activities needed to learn successfully. This personality represents that inner voice that issues commands during reading: "Slow down! This is pretty tough going!" "Hold it here! This doesn't make any sense. Better re-read." Or "This stuff doesn't look very important. I'll just skim over it quickly and get into the next section." Effective learners talk to themselves.

Researchers call this internal monologue *metacognition*—the ability to think about thinking. Metacognition involves a self-awareness of what one is doing and how it is going. It also reflects an ability to switch gears and try something else when learning breaks down, such as when a reading passage is proving particularly difficult. Ineffective readers approach print passively and continue to plow ahead, even if nothing is making sense. But ineffective readers can be taught how to activate the control center in their minds that directs their learning.

One strategy that triggers students to think about how their reading is proceeding is the Self-Monitoring Approach to Reading and Thinking (SMART) (Vaughan & Estes, 1986).

Using the Strategy

SMART is based on the premise that successful reading begins with recognizing what is understood and not understood in a passage. Using this strategy involves the following steps:

1 Select a passage of four or five paragraphs that you find personally challenging and ask students to follow along as you think aloud about your reading. (It may help to enlarge the passage and place it on an overhead transparency.) After reading a few sentences or a paragraph, comment aloud that you understand this section and make a check mark (√) in the margin. Continue on, modeling a part that seems confusing by writing a question mark (?) next to the sentence or paragraph. Tell students that there is something about it you do not fully understand. For example, a short passage about rugby, a game unfamiliar to most students, could serve as an excellent think-aloud using these techniques:

Rugby is a type of football that is popular in the United Kingdom. Rugby matches consist of two 40-minute periods of play, with a 5-minute halftime break. A match begins with a kickoff, from the center of the halfway line, of an oval-shaped ball somewhat larger than a U.S. football. Each team, which consists of 8 forwards and 7 backs, attempts to ground the ball in the opposing team's goal area. Action is generally continuous, although after a penalty, play is resumed by a *scrummage*. In a tight scrummage, a player rolls the ball into a tunnel formed by the opposing team's forwards, who are linked together with their arms about each other's waists. As they push, both teams attempt to heel the ball.

STRATEGY INDEX
Cognitive Processes
Activating/Focusing
Selecting/Organizing
Integrating/Applying
Text Frames
Cause/Effect
Concept/Definition
Problem/Solution
Compare/Contrast
Proposition/Support
Goal/Action/Outcome
Student Activities
Developing Vocabulary
Brainstorming of Ideas
Learning Cooperatively
Promoting Discussion
Interactive Reading
Encouraging Writing
Graphic Representation
Building Study Skills

Parts of this passage will probably make sense, but at other points a pause is needed so you can record a question mark to highlight material that needs clarification.

2 After reading the entire passage, model to students how to paraphrase material in words that make sense to them. Look at each (?) recorded in the margin. Brainstorm with students what could be done to make sense of those parts. Observe that some question marks may make sense after the entire passage is read. If so, change them to check marks. List and discuss students' suggestions for dealing with remaining question marks.

3 Introduce the SMART protocol to students (see Read SMART!). Model the steps under Troubleshoot using a new passage, perhaps from the textbook, as students follow along. Emphasize strategies that students can try before they ask for help, and that successful readers return to clear up each question (?).

READ SMART!

1. **Read**. Read a section of the text. Using a pencil, lightly place a check mark (√) next to each paragraph that you understand. Place a question mark (?) next to each paragraph that contains something you do not understand.

2. **Self-Translate**. At the end of each section, stop and explain to yourself, in your own words, what you read. Look back at the text as you go over the material.

3. **Troubleshoot**. Go back to each (?) and see if you can now make sense of the paragraph.

   a. **Re-read** the trouble spot to see if it now makes sense. If it still does not make sense:

   b. **Pinpoint** a problem by figuring out why you are having trouble:
      • Is it a difficult word or unfamiliar vocabulary?
      • Is it a difficult sentence or confusing language?
      • Is it a subject about which you know very little?

   c. **Try** a Fix-Up Strategy:
      • Use the glossary or some other vocabulary aid.
      • Look over the pictures or other graphics.
      • Examine other parts of the chapter (summary, review section, diagrams, or other features).

   d. **Explain** to yourself exactly what you do not understand or what confuses you.

   e. **Get Help**. Ask the teacher or a classmate.

---

4 Have students read a passage on their own using the check mark and question mark system. Have them work through the SMART protocol with a partner, verbalizing what is understood and not understood, and working together through any problems. Emphasize that before asking for help students should be able to (1) specify the source of their problem (an unfamiliar word, an unclear sentence, or a need for more examples), and (2) explain how they tried to solve their problem.

Advantages

- Students are provided with a system that helps them actively monitor their reading success.

- Students learn to verbalize what they do and do not understand in a reading.

- Students are encouraged to persist until an entire reading makes sense. Students have specific steps to use to clear up trouble spots.

- Students become involved in summarizing the material in their own words, thus helping them to remember as well as understand.

This strategy is adaptable to most subject areas and is appropriate for elementary through high school level students. It is especially effective in cooperative group or tutorial settings.

Reference

Vaughan, J., & Estes, T. (1986). *Reading and reasoning beyond the primary grades*. Boston: Allyn & Bacon.

Story Impressions

Teen athletes...concussions...soccer, football, volleyball...susceptible...head injury...62,800...headaches, sleep disorders...high risk...learning disabilities.

Can you piece together the storyline implied by the preceding chain of key words excerpted from a recent newspaper article? In all likelihood, by connecting these terms and drawing from what you already know about them, you can successfully infer the focus of this public health report.

As you surmised, the article raises cautions about concussions suffered by teen athletes, especially those participating in sports such as soccer, football, and volleyball. Adolescents are more susceptible to head injury from concussions, and a recent study estimated that 62,800 adolescents receive at least mild sports-related concussions each year. Symptoms of a concussion include headaches and sleep disorders, and students with learning disabilities are especially at risk for lingering brain injury resulting from concussions.

The chain of key words that was provided prompted you to access what you know about sports concussions, and perhaps your curiosity was piqued about what the article said about dangers for teen athletes. You were able to form an impression of the text before you actually read it.

Using the Strategy

Story Impressions (McGinley & Denner, 1987) is a strategy that introduces significant terms and concepts to students before they encounter them in an assignment. Using the strategy involves the following steps:

1 Preview a text section or story, and identify a series of terms or two- or three-word phrases related to significant information or plot events. List the terms as they are presented in the text, in the order students will encounter them while reading. This step cues students to the sequence of events or cause/effect relationships. Create a student worksheet with the terms arranged in a vertical column, connected by arrows to indicate order (see Story Impressions for Earth Science). For example, to prepare students for a textbook passage on geysers, select a chain of terms and phrases that emphasize how volcanic activity leads to the heating of groundwater, which can sometimes create geysers.

2 Have students work with partners to brainstorm possible connections to the chain of clues on their worksheets. Using what they might know about some of the terms, encourage them to make predictions about both the content of the text and the meanings of unfamiliar key words. In the earth science example, students can tap their knowledge about how volcanic activity generates heat and brainstorm possible connections to geysers. Some students will realize that heated water builds up pressure, which explains the phenomena of geysers such as Old Faithful in Yellowstone National Park, Wyoming. Students may also need to form conjectures of the meanings of terms such as *igneous*, *fissure*, and *constricted* as they work on their predictions.

3 Have students draft their own impression of what a text might contain. First, inform them of the context for the terms—textbook passage, short story, newspaper article, or biographical excerpt. Ask students to create a possible version of this text, based on their knowledge of the key terms and their hunches about unknown items. In the box adjacent to the word chains, have students write a paragraph representing their prediction of the text. All terms from the chain must be used in this paragraph, and students should integrate them into their writing in the order that they appear on the list. Have partners share their prediction summaries with the entire class. For example, a pair of earth science students might use their partial knowledge of terms to record this impression:

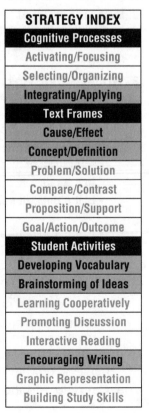

STRATEGY INDEX
Cognitive Processes
Activating/Focusing
Selecting/Organizing
Integrating/Applying
Text Frames
Cause/Effect
Concept/Definition
Problem/Solution
Compare/Contrast
Proposition/Support
Goal/Action/Outcome
Student Activities
Developing Vocabulary
Brainstorming of Ideas
Learning Cooperatively
Promoting Discussion
Interactive Reading
Encouraging Writing
Graphic Representation
Building Study Skills

Volcanic activity pushes igneous rocks out of the center of the earth. The high temperature there heats groundwater to the boiling point, and it becomes steam. This steam has pent up pressure which causes it to fissure and then change to hot springs. The hot springs come out of the ground in a constricted tube with an eruption. This is called a geyser, like Old Faithful in Yellowstone.

4 Now that students have encountered key terms and concepts, activated relevant prior knowledge, and entertained predictions about the material, have them test their impressions by reading a text selection or story. As they read, have them check off the terms in the chain that they used accurately in their prediction summaries. To solidify new learning, have students write a second summary paragraph, again using all the terms in the order they are represented in the chain. Have them contrast their prediction summaries with the ones they wrote after reading the article to highlight any similarities between their impressions and the actual text.

For example, students studying U.S. history in the early 20th century were given a story impression for a textbook section on Theodore Roosevelt's presidency. After reading the passage, students revisited key terms,

STORY IMPRESSIONS FOR EARTH SCIENCE

Chain of Events	Your version of what the textbook might say: Write a paragraph using the chain words in order.
volcanic activity	
↓	
igneous rock	
↓	
temperature	
↓	
groundwater	
↓	
boiling	
↓	
steam	
↓	
pent up pressure	
↓	
fissure	
↓	
hot springs	
↓	
constricted tube	
↓	
eruption	
↓	
geyser	
↓	
Old Faithful	

STORY IMPRESSIONS FOR HISTORY
Roosevelt Era

Key Terms	Story Summary: After reading Section 2—Write your summary paragraph about Theodore Roosevelt below. Add 5 additional terms from Section 2; write them in the place you feel these terms belong in the left column. Again, you must use all the terms in your summary (including your 5 new ones) in the order that they appear on the list.
Teddy Roosevelt ↓ progressive ↓ Square Deal ↓ reform ↓ corruption ↓ regulate ↓ trust buster ↓ law suits ↓ consumer ↓ dangerous ↓ Food & Drug Act ↓ National Parks ↓ reclamation	

added new terms deemed significant to the time period, and developed a summary paragraph that demonstrated their understanding of the passage (see Story Impressions for History).

A story impressions chain makes an excellent prompt for essay exams. Students can be asked to synthesize their learning by linking together key information into a meaningful summary statement of the material from a unit of study.

Advantages

- Students are introduced to essential terminology and information before they become immersed in reading.
- Students marshal what they know about a topic and brainstorm possible connections to the new material.
- Students receive guidance in two comprehension tasks that are often difficult: determining importance and summarizing.
- Students have an opportunity to verbalize their learning in writing and can contrast what they knew before reading with what they know now.
- After sufficient practice, students can be asked to create their own chains of key terms—as a comprehension activity and for use as story impressions to prepare their classmates for a new selection.

Reference

McGinley, W., & Denner, P. (1987). Story impressions: A prereading/writing activity. *Journal of Reading, 31,* 248–253.

Story Mapping

Once upon a time... Could you please read me a story, Dad? Did you hear the story about the ice fisherman who... You'll never believe what happened last night! Let me tell you the whole story....

Stories—we grew up hearing them as children. We read them throughout our schooling. We relax while enjoying them in novels we read for pleasure. We experience them on television and in movie theaters, and we tell them to our friends. Much of the way we view the world around us is organized into stories.

Children encounter narrative text very early in their lives, and they begin to internalize the common elements found in most stories. Story Mapping (Beck & McKeown, 1981) is a strategy that helps students use their knowledge of narrative structure to analyze stories. Story Maps feature graphic representations of key story elements. The resulting visual outline helps students build a coherent framework for understanding and remembering a story.

Using the Strategy

Story Maps can be created for both short stories and longer works of fiction, such as novels. Using the strategy involves the following steps:

1 Reinforce with students the key elements of a story. For example, introduce story structure by posing the following question: I'm going to read you a story. What would you want to know about this story? Students would likely comment that they want to know who the story is about, what happens in the story, where the story takes place, and how the story ends. These common elements of narrative structure can be presented as a Story Star on an overhead transparency (see Story Star). Note how each of the above questions can be reworded to reflect the basic elements of a story: *Who?* refers to characters, *Where?* and *When?* involve setting and mood, *What happens?* details events of the plot, *How did it end?* involves the resolution of the story's conflict. *Why* questions get at the author's theme of the story.

2 Read to students a story that you have selected for its clear illustration of story structure. When you have finished the story, hand out blank Story Maps (see Appendix, page 166) to each student. Have them fill in the key information from the story as you model this process on an overhead transparency. Emphasize the recording of only major events—those that move the plot along—and establish the initiating event that sets the story into motion. (Instruct student to circle the number of this event on their maps.) Students expect a story to feature some sort of conflict, and how that conflict gets resolved is what makes a story interesting. As part of the modeling, review the basic kinds of conflict inherent in fictional literature:

- *within a person* (a character is struggling with him or herself, trying to figure out what to do);

- *between people* (a character has some sort of problem with others that needs to be addressed); and

- *between people and nature* (a character is presented with a difficult natural situation that he or she must overcome—threatening animals, treacherous weather, a dangerous environment, or a disaster such as a fire).

For example, ninth graders reading the Stephen King short story, "Battleground," first identify the characters (the hired killer, Renshaw, and the tiny soldiers), and the setting (Renshaw's San Francisco apartment). They note that the action is initiated by the arrival of a box of miniature soldiers to Renshaw's apartment, and they record the other major events leading to the climax—when Renshaw attacks his tiny assailants from the ledge outside his window. Subsequent action includes an explosion, Renshaw's death, and the on-

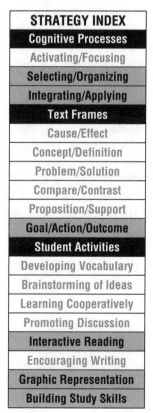

STRATEGY INDEX
Cognitive Processes
Activating/Focusing
Selecting/Organizing
Integrating/Applying
Text Frames
Cause/Effect
Concept/Definition
Problem/Solution
Compare/Contrast
Proposition/Support
Goal/Action/Outcome
Student Activities
Developing Vocabulary
Brainstorming of Ideas
Learning Cooperatively
Promoting Discussion
Interactive Reading
Encouraging Writing
Graphic Representation
Building Study Skills

STORY STAR

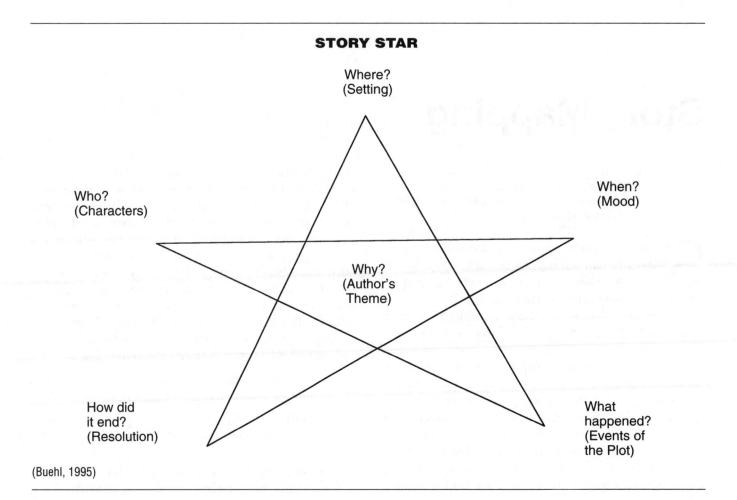

Where?
(Setting)

Who?
(Characters)

When?
(Mood)

Why?
(Author's
Theme)

How did
it end?
(Resolution)

What
happened?
(Events of
the Plot)

(Buehl, 1995)

lookers' discovery of a message about a scale-model atomic bomb, which had arrived unbeknownst to Renshaw with the tiny soldiers. Students identify the conflict as *between people*, and observe that this conflict is resolved with Renshaw's death (see Story Map for "Battleground").

3 Model with students how to use the organized information in the Story Map to determine the author's theme. Emphasize that the conflict and the way it is resolved provide a great deal of insight into possible points the author may have wished to communicate through the story. Students will recognize in "Battleground" that the tables are ironically turned on the major character. Renshaw is an assassin who gets his due. Students might articulate the theme as, What goes around comes around, or The hunter can easily become the hunted, or Those who live by violence die by violence.

4 Demonstrate how significant questions that can be asked about a story conform to the structure displayed in the Story Map. Significant questions should relate to the setting, character development, events of the plot, the conflict and its resolution, and

the author's possible themes. Questions may also focus on the author's craft, such as the use of language and literary devices used in developing the story's components. For example, questions for "Battleground" might highlight the irony of a wily killer being outwitted by someone he has victimized. Questions about specific events in the rising action could establish how Renshaw's mood changed from annoyance to anger to desperation. Ask students to articulate author themes based on support cited from the text.

5 Have students use the Story Map to analyze a short story that they read independently. After reading, have the students work with a partner to complete a new Story Map. Solicit possible statements from the whole group about the author's theme, and discuss the rationale for each statement based on information from the story.

Advantages

- Students are provided with a visual framework for understanding and analyzing stories, and their knowledge of story structure is reinforced

STORY MAP FOR "BATTLEGROUND"

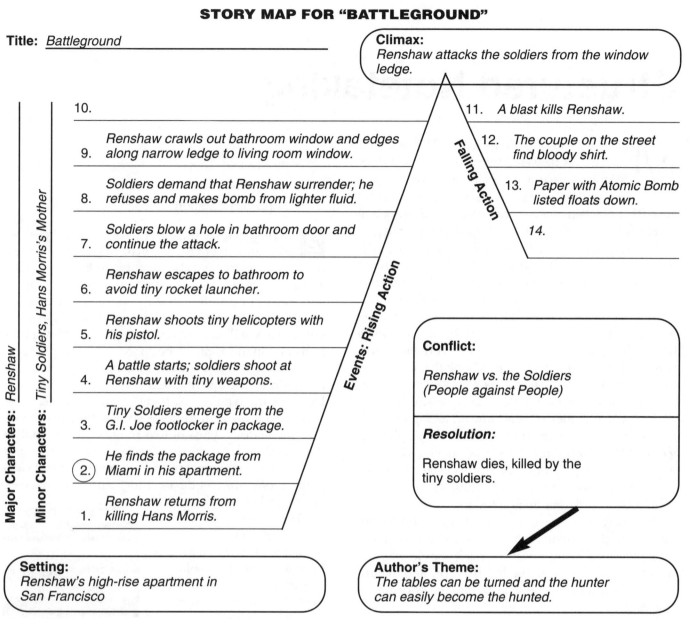

Title: _Battleground_

Climax:
Renshaw attacks the soldiers from the window ledge.

Major Characters: _Renshaw_

Minor Characters: _Tiny Soldiers, Hans Morris's Mother_

10.

9. _Renshaw crawls out bathroom window and edges along narrow ledge to living room window._

8. _Soldiers demand that Renshaw surrender; he refuses and makes bomb from lighter fluid._

7. _Soldiers blow a hole in bathroom door and continue the attack._

6. _Renshaw escapes to bathroom to avoid tiny rocket launcher._

5. _Renshaw shoots tiny helicopters with his pistol._

4. _A battle starts; soldiers shoot at Renshaw with tiny weapons._

3. _Tiny Soldiers emerge from the G.I. Joe footlocker in package._

2. _He finds the package from Miami in his apartment._

1. _Renshaw returns from killing Hans Morris._

Events: Rising Action

Falling Action

11. _A blast kills Renshaw._

12. _The couple on the street find bloody shirt._

13. _Paper with Atomic Bomb listed floats down._

14.

Conflict:

Renshaw vs. the Soldiers (People against People)

Resolution:

Renshaw dies, killed by the tiny soldiers.

Setting:
Renshaw's high-rise apartment in San Francisco

Author's Theme:
The tables can be turned and the hunter can easily become the hunted.

(Buehl, 1995)

as a foundation for the successful reading of narrative text.

- Questions for guiding and discussing stories that are derived from the elements of story structure lead to more coherent and integrated comprehension from students. Students improve their ability to predict probable questions for a particular story.

- Students become practiced in using story structure as a basis for the creation of their own stories. Students also have a clear model for the writing of summaries and other reactions to the stories they read.

This strategy is appropriate for most narrative text. It can be modified for use with some types of expository material, such as biographies and autobiographies.

References

Beck, I., & McKeown, M. (1981). Developing questions that promote comprehension: The story map. _Language Arts, 58,_ 913–918.

Buehl, D. (1995). _Classroom strategies for interactive learning._ Madison, WI: Wisconsin State Reading Association.

Other Work Cited

King, S. (1978). _Battleground, in Nightshift._ New York: Doubleday.

Structured Notetaking

"Make sure you take notes on this!" This oft-heard directive is delivered by teachers almost daily to students learning from print, classroom presentations and discussions, and from video. Teachers know that notetaking is a prerequisite for remembering and learning, and that it is an essential study strategy.

Yet teachers are frequently disappointed with the results of student notetaking. Student notes often are disorganized and lack important information. Students are frequently confused as to what to write down and what to leave out. Some students associate notetaking with mindlessly copying material verbatim from a book, the chalkboard, or from an overhead transparency. The result may be a notebook that contains a lot of writing but is ineffective as a resource for study.

Structured Notetaking (Smith & Tompkins, 1988) is a strategy that guides students toward taking more effective notes. The strategy makes use of graphic organizers, a powerful means of representing ideas and information. Graphic organizers provide students with a visual framework for making decisions about what should be included in their notes and impose a structure on student notes that make them useful for future referral. Structured Notetaking is an excellent strategy to use in all aspects of classroom learning in which notetaking is desirable—from printed materials, video, teacher presentations, and class or group discussions.

Using the Strategy

Structured Notetaking involves creating graphic outlines that serve as organized study guides for students as they take their notes. Eventually students will be able to devise their own structured notes as an independent study skill. Using this strategy involves the following steps.

1 Preview the content students will be learning and identify the organizational structure that is best represented in the material. The following six text frames address common ways that information is organized (see Text Frames in Chapter 2):

- Problem/Solution
- Compare/Contrast
- Cause/Effect
- Proposition/Support
- Goal/Action/Outcome
- Concept/Definition

2 Create a graphic organizer using boxes, circles, arrows, and other visual structures that emphasize a particular text frame. Label with frame language, such as causes/effects, similarities/differences, or problem/causes of problem/possible solutions. Distribute this graphic organizer to students as a notetaking study guide. They will take notes by recording relevant information in the appropriate spaces in the graphic outline. Before students begin the structured notes, call attention to the specific text frame being followed. Highlight the type of text frame being used each time you provide structured notes so that students recognize the various types of text frames and internalize their use. Students need to be aware that boxes and circles are not randomly placed on a page, but that each graphic organizer is devised to help them perceive meaningful connections.

For example, a selection for a science class about endangered animals may adhere to a problem/solution text frame. Provide students with Endangered Animals graphic outlines to be filled in with their notes from the reading (see Structured Notetaking for Science: Endangered Animals). The first endangered animal in the selection is the dolphin. As they read, have students select information that fits into the four boxes in the graphic ("dolphins get caught in underwater tuna nets," "commercial fisheries are causing the problem," "we can buy tuna with the 'dolphin-safe' designation," and "we can lobby for international fishing

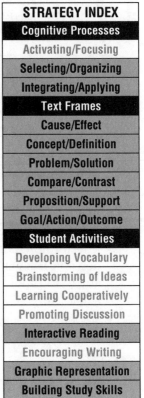

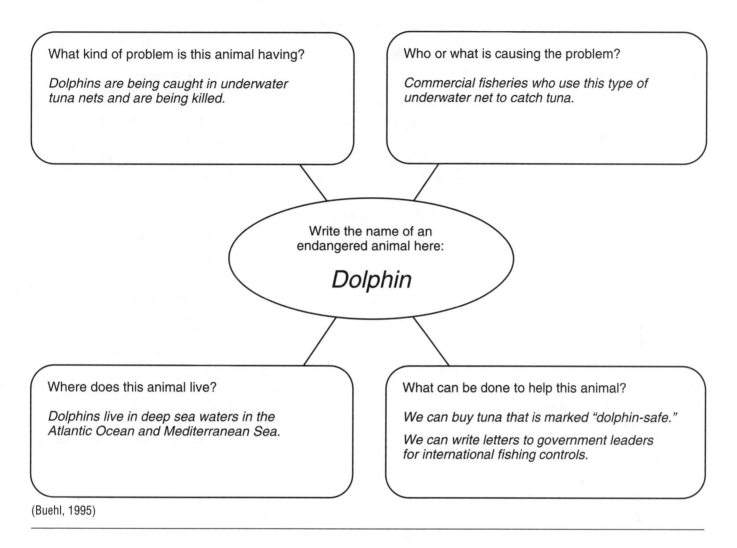

What kind of problem is this animal having?

Dolphins are being caught in underwater tuna nets and are being killed.

Who or what is causing the problem?

Commercial fisheries who use this type of underwater net to catch tuna.

Write the name of an endangered animal here:

Dolphin

Where does this animal live?

Dolphins live in deep sea waters in the Atlantic Ocean and Mediterranean Sea.

What can be done to help this animal?

We can buy tuna that is marked "dolphin-safe."

We can write letters to government leaders for international fishing controls.

(Buehl, 1995)

regulations"). Ask students to continue reading and complete a second graphic organizer for the next endangered animal.

3 Structured Notetaking provides a number of opportunities for students to collaborate. When introducing the strategy, have students work in pairs while reading a passage. As part of this process, ask students to justify to their partners decisions on what to select and where to place it in the graphic outline. For example, history students viewing a video program on the migration of African Americans from the rural, southern United States to northern cities in the early 20th century are provided with a graphic organizer that presents both cause/effect and compare/contrast text frames (see Structured Notes for History Video). As students view the video, have them first individually record information that describes life in the rural South and the contrasting life in Chicago, Illinois. Students also are cued into seeking the causal factors that encouraged African Americans to relocate to northern urban areas. Instruct them to write quickly and not to worry about legibility and completeness.

When the video is over, put students in pairs or small groups and provide them a second blank copy of the graphic organizer. Instruct students to compare notes from the video with their classmates to develop a more thorough set of structured notes. Collect and photocopy the final exemplary notes for each member of the group.

4 As students gain practice using structured notes, they will begin to develop their own graphic organizers to structure their notes (Jones, Pierce, & Hunter, 1988/1989). At first, help students to identify the most appropriate text frame for student-created

STRUCTURED NOTES FOR HISTORY VIDEO

**Factors that Encouraged
African Americans to Move
North to Chicago**

**Life in the South
Before Migration
North**

- *Many lived in shacks*
- *Poor food*
- *Segregation*
- *Low wages*
- *Few jobs*
- *Jim Crow laws*
- *KKK harassment*
- *Poor schools*
- *Second class status*
- *Discrimination*
- *Boll Weevil ruined cotton*
- *Racial violence*
- *Lack of protection from courts and law*

- *Recruited to north by factories needing laborers.*
- *Were protected with free transportation (railroads).*
- *Agents sent south encouraged African Americans to come north.*
- *World War I caused need for workers and brought about new jobs and new factories.*
- *New laws restricted immigration from other countries.*
- *The Chicago Defender newspaper spoke to African Americans.*
- *Hangings and lynchings were increasing in the south.*

**Life in Chicago
for African Americans**

- *Last hired, first fired.*
- *Had jobs but little money.*
- *Postwar depression put people out of work.*
- *Created neighborhoods for all African Americans.*
- *Housing shortages.*
- *Culture flourished—music, food, churches.*
- *African American city leaders and business leaders emerged.*
- *Competed for jobs with returning WWI soldiers.*
- *Race riots, bombs, killings*

(Buehl, 1995)

notes, a task that they will become increasingly able to accomplish independently.

Advantages

- Students are able to see relationships between ideas as they take notes—they realize that notetaking is more than writing down isolated pieces of information.
- Students are able to take notes that are coherent and easy to use for study and future learning.
- Students are provided with organizational models that illustrate the basic structure of the information they are learning.
- Structured notes emphasize visual representation of information, which facilitates memory of the material.

- Student-created structured notes stimulate creativity and make notetaking a more enjoyable activity.

This strategy can be adapted for elementary through high school levels and can be used successfully with materials in all content areas.

References and Suggested Reading

Armbruster, B., & Anderson, T. (1982). *Idea mapping: The technique and its use in the classroom* (Reading Education Report No. 36). Urbana, IL: University of Illinois, Center for the Study of Reading.

Buehl, D. (1995). *Classroom strategies for interactive learning.* Madison, WI: Wisconsin State Reading Association.

Jones, B., Pierce, J., & Hunter, B. (1988/1989). Teaching students to construct graphic representations. *Educational Leadership, 46,* 20–25.

Smith, P., & Tompkins, G. (1988). Structured notetaking: A new strategy for content area readers. *Journal of Reading, 32,* 46–53.

Template Frames

Dear Grandma, thank you for the T-shirt you got me on your trip to Alaska. I really like the funny picture of the grizzly bear on it, and red is my favorite color. I have been wearing my shirt to school and all my friends are asking when I went to Alaska! Thanks for remembering me on your vacation.

Think about assisting a child who is writing a thank-you note. You might find yourself prompting the child on what a good thank-you note should include. In addition to thanking someone, the note should identify the gift, express appreciation, and perhaps comment on how the gift is being used. A conclusion usually recognizes the gift-giver for his or her thoughtfulness.

In other words, there is an internal structure to this specific communication—the thank-you note—which you are teaching to this child. In effect, you have in your mind a template for a thank-you note that can be adapted to other written communications: a sympathy note, an invitation, a letter of complaint, a mail-order purchase, and others. Each mandates a different structure or template that you have internalized for use as the situation dictates.

Using the Strategy

A template is an outline or a pattern used to re-create something. Templates are used in quilting, woodworking projects, genealogy charts, computer applications, and of course, writing. However, because templates for writing are mental structures, many students never see or use them. Their writing lacks coherence, with information randomly stated and key parts missing. Teachers can use templates as a strategy to develop students' ability to handle a variety of classroom writing tasks. Templates are especially valuable in helping students cope with essay exams. Using the strategy involves the following steps:

1 Share with students exemplary models (either created or collected) of the kind of writing you expect. Well-written examples will exhibit a clear text-frame organization, such as cause/effect, compare/contrast, proposition/support, problem/solution, or concept/definition. To reveal the structure of the template, underline key elements of the writing, such as

topic sentence, text-frame language, transitions, and summary or conclusion. This will make the template explicit for students. For example, the following essay illustrates a cause/effect template for students studying weathering in earth science:

Question: Explain the causes of mechanical weathering and describe its effects on rocks.

Answer: <u>Mechanical weathering is caused by water, by plants, and by animals. First,</u> water <u>causes</u> weathering <u>in two ways</u>: by freezing and by wetting and drying. Freezing water forms ice in cracks of rocks, which splits them apart. Water <u>also causes</u> weathering <u>because</u> when some rocks get wet they expand and when they dry they shrink. <u>This leads to</u> rocks breaking up. <u>Secondly,</u> plants <u>cause</u> weathering when their roots grow into cracks in rocks and <u>then</u> break them up. <u>Thirdly,</u> animals dig holes in the ground, which expose rocks to water, which weathers them. <u>As a result of mechanical weathering,</u> rocks are broken into smaller pieces but keep their same chemical composition.

2 Provide students with a template containing the key elements of a paragraph to use as an outline for a writing task. This will guide them in constructing an organized written response. Key words that forecast the text organization of the paragraph are emphasized:

- comparison (similarly, likewise, in like manner),
- contrast (but, yet, however, on the other hand, on the contrary),
- concept/definition (for example, furthermore, such as),
- problem/solution (for this reason, therefore, instead of),

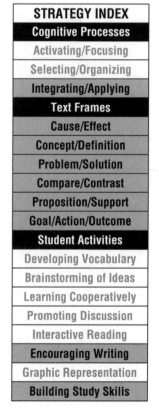

STRATEGY INDEX
Cognitive Processes
Activating/Focusing
Selecting/Organizing
Integrating/Applying
Text Frames
Cause/Effect
Concept/Definition
Problem/Solution
Compare/Contrast
Proposition/Support
Goal/Action/Outcome
Student Activities
Developing Vocabulary
Brainstorming of Ideas
Learning Cooperatively
Promoting Discussion
Interactive Reading
Encouraging Writing
Graphic Representation
Building Study Skills

- proposition/support (in conclusion, if, indicate, suggest),
- cause/effect (because, consequently, since, then, as a result), and
- goal/action/outcome (steps, first, second, next, finally).

The following is a template frame for students responding to an essay question on a history test:

Question: What problems did prairie farmers encounter and what did they do to solve their problems?

Answer: Prairie farmers encountered a number of problems that made their life on the plains very difficult. First _____. Another problem _____. _____ was a third challenge they had to face, because _____. The farmers tried to solve their problems by _____. They also _____. Finally, _____.

Emphasize to students not to treat the template frame as a fill-in-the-blank exercise. Instead, instruct them to use the cues provided in the template as a guide to rewriting answers in a paragraph format. Some students will customize the template to fit their ideas and writing style. Encourage them to expand their paragraphs with additional sentences and information. The purpose of the template is not to render students' writing as mechanical and formalistic, but to help them to construct a coherent, well-formed essay.

3 As students become practiced in using template frames, ask them to assume more responsibility for organizing their writing by (a) having them work in cooperative groups to develop a template frame for a question to be answered, (b) having the class choose the template they feel would work best for the essay, or (c) offering three possible template options.

Advantages

- Students learn how to craft well-written responses that can be personalized as they become more sophisticated writers.
- Students are given an organized way of getting started when confronted with demanding writing tasks.
- Students learn to use key transition elements that reflect appropriate text frames, such as cause/effect or proposition/support.

Template frames also can be used to structure the writing of lab reports in science, character analysis in language arts, book critiques, position papers, and other types of student writing.

Suggested Reading

Santa, C., Havens, L., & Macumber, E. (1996). *Creating independence through student-owned strategies*. Dubuque, IA: Kendall/Hunt.

Vocabulary Overview Guide

The vagaries of Andrew's life before he returned to Oregon and joined the family business are rarely mentioned these days.

Vagaries? Can you recollect seeing this word before? Could you offer a hunch as to its meaning? Would you feel confident using this word in your speaking and writing? For many people, a word such as *vagaries* lies on the periphery of their vocabularies. The word may be somewhat familiar, perhaps encountered infrequently during reading, but most people have never had the urge to look it up in a dictionary.

Instead, they develop an increasingly meaningful concept of this word through context. Initially, proficient readers would look at the word for possible etymological connections (Does *vagary* fit with *vague*, or is *vagrant* a better match? How about *vagabond*?). Then they would track subsequent sightings of vagary and begin to construct a working definition based on its appearance in multiple contexts: "The vagaries of government policy toward the homeless..." or "The vagaries of his jokes until they hit the punch line...." Eventually, readers would refine their understanding that vagary refers to aimless and unpredictable wandering or actions.

As teachers, we know that vocabulary development is a critical component of reading comprehension. But many of the activities we use with students to improve their vocabularies are not as successful as we would like. Students who are given lists of words to look up and study admit that they forget most of them once the test is over. The Vocabulary Overview Guide (Carr, 1985) is a structured activity that involves students in taking personal responsibility for identifying and learning useful new words from their reading.

Using the Strategy

The Vocabulary Overview Guide is a graphic organizer that includes a meaningful clue in addition to a definition (see Appendix, page 167). This strategy conditions students to look for key words as they read and it provides a system for studying the words so that they are retained over time. Using the strategy involves the following steps:

1 Begin with activities that encourage students to deal with vocabulary in context rather than as isolated definitions. Textbooks in all disciplines make extensive use of context-embedded aids to introduce technical vocabulary, and these clues can help students place the usage of unfamiliar terms. To sensitize students to analyzing contextual clues, rewrite brief passages from materials students typically read in your class, substituting nonsense terms for actual words. The following example would be appropriate for students in a language arts setting:

> Cautiously, Amanda reached for her spoon. The thick, green mass on her plate did not look or smell appetizing. She was certain that she would find the lumpy, gooey dish distasteful, yet she was determined to try it. Amanda raised a spoonful to her mouth, but she couldn't help immediately *whagging* it.
>
> To *whag* means to (a) swallow (b) enjoy (c) spit out (d) taste.

All the choices have something to do with eating, but only *spit out* fits with the entire passage and the various semantic and syntactic clues that are provided. This nonsense word activity conditions students to tune automatically into these various clues.

2 Researchers argue that relying on context alone is often inadequate. Students may misread contextual clues, or the specific context may be open to several varied interpretations of a word's possible meaning. To help students react to a word in a variety of contexts, provide multiple instances of the word in action. For example, students in a social studies class might initially see the word *chide* in a newspaper article: "Critics chided the government for the slow re-

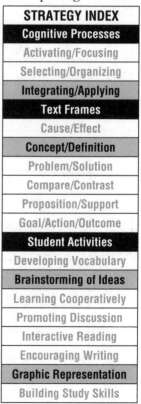

STRATEGY INDEX
Cognitive Processes
Activating/Focusing
Selecting/Organizing
Integrating/Applying
Text Frames
Cause/Effect
Concept/Definition
Problem/Solution
Compare/Contrast
Proposition/Support
Goal/Action/Outcome
Student Activities
Developing Vocabulary
Brainstorming of Ideas
Learning Cooperatively
Promoting Discussion
Interactive Reading
Encouraging Writing
Graphic Representation
Building Study Skills

sponse to requests for disaster aid." In addition to this contextual example of *chide*, ask students to examine additional instances:

> Jeremy was tired of his parents constantly chiding him for the messy state of his room.

> Her friends chided Sarah into apologizing for the rude remark.

> The principal chided the students for their noisy behavior in the hallway.

Ask students to determine the tone of the context. Does it seem to be positive, negative, or neutral? Does *chide* seem like something you would like someone to do to you? Next, ask them to try to substitute a word or phrase that seems to work within the general parameters of the context. For example, what word might critics use to tell the government that it was responding too slowly to disaster aid requests? How about *criticized? Condemned? Blamed? Scolded?* Which word fits best in the other contexts? As students explore each context, they will realize that although all their guesses might work with the first context, the subsequent sentences cause them to narrow and refine their work-

ing definitions (scold—to goad someone into action). They develop a much richer and more complex understanding of a useful word than if they had merely attempted to memorize a possibly obscure dictionary definition.

3 Select a reading assignment that contains several useful words for your students to learn. After they read a selection, model the Vocabulary Overview Guide using an overhead transparency or chalkboard. For example, key words in a short story on ghosts might include *eerie, tormented, apparition, legend, premonition,* and *supernatural.* Discuss with students the main topic or theme of the selection, and note how the words selected connect to this topic or theme. Identify with students the important categories within this topic. Under the topic of ghosts, you may decide on: What are ghosts like? (Appearance), How do people react to ghosts? (People), and Why are there ghosts? (Explanation) as your categories. Write these categories on the Overview Guide, and arrange the key words on the guide under the appropriate category (see Vocabulary Overview Guide for Ghosts).

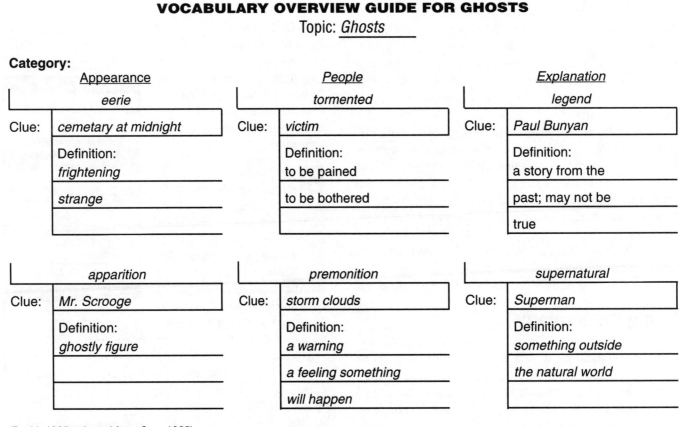

VOCABULARY OVERVIEW GUIDE FOR GHOSTS
Topic: *Ghosts*

Category:

	Appearance		*People*		*Explanation*
	eerie		*tormented*		*legend*
Clue:	*cemetary at midnight*	Clue:	*victim*	Clue:	*Paul Bunyan*
	Definition: *frightening* *strange*		Definition: *to be pained* *to be bothered*		Definition: *a story from the past; may not be true*
	apparition		*premonition*		*supernatural*
Clue:	*Mr. Scrooge*	Clue:	*storm clouds*	Clue:	*Superman*
	Definition: *ghostly figure*		Definition: *a warning* *a feeling something will happen*		Definition: *something outside the natural world*

(Buehl, 1995; adapted from Carr, 1985)

4 Assign several students to examine the context of each new word in the text and assign others to look up dictionary definitions. Have them discuss working definitions for each term. Working definitions are not single-word synonyms from a dictionary entry, but are more expansive definitions based on a sense of the context in which the word can be used. Enter these definitions on the Vocabulary Overview Guides.

Brainstorm with students possible clues to help them learn each new word. These clues will help link new words to their background knowledge. For example, students may decide that *eerie* might describe how they would feel being in a cemetery at midnight. This becomes their meaningful clue for remembering this word. Encourage students to personalize their clues. A clue that works for one student may not connect with another. For example, students unfamiliar with Dickens's *A Christmas Carol* will not find the clue of *Mr. Scrooge* helpful for remembering the meaning of *apparition*; however, the movie *Ghostbusters* could be just the clue to trigger this word.

Encourage students to develop a strong association between new words and clues that trigger a sense of their meanings. For instance, a student learning the word *extinct* may select *dinosaurs* as a clue to the meaning "no longer living." A student learning *biceps* may decide on *Arnold Schwarzenegger* as a meaningful clue. As students study new words on the Overview Guide, ask them to cover the definitions to see if their clues are sufficient to help them recall the word's meaning.

5 Gradually move students toward accepting more responsibility for selecting, categorizing, and defining new key words from a reading. Transition them from identifying some new words with the whole class to assigning these tasks in small groups or with student pairs. Finally, have individual students construct their own Vocabulary Overview Guides based on a reading assignment.

Advantages

- Students develop ownership of new words that they encounter and learn.
- Students are provided with a well-organized structure for keeping track of and studying key words.
- Students come to regard vocabulary learning as more than looking up definitions in a dictionary, and they look for ways to link the new word with what they already know.
- Students are more motivated to learn words that they have personally selected from a reading.

The Vocabulary Overview Guide is a strategy adaptable to all content areas, including science, social studies, and math.

References

Buehl, D. (1995). *Classroom strategies for interactive learning.* Madison, WI: Wisconsin State Reading Association.

Carr, E.M. (1985). The vocabulary overview guide: A metacognitive strategy to improve vocabulary comprehension and retention. *Journal of Reading, 28,* 684–689.

Word Family Trees

Can you guess this word? It once referred to a scrap of food given to someone less fortunate. The word, initially a Latin term, was later adopted by the French in medieval times to signify a lump of bread or other leavings of a meal provided to a beggar. The English expanded the word's usage from "a gift begged" to "a present." Along the way, the word has taken on a decidedly negative connotation. The modern meaning is to offer a gift, sometimes substantial, to influence someone's behavior.

The word? *Bribe.* What an interesting etymological journey—from a small gesture of generosity to a calculating act of corruption. One can almost speculate the circumstances that led the word *bribe* to be associated today with a different type of beggar.

Clearly, a word such as *bribe* has a deep and involved meaning. We understand the word far beyond any terse dictionary definition. All sorts of connections may come to mind: a parent who offers a child candy to quell a tantrum; a favor from a sibling for keeping quiet about a family rule infraction; a payment made to a decision maker to influence the awarding of a contract; a campaign contribution handed to a politician to further a group's political (or financial) agenda. Bribe is a rich concept with many layers of meaning; it is not a mere vocabulary word.

Students, however, often view vocabulary learning in a very narrow sense. They look up a new word in a dictionary, perhaps obtaining only a foggy notion of its meaning or grasping quickly at a possible synonym. If they must master the word for a vocabulary quiz, they memorize it as an act of short-term learning, forgetting it soon after and never incorporating it into their speaking and writing. Students often attempt to learn vocabulary words as facts (definitions), not as concepts. Encouraging students to be word browsers, to become playfully engaged with new vocabulary, can help reinforce that true vocabulary acquisition involves more than quick trips to a dictionary.

The Word Family Tree (Buehl, 1999) is strategy that involves students in connecting a key term to its origins, to related words that share a common root, to words that serve a similar function, and to situations in which one might expect the word to be used.

Using the Strategy

Introduce the Word Family Tree graphic organizer as a means of vocabulary study (see Appendix, page 168). As an analogy, refer to a genealogical family tree to prepare students for this activity. Family trees list an individual's ancestors, direct descendants, and other relatives, such as cousins, aunts, and uncles, while the Word Family Tree lists the "relatives" of a word. Using this strategy involves the following steps:

1 Begin with activities that pique students' interest in word origins. Key terms from a unit of study or other frequently occurring words are excellent candidates for etymological exploration. For example, a What's the Word Connection? exercise establishes that a word's history can provide insight into its current meanings:

What's the word connection—

— between bow and arrow, and to be very drunk?

— between a person who sits beside you at a meal and flatters you, and an organism that lives off others?

— between a baptism sponsor and someone who spreads small talk about you?

Invite student speculations, providing them with the original word forms: the Greek *toxon* (bow and arrow), the Greek *parasitos* (para—beside and sitos—wheat, grain, or food), and the Anglo-Saxon *godsibb* (God and sib—a relation). Students will notice root forms and may be able to provide modern equivalents: *intoxicate, parasite,* and *gossip.* Along the way, students will discover that the Greeks dipped arrows in poison, and to be poisoned was to be intoxicated; that originally parasites were folks who wheedled meals (and even-

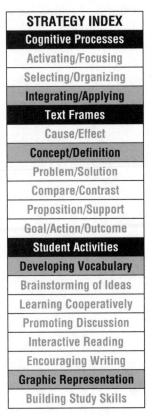

STRATEGY INDEX

Cognitive Processes
Activating/Focusing
Selecting/Organizing
Integrating/Applying
Text Frames
Cause/Effect
Concept/Definition
Problem/Solution
Compare/Contrast
Proposition/Support
Goal/Action/Outcome
Student Activities
Developing Vocabulary
Brainstorming of Ideas
Learning Cooperatively
Promoting Discussion
Interactive Reading
Encouraging Writing
Graphic Representation
Building Study Skills

tually their living) by "buttering up" wealthy benefactors; and that originally gossips were individuals very close to a family (sibling is derived from the same root), regarded as talkative and ready sources for information. Today, a gossip spreads idle talk and rumors, and the connotation has changed from praiseworthy to pejorative.

2 Introduce students to the Word Family Tree by using the word *acquiesce* encountered in a history

text. Show how the word is linked to a meaningful root to help them gain insight into likely contexts where the word might appear (see Word Family Tree for *Acquiesce*).

3 Select a group of target words for students to investigate, which could be pivotal words in a short story, key terms in a unit of study, or general high-utility vocabulary words. For example, key terms in a biology unit might include *genetics, mutation, recessive,*

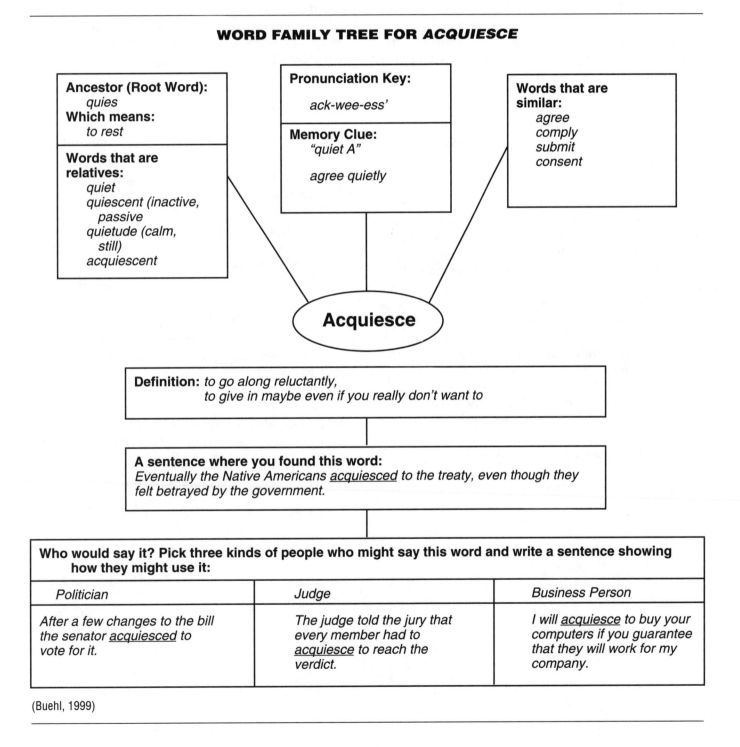

WORD FAMILY TREE FOR *ACQUIESCE*

Ancestor (Root Word):
  quies
Which means:
  to rest

Words that are relatives:
  quiet
  quiescent (inactive, passive
  quietude (calm, still)
  acquiescent

Pronunciation Key:
  ack-wee-ess'

Memory Clue:
  "quiet A"

  agree quietly

Words that are similar:
  agree
  comply
  submit
  consent

Acquiesce

Definition: *to go along reluctantly, to give in maybe even if you really don't want to*

A sentence where you found this word:
Eventually the Native Americans <u>acquiesced</u> to the treaty, even though they felt betrayed by the government.

Who would say it? Pick three kinds of people who might say this word and write a sentence showing how they might use it:

Politician	Judge	Business Person
After a few changes to the bill the senator <u>acquiesced</u> to vote for it.	*The judge told the jury that every member had to <u>acquiesce</u> to reach the verdict.*	*I will <u>acquiesce</u> to buy your computers if you guarantee that they will work for my company.*

(Buehl, 1999)

inherited, and *dominant*. Although students will encounter other biological terminology, selected words should represent essential concepts to be learned. The history passage that included *acquiesce* might also feature key words such as *imperialism*, *treaty*, and *colonialism*. Have students work with partners or in cooperative groups to complete Word Family Trees for target words, using appropriate resources including textbooks, a thesaurus, dictionary, or other vocabulary-rich sources. Part of the activity involves brainstorming to determine what kinds of people might be heard using the word and devising possible sentences for those contexts. Ask students to brainstorm possible mnemonic clues to help remember the meaning of the word. In the biology example, students investigating the Word Family Tree for *genetics* may uncover a rich array of relatives all derived from the same origin: *gene, genealogy, gender, genius*, and *generate*.

Allow time for students to share Word Family Trees with classmates to discover other related words, possible synonyms, and useful contexts where the word might make an appearance.

4 Integrate consideration of word origin as a regular routine in classroom learning. Encourage students to raise their own questions about possible word backgrounds, and to consult sources other than abridged dictionaries to enrich their vocabulary understanding. For example, a music teacher may ask, Can you remember the difference between a *sonata* and a *concerto*? What would you hear if you listened to a compact disc of Prokofiev's *1st Violin Concerto*—a soloist playing with piano accompaniment, or the soloist with full orchestral backing? Students completing Word Family Trees on the two terms would realize that word origins provide a clue for remembering the two forms of classical music composition. The word *concerto* is derived from the same Latin root *concertare*—to organize or arrange, as *concert*—to act together, to work in harmony: It will take the *concerted* effort of our entire community to revitalize the down-

town area. A *concerto* is a composition that requires the soloist(s) to work together with a symphony orchestra to produce music.

Students creating a family tree for *sonata* will discover that the ancestor is the root *sonare*—to sound. Close relatives that share this origin are *sound*, *sonar*, *sonic*, *sonnet*, and *sonorous*. Similar words include *solo* and *recital*.

As in this example, music teachers would find many opportunities to use Word Family Trees to help students master key musical terms. Students familiar with the use of the term *concert* as a public musical performance, who realize that the root also means cooperative behavior, add a dimension to their knowledge that helps them to recall the meaning of the term *concerto* as well.

Advantages

- Students develop a thorough understanding of important vocabulary.

- Students come to see the organic nature of vocabulary, as word meanings have grown and changed over the years.

- Students begin to identify useful word roots and notice connections among words derived from similar origins.

- Students are more likely to remember new words and feel confident in using them when they write and talk.

- Students are encouraged to raise questions of their own about possible word backgrounds, and to consult sources other than abridged dictionaries to enrich their vocabulary understanding.

Reference and Suggested Reading

Buehl, D. (1999). Word family trees: Heritage sheds insight into words' meaning and use. *WEAC News & Views, 35*(2), 14.
Klemp, R. (1994). Word storm: Connecting vocabulary to the student's database. *The Reading Teacher, 48*, 282.

You Ought to Be in Pictures

Remember paging through an old family photo album? As you gazed at pictures of your kinfolk, taken perhaps a century or more ago, you probably found yourself pausing periodically and imagining what life was like for those people. What were the daily conditions growing up on a dairy farm in rural Wisconsin in 1896? How has the landscape changed since then? What was the country like for your great-grandparents who emigrated to the United States in the 1880s? Who in a particular photo is most like you?

Photographs can evoke a sense of mood and convey meaningful information that communicates far beyond written description. The old adage, "a picture is worth a thousand words," explains why textbook editors undertake the expense of including many photographs and other visuals in the layout of a chapter. Unfortunately, students taking the "quick trip" through a textbook section—endeavoring to finish the reading and complete the assignment—may overlook these rich sources of insight about the content. In addition, students may regard the textbook as personally uninviting and distant, as merely paragraphs of dense information. Taking time to guide students through a thoughtful examination of photographs can help them connect to concepts and successfully tackle learning new material. You Ought to Be In Pictures (Buehl, 2000) is a strategy that encourages students to imagine themselves within the context of a photograph.

Using the Strategy

You Ought to Be in Pictures prepares students to read a passage using pictures to process new learning through extensive use of mental imagery. Using the strategy involves the following steps:

1 Look for vivid photographs that connect with some aspect of your curriculum. Some outstanding photographs already may be provided in the textbook students are reading. Check other textbooks, reference sources, and newspapers and magazines. Search for photographs to which your students can make a personal connection. To display photographs, make slides or use an overhead transparency. A scanner will allow you to make a computerized image, which can be shown via a computer projector or be printed onto an overhead transparency.

2 Select a photograph that will introduce or extend important ideas or concepts for a unit of study. Guide students in their viewing of the photograph by stimulating their mental imagery and suggesting a personal connection to events portrayed in the picture. For example, to prepare students in a history course for studying the Great Depression of the 1930s, identify a photograph that illustrates some key themes of the time period (see Dorothea Lange photo). Take students through the following guided imagery exercise (see Guided Imagery, page 59).

During the period of the Great Depression, many people, especially farmers, lost their land and were forced out on the road. You are looking at a Library of Congress photograph of a homeless family in Oklahoma in the 1930s.

First, examine the location of the photograph and note as many details as possible. What do you observe about the countryside? About the land? The plants and vegetation? The road? What time of year might it be? What does the climate appear to be like? What type of day does it seem to be?

Now focus closely on each person in the photograph. Pay particular attention to what each person is wearing. Look at the way family members carry themselves, their posture, their facial expressions.

Next, choose one individual in the photograph and imagine you are this person. What might you be thinking while this was happening? Describe what you might be feeling, what emotions you might be experiencing. What has the day been like for you? Imagine what might have happened before the scene presented in the photo. What do you see happening later during this day and following days?

3 Guided imagery using photographs provides an excellent opportunity for students to record observa-

STRATEGY INDEX
Cognitive Processes
Activating/Focusing
Selecting/Organizing
Integrating/Applying
Text Frames
Cause/Effect
Concept/Definition
Problem/Solution
Compare/Contrast
Proposition/Support
Goal/Action/Outcome
Student Activities
Developing Vocabulary
Brainstorming of Ideas
Learning Cooperatively
Promoting Discussion
Interactive Reading
Encouraging Writing
Graphic Representation
Building Study Skills

tions and thoughts in writing. Using the Depression example, give students the following writing prompt:

It is now many years later. You are showing this photograph to a grandchild. What would you tell this child about your memories of that day? Write what you would share as an entry in your notebook.

4 After students respond in writing, ask for volunteers to read their entries to the class. Students who have chosen the same individual with whom to identify will hear and compare classmates' musings about that individual during that difficult time. Students will delve into the Great Depression unit with much more empathy for the great personal dramas of the time and more personal involvement in the material.

This strategy can be adapted for use with photographs that do not feature people. For example, with science pictures, suggest that students are personally witnessing what is portrayed in the photo and guide them through noticing details as if they were actually viewing the scene.

Advantages

- Students become personally engaged in learning through their imaginations.
- Students develop empathy for others as they make connections to learning through photographs.
- Students encounter key ideas before reading, are likely to be motivated to learn more about the topic, and are primed to learn from text materials that may otherwise be regarded as cold and impersonal.

References

Buehl, D. (2000). You ought to be in pictures: Using photos to help students understand past. *WEAC News and Views*, *35*(8), 14.

Lange, D. (1938). *American memory collection* [Online]. Library of Congress. Available: www.memory.loc.gov

THE DEPRESSION IN OKLAHOMA

Dorothea Lange, 1938

Appendix

Analogy Graphic Organizer

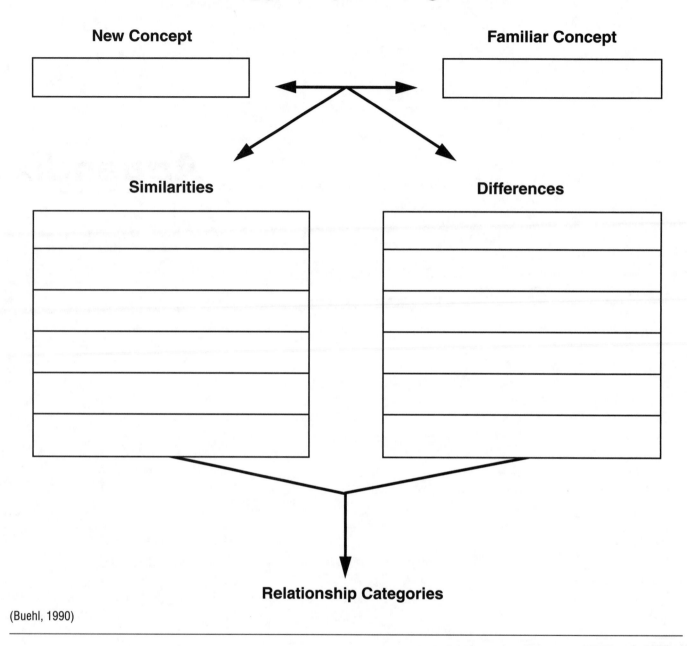

New Concept

Familiar Concept

Similarities

Differences

Relationship Categories

(Buehl, 1990)

Character Analysis Grid

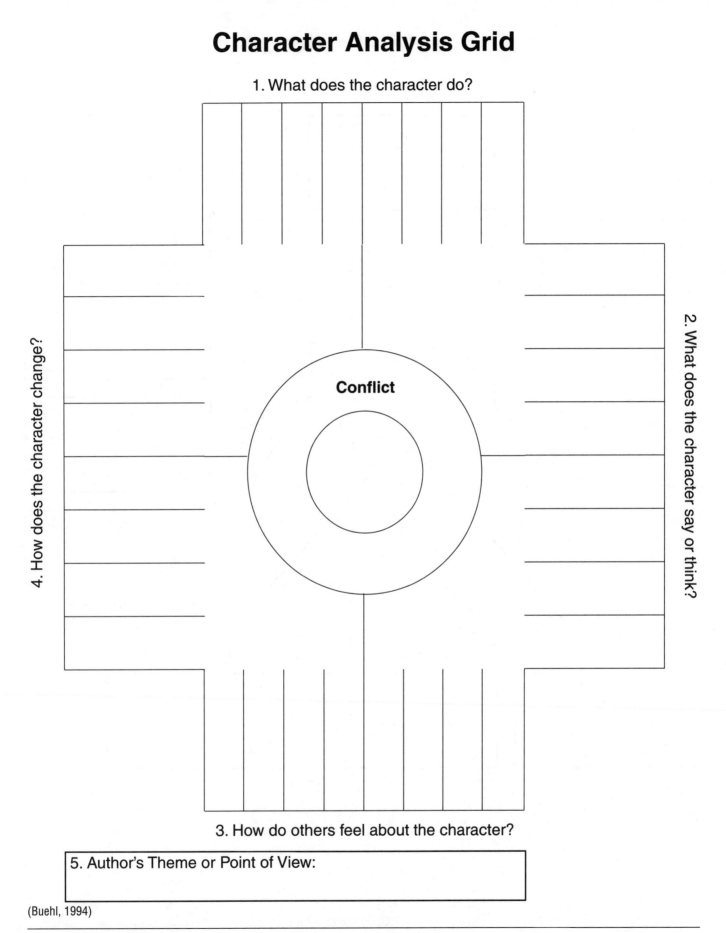

1. What does the character do?

2. What does the character say or think?

Conflict

4. How does the character change?

3. How do others feel about the character?

5. Author's Theme or Point of View:

(Buehl, 1994)

Concept/Definition Map

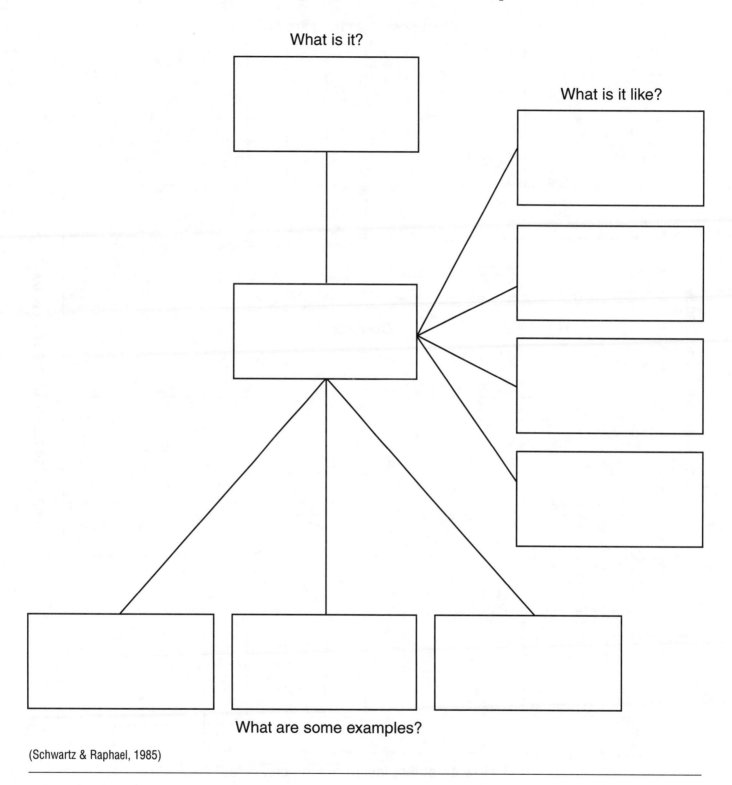

What is it?

What is it like?

What are some examples?

(Schwartz & Raphael, 1985)

Different Perspectives Graphic Outline

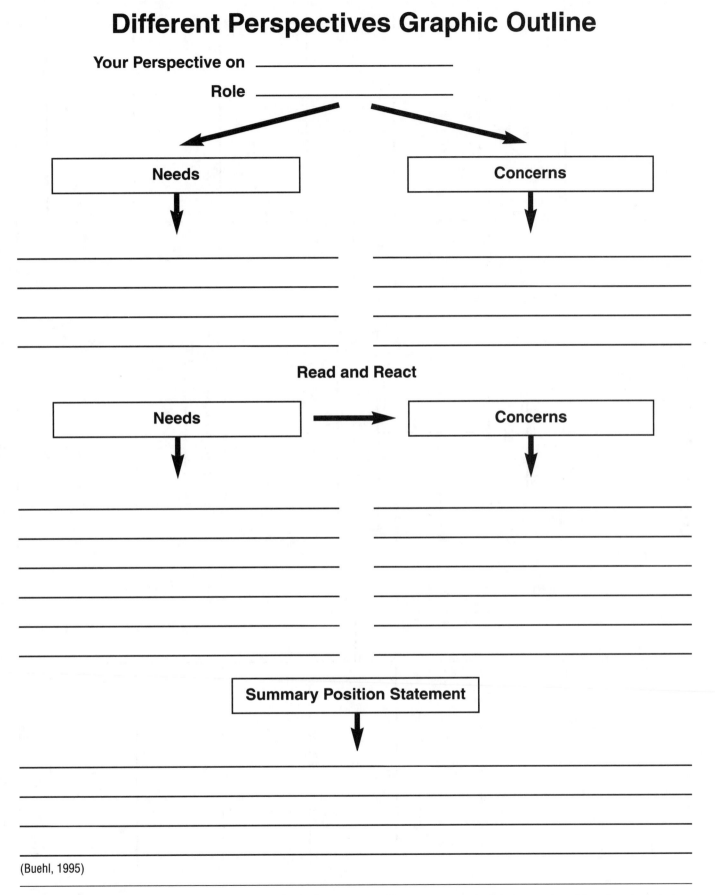

Your Perspective on _____

Role _____

Needs

Concerns

Read and React

Needs

Concerns

Summary Position Statement

(Buehl, 1995)

Discussion Web

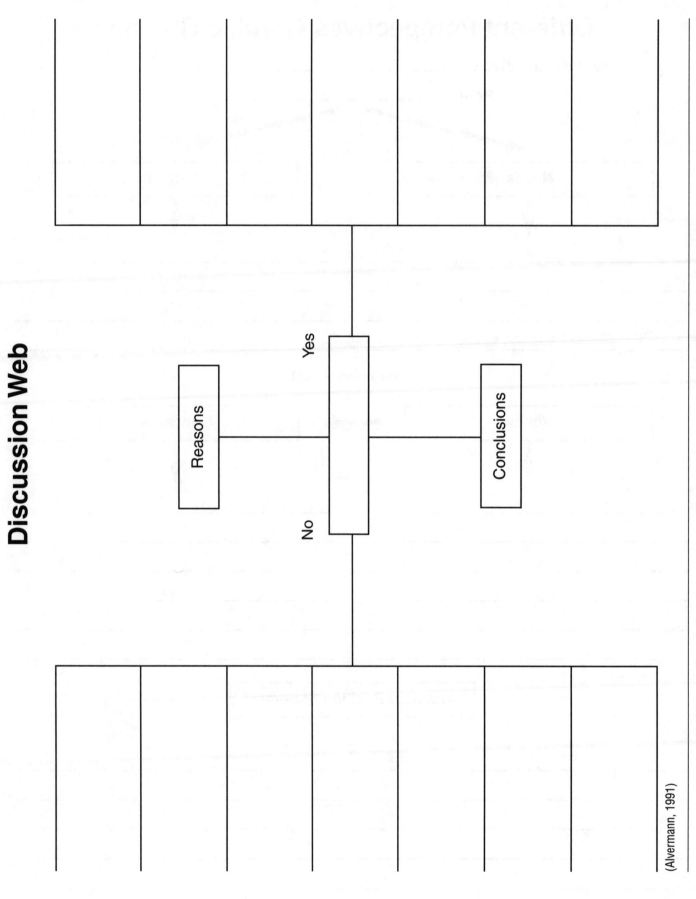

Reasons | Yes / No | Conclusions

Fact Pyramid

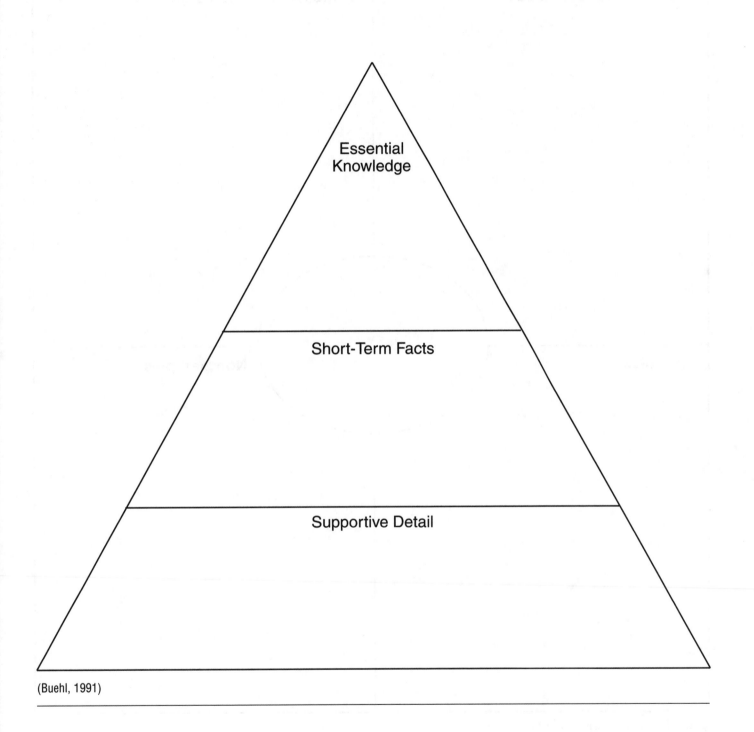

Essential
Knowledge

Short-Term Facts

Supportive Detail

(Buehl, 1991)

Frayer Model

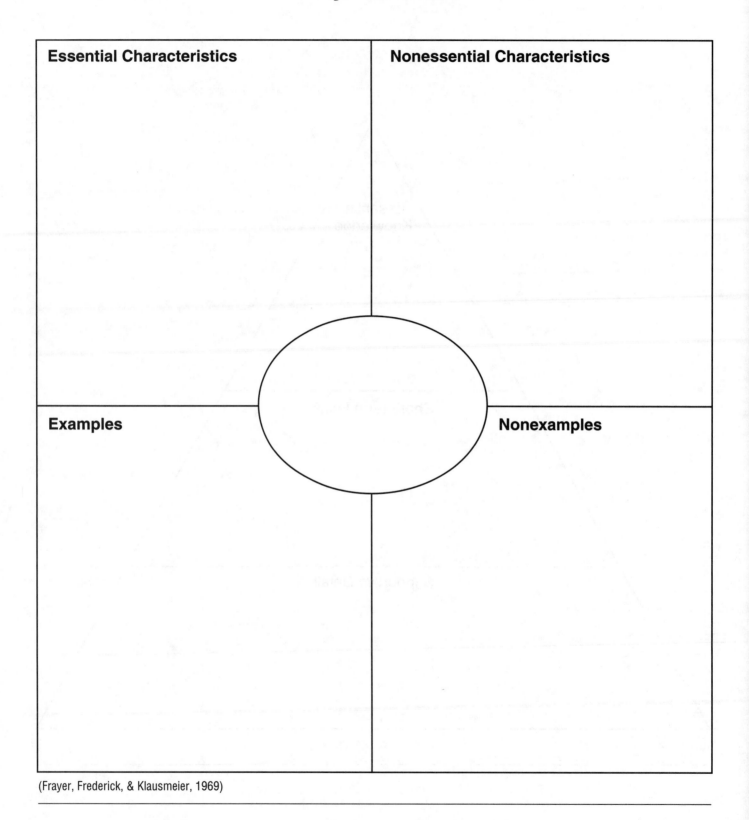

Essential Characteristics	Nonessential Characteristics

Examples	Nonexamples

(Frayer, Frederick, & Klausmeier, 1969)

History Change Frame Graphic Organizer

Group?	Group?	Group?
What problems did they face?	What problems did they face?	What problems did they face?
What changes caused these problems?	What changes caused these problems?	What changes caused these problems?
What did they do to solve the problems?	What did they do to solve the problems?	What did they do to solve the problems?

(Buehl, 1992)

Classroom Strategies for Interactive Learning, 2nd Ed., by Doug Buehl ©2001. Newark, DE: International Reading Association.
May be copied for classroom use.

History Memory Bubbles

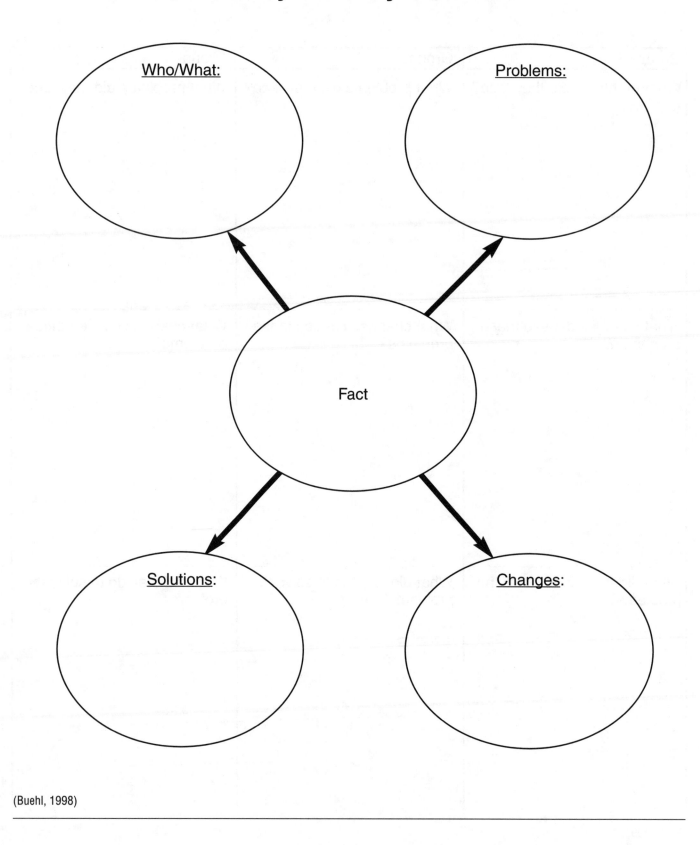

Who/What:

Problems:

Fact

Solutions:

Changes:

(Buehl, 1998)

I-Chart

Topic:	Q1:	Q2:	Q3:	Q4:	Other Interesting Facts	New Questions
What We Know:						
Source:						
Source:						
Source:						
Summaries						

(Hoffman, 1992)

Proposition/Support Outline

Proposition:

Support:

1. Facts

2. Statistics

3. Examples

4. Expert Authority

5. Logic and Reasoning

(Buehl, 1992)

Science Connection Overview

What's Familiar?

What's the Connection? Skim and survey the chapter for things that are familiar and that connect with your life or world. List them below:

What topics are covered?

Read the Summary. What topic areas seem to be the most important?

What questions do you have?

Questions of Interest. What questions do you have about this material that may be answered in the chapter?

How is it organized?

Chapter Organization: What categories of information are provided in this chapter?

Translate

Read and Translate: Use 3 × 5 cards for vocabulary.

(Buehl, 1992)

Semantic Feature Analysis Grid

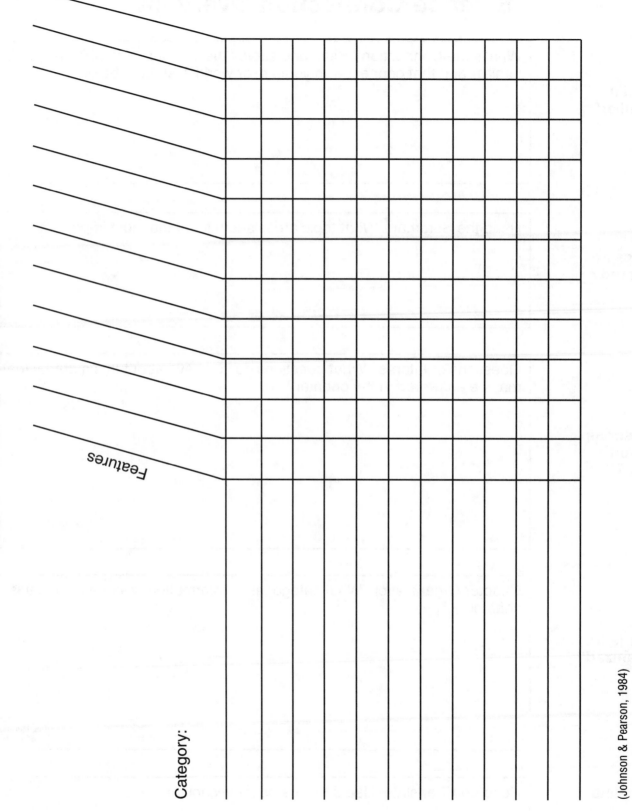

Features

Category:

The Sequential Roundtable Alphabet

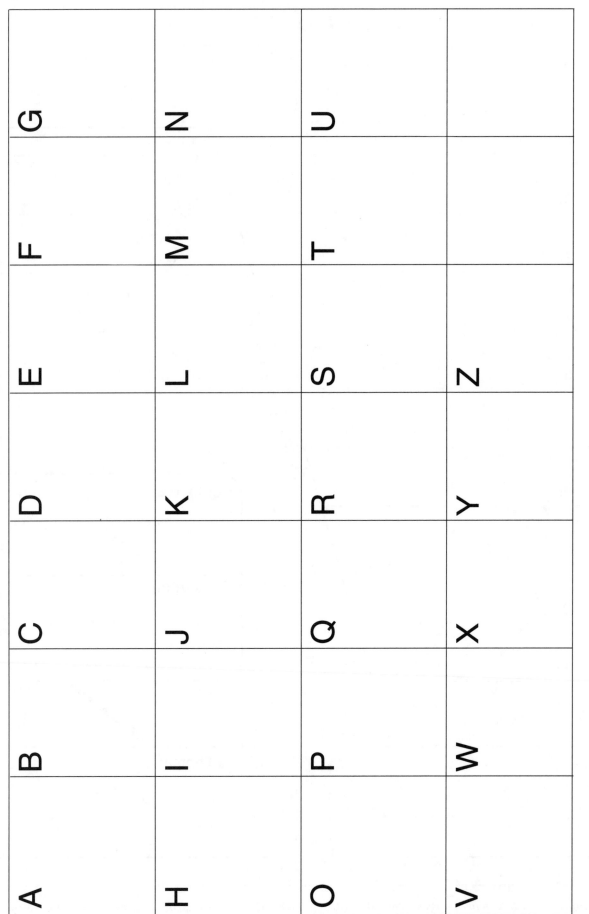

A	B	C	D	E	F	G	
H	I	J	K	L	M	N	
O	P	Q	R	S	T	U	
V	W	X	Y	Z			

(Ricci & Wahlgren, 1998)

Classroom Strategies for Interactive Learning, 2nd Ed., by Doug Buehl ©2001. Newark, DE: International Reading Association.
May be copied for classroom use.

Story Map

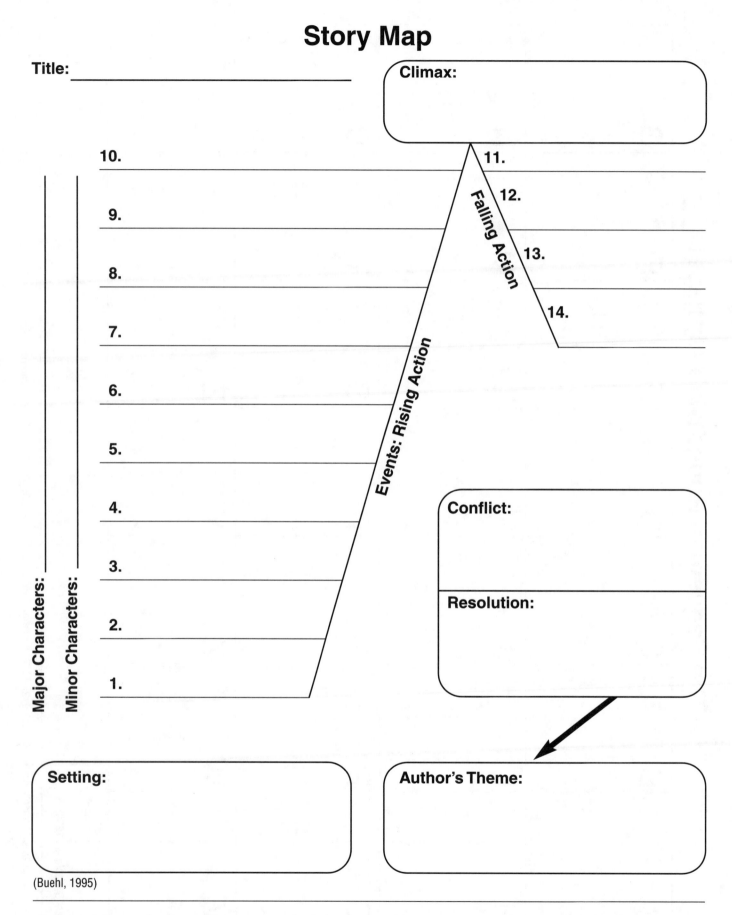

Title: _____

Climax:

10. _____

11.

Falling Action

12.

9. _____

13.

8. _____

14.

7. _____

Events: Rising Action

6. _____

5. _____

Conflict:

4. _____

Resolution:

3. _____

2. _____

1. _____

Major Characters:

Minor Characters:

Setting:

Author's Theme:

(Buehl, 1995)

Vocabulary Overview Guide

Topic: _____

Category:

_____   _____   _____

Clue: _____   Clue: _____   Clue: _____

　　Definition: _____   　　Definition: _____   　　Definition: _____

　　_____   　　_____   　　_____

　　_____   　　_____   　　_____

Clue: _____   Clue: _____   Clue: _____

　　Definition: _____   　　Definition: _____   　　Definition: _____

　　_____   　　_____   　　_____

　　_____   　　_____   　　_____

Clue: _____   Clue: _____   Clue: _____

　　Definition: _____   　　Definition: _____   　　Definition: _____

　　_____   　　_____   　　_____

　　_____   　　_____   　　_____

Clue: _____   Clue: _____   Clue: _____

　　Definition: _____   　　Definition: _____   　　Definition: _____

　　_____   　　_____   　　_____

　　_____   　　_____   　　_____

(Carr, 1985)

Word Family Tree

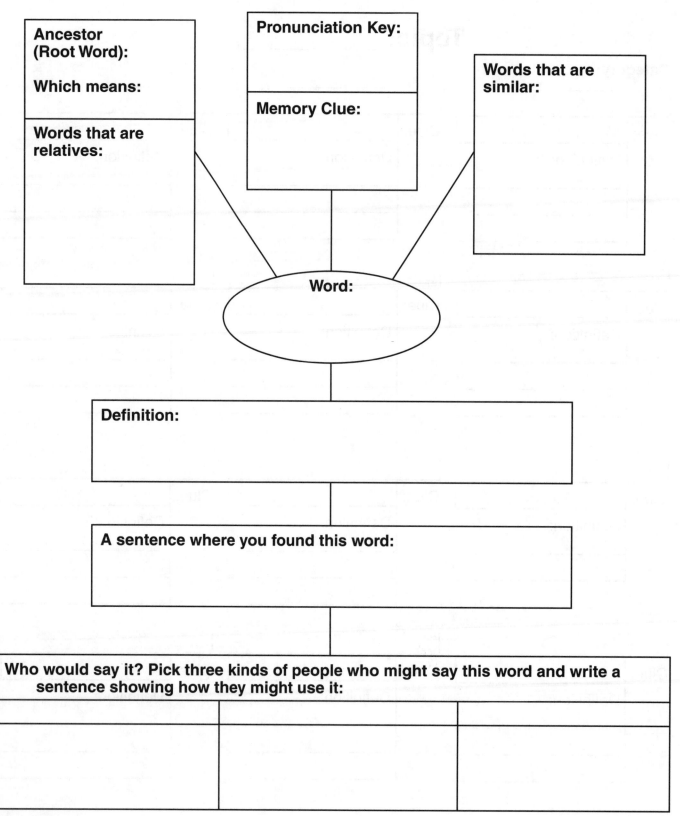

Ancestor (Root Word):

Which means:

Words that are relatives:

Pronunciation Key:

Memory Clue:

Words that are similar:

Word:

Definition:

A sentence where you found this word:

Who would say it? Pick three kinds of people who might say this word and write a sentence showing how they might use it:

(Buehl, 1999)

REFERENCES AND SUGGESTED READING

Anderson, T., & Armbruster, B. (1984). Studying. In P.D. Pearson (Ed.), *Handbook of reading research*. New York: Longman.

Armbruster, B., & Anderson, T. (1982). *Idea mapping: The technique and it's use in the classroom* (Reading Education Report No. 36). Urbana, IL: University of Illinois, Center for the Study of Reading.

Aronson, E., Stephen, C., Sikes, J., Blaney, N., & Snapp, M. (1978). *The jigsaw classroom*. Beverly Hills, CA: Sage Publications.

Alvermann, D. (1991). The discussion web: A graphic aid for learning across the curriculum. *The Reading Teacher, 45*, 92–99.

Anders, P.L., & Bos, C.S. (1986). Semantic feature analysis: An interactive strategy for vocabulary development and text comprehension. *Journal of Reading, 29*, 610–616.

Barron, R. (1969). The use of vocabulary as an advance organizer. In H. Herber & P. Sanders, *Research in reading in the content areas: First year report* (pp. 29–39). Syracuse, NY: Syracuse University.

Bean, T., Singer, H., & Cowan, S. (1985). Analogical study guides: Improving comprehension in science. *Journal of Reading, 29*, 246–250.

Beck, I., & McKeown, M. (1981). Developing questions that promote comprehension: The story map. *Language Arts, 58*(8), 913–918.

Beck, I.L., McKeown, M.G., Hamilton, R.L., & Kucan, L. (1997). *Questioning the author: An approach for enhancing student engagement with text*. Newark, DE: International Reading Association.

Blachowicz, C. (1993, November). *Developing active comprehenders*. Paper presented at the Madison Area Reading Association, Madison, Wisconsin.

Buehl, D. (1991). Fact pyramids. *New perspectives: Reading across the curriculum*. Madison, WI: Madison Metropolitan School District, 7(6), 1–2.

Buehl, D. (1991). Frames of mind. *The Exchange. Newsletter of the IRA Secondary Reading Interest Group, 4*(2), 4–5.

Buehl, D. (1992). A frame of mind for reading history. *The Exchange. Newsletter of the IRA Secondary Reading Interest Group, 5*(1), 4–5.

Buehl, D. (1992). The connection overview: A strategy for learning in science. *WSRA Journal, 36*(2), 21–30.

Buehl, D. (1992). Outline helps students analyze credibility of author's premise. *WEAC News & Views, 28*(1), 8.

Buehl, D. (1993). Magnetized: Students are drawn to technique that identifies key words. *WEAC News & Views, 29*(4), 13.

Buehl, D. (1994). Persona: Character analysis sheds light on story's meaning. *WEAC News & Views, 29*(10), 21.

Buehl, D. (1994). You said it: Colorful quotes can be the voice of a character's soul. *WEAC News & Views, 29*(11), 21.

Buehl, D. (1995). *Classroom strategies for interactive learning*. Schofield, WI: Wisconsin State Reading Association.

Buehl, D. (1998). Making math make sense: Tactics help kids understand math language. *WEAC News and Views, 34*(3), 17.

Buehl, D. (1998). Memory bubbles: They help put information into context. *WEAC News and Views, 33*(7), 13.

Buehl, D. (1999). Word family trees: Heritage sheds insight into words' meaning and use. *WEAC News & Views, 35*(2), 14.

Buehl, D. (2000). Breaking it down: Understanding the question leads to a better answer. *WEAC News and Views, 35*(6), 14.

Buehl, D. (2000). You ought to be in pictures: Using photos to help students understand past. *WEAC News and Views, 35*(8), 14.

Buehl, D., & Hein, D. (1990). Analogy graphic organizer. *The Exchange. Secondary Reading Interest Group Newsletter, 3*(2), 6.

Buzan T. (1983). *Use both sides of your brain* (Rev. ed.). New York: Dutton.

Carr, E.M. (1985). The vocabulary overview guide: A metacognitive strategy to improve vocabulary comprehension and retention. *Journal of Reading, 28*, 684–689.

Carr, E.M., & Ogle, D. (1987). K-W-L plus: A strategy for comprehension and summarization. *Journal of Reading, 30*, 626–631.

Cook, D. (Ed.). (1986). *A guide to curriculum planning in reading*. Madison, WI: Wisconsin Department of Public Instruction.

Cook, D. (Ed.). (1989). *Strategic learning in the content areas*. Madison, WI: Department of Public Instruction.

Costa, A. (1997). *Teaching for intelligent behavior*. Davis, CA: Search Models Unlimited.

Cunningham, D., & Shablak, S. (1975). Selective reading guide-o-rama: The content teacher's best friend. *Journal of Reading, 18*, 380–382.

Duke, N., & Pearson, P.D. (2000, June). *Effective practices for developing reading comprehension*. Paper presented at Madison Literacy Institute, Madison, Wisconsin.

Frayer, D., Frederick, W., & Klausmeier, H. (1969). *A schema for testing the level of cognitive mastery* (Working Paper No. 16). Madison, WI: Wisconsin Research and Development Center.

Fulwiler, T. (1980). Journals across the disciplines. *The English Journal, 69*(9), 14–19.

Gaither, P. (1997, May). *Caught in the act: Strategies to engage readers with informational text*. Paper presented at the 47th Annual Convention of the International Reading Association, Atlanta, Georgia.

Gambrell, L., Kapinus, B., & Wilson, R. (1987). Using mental imagery and summarization to achieve independence in comprehension. *Journal of Reading, 30*, 638–642.

Hayes, D. (1989). Helping students GRASP the knack of writing summaries. *Journal of Reading, 33*, 96–101.

Herber, H. (1978). *Teaching reading in content areas* (2nd ed.). Englewood Cliffs, NJ: Prentice-Hall.

Hoffman, J. (1992). Critical reading/thinking across the curriculum: Using I-charts to support learning. *Language Arts, 69*, 121–127.

Johnson, D., & Pearson, P.D. (1984). *Teaching reading vocabulary* (2nd ed.). New York: Holt, Rinehart and Winston.

Jones, B., Pierce, J., & Hunter, B. (1988/1989). Teaching students to construct graphic representations. *Educational Leadership, 46*, 20–25.

Jones, B., Palincsar, A., Ogle, D., & Carr, E. (1987). *Strategic teaching and learning: Cognitive instruction in the content areas*. Alexandria, VA: Association for Supervision & Curriculum Development.

Joyce, B., & Weil, M. (1986). *Models of teaching*. Englewood Cliffs, NJ: Prentice-Hall.

Kennedy, M. (May, 1991). Policy issues in teacher education. *Phi Delta Kappan, 72*(9), 658–665.

Kinkead, D., Thompson, R., Wright, C., & Gutierrez, C. (1992). Pyramiding: Reading and writing to learn social studies. *The Exchange. Newsletter of the IRA Secondary Reading Interest Group, 5*(2), 3.

Klein, M. (1988). *Teaching reading comprehension and vocabulary: A guide for teachers*. Englewood Cliffs, NJ: Prentice Hall.

Klemp, R. (1994). Word storm: Connecting vocabulary to the student's database. *The Reading Teacher, 48*, 282.

Langer, J. (1981). From theory to practice: A prereading plan. *Journal of Reading, 25*, 152–156.

Lazear, D. (1991). *Seven ways of teaching: The artistry of teaching with multiple intelligences*. Palatine, IL: Skylight.

Levin, J. (1983). Pictorial strategies for school learning. In M. Pressley & J. Levin (Eds.), *Cognitive strategy research: Educational applications*. New York: Springer-Verlag.

Marzano, R., Pickering, D., Arredondo, D., Blackburn, G., Brandt, R., & Moffett, C. (1992). *Dimensions of learning teacher's manual*. Alexandria, VA: Association for Supervision & Curriculum Development.

Marzano, R., Pickering, D., Arredondo, D., Blackburn, G., Brandt, R., & Wood, K. (1988). Guiding students through informational text. *The Reading Teacher, 41*, 912–920.

McGinley, W., & Denner, P. (1987). Story impressions: A prereading/writing activity. *Journal of Reading, 31*, 248–253.

McLaren, J., Rotundo, L., & Gurley-Dilger, L. (1991). *Heath biology*. Lexington, MA: D.C. Heath.

McNeil, J. (1984). *Reading comprehension: New directions for classroom practice*. Glenview, IL: Scott, Foresman.

McTighe, J., & Lyman, F. (1988). Cueing thinking in the classroom: The promise of theory-embedded tools. *Educational Leadership, 45*(7), 18–24.

Moffett, C. (1992). *Dimensions of learning teacher's manual*. Alexandria, VA: Association for Supervision & Curriculum Development.

Moore, D., Bean, T., Birdyshaw, D., & Rycik, J. (1999). *Adolescent literacy: A position statement for the Commission on Adolescent Literacy of the International Reading Association*. Newark: DE: International Reading Association.

Moore, D., & Moore, S. (1986). Possible sentences. In E. Dishner, T. Bean, J. Readence, & D. Moore (Eds.), *Reading in the content areas: Improving classroom instruction* (2nd ed.). Dubuque, IA: Kendall/Hunt.

Ogle, D. (1986). K-W-L: A teaching model that develops active reading of expository text. *The Reading Teacher, 39*, 564–570.

Peters, C. (1979). The effect of systematic restructuring of material upon the comprehension process. *Reading Research Quarterly, 11*, 87–110.

Pittelman, S., Heimlich, J., Berglund, R., & French, M. (1991). *Semantic feature analysis: Classroom applications*. Newark, DE: International Reading Association.

Pressley, M., Symons, S., McDaniel, M., Snyder, B., & Turnure, J. (1988). Elaborative interrogation facilitates acquisition of confusing facts. *Journal of Educational Psychology, 80*(3), 268–278.

Raphael, T.E. (1982). Question-answering strategies for children. *The Reading Teacher, 36*, 186–190.

Raphael, T. (1986). Teaching question answer relationships, revisited. *The Reading Teacher, 39*, 516–522.

Readence, J., Bean, T., & Baldwin, R. (1989). *Content area reading: An integrated approach* (3rd ed.). Dubuque, IA: Kendall/Hunt.

Readence, J., Moore, D., & Rickelman, R. (1989). *Prereading activities for content area reading and learning* (2nd ed.). Newark, DE: International Reading Association.

Ricci, G., & Wahlgren, C. (1998, May). *The key to know "PAINE" know gain*. Paper presented at the 43rd Annual Convention of the International Reading Association, Orlando, Florida.

Santa, C. (1988). *Content reading including study systems*. Dubuque, IA: Kendall/Hunt.

Santa, C., & Havens, L. (1991). Learning through writing. In C. Santa & D. Alvermann (Eds.), *Science learning: Processes and applications*. Newark, DE: International Reading Association.

Santa, C., Havens, L., & Macumber, E. (1996). Creating independence through student-owned strategies. Dubuque, IA: Kendall/Hunt.

Schwartz, R., & Raphael, T. (1985). Concept of definition: A key to improving students' vocabulary. *The Reading Teacher, 39*, 198–205.

Shearer, B. (1998, February). *Student-directed and focused inquiry*. Paper presented at the Wisconsin State Reading Association Conference, Milwaukee, Wisconsin.

Smith, P., & Tompkins, G. (1988). Structured notetaking: A new strategy for content area readers. *Journal of Reading, 32*, 46–53.

Solon, C. (1980). The pyramid diagram: A college study skills tool. *Journal of Reading, 23*, 594–597.

Taba, H. (1967). *Teacher's handbook for elementary social studies*. Reading, MA: Addison-Wesley.

Thelen, J. (1982). Preparing students for content rading assignments. *Journal of Reading, 25*, 544–549.

Tierney, R., Readence, J., & Dishner, E. (1990). *Reading strategies and practices: A compendium* (3rd ed.). Boston: Allyn & Bacon.

Trelease, J. (1989). *The new read-aloud handbook*. New York: Penguin.

Vacca, R., & Vacca, J. (1999). *Content area reading: Literacy and learning across the curriculum* (6th ed.). New York: Longman.

Vaughan, J., & Estes, T. (1986). *Reading and reasoning beyond the primary grades*. Boston: Allyn & Bacon.

Williams, D. (1986, May). Unlocking the question. In H. Carr (Chair), *Using research to support teacher change and student progress in the content areas*. Paper presented at the 31st Annual Convention of the International Reading Association, Philadelphia, Pennsylvania.

Wood, E., Pressley, M., & Winne, P. (1990). Elaborative interrogation effects on children's learning of factual content. *Journal of Educational Psychology, 82*(4), 741–748.

Wood, K. (1988). Guiding students through informational text. *The Reading Teacher, 41*, 912–920.

Wood, K., Lapp, D., & Flood, J. (1992). *Guiding readers through text: A review of study guides*. Newark, DE: International Reading Association.